INDIA'S CONTRIBUTION TO THE GREAT WAR

INDIA'S CONTRIBUTION TO THE GREAT WAR

Introduction by

Col. Harjeet Singh

PENTAGON PRESS

India's Contribution to the Great War

First Published in 1923
Reissued 2014

ISBN 978-81-8274-782-1

Published by
PENTAGON PRESS
206, Peacock Lane, Shahpur Jat,
New Delhi-110049
Phones: 011-64706243, 26491568
Telefax: 011-26490600
email: rajan@pentagonpress.in
website: www.pentagonpress.in

Branch:
Prime Arcade
Office #11
1154 Saifee Street
Opp. M.G. Road, Camp
Pune-411001
Email: pentagonpresspune@gmail.com

Printed at Avantika Printers Private Limited.

CONTENTS

Appendices

INTRODUCTION

The First World War (1914-1918) or the Great War for Civilisation, as it was known at the time, was a watershed event in modern world history. The events of that conflict changed the social and political map of the world forever. Its repercussions reverberate through time and many contemporary conflicts, particularly in the Middle East, trace their roots directly to the fallout of that war.

India, though a colony at the time, actively supported the war effort in its bid to gain Dominion status. Mainstream political opinion in 1914 was of the view that if India desired greater responsibility and political autonomy, it must be willing to share in the burden of imperial defence. As a result, India contributed immensely to the war effort in terms of both men and material.

The details of India's contribution in terms of men, material and money are not generally known. In this context, this official publication helps in bringing these details to the fore. It is a record worthy of recounting to show the immense contribution as well as sacrifices made for a war which was not India's. Her soldiers served with credit and honour in numerous battlefields around the globe: in France and Belgium, in Aden, East Africa, Gallipoli, Egypt, Mesopotamia, Palestine, Persia, Salonika, Russia, and even in China. By the end of the war 1,100,000 Indians had served overseas at the cost of 60,000 dead. They earned over 9,200 decorations for gallantry including 11 VCs. These figures include the contribution of over 26,000 Imperial Service troops who were a part of the armies of the semi-autonomous Princely States. It must also be remembered that the responsibility for peace on the North Western Frontier remained of paramount importance and troops remained deployed there throughout the period of the war and later.

At the end of the Great War, Sir James Willcocks, wrote a laudatory account of what his troops had achieved. He had little need to justify telling his story. For the first year of the war, he had commanded the Indian Corps in France, whose soldiers had fought and died in most of the great battles on the Western Front. But Willcocks prefaced his account with an especial plea. The soldiers of Britain and the white Dominions, he thought, would easily find chroniclers willing to tell their tale. India's soldiers, he suggested, 'will furnish no writers to thrill the generations to come; they will just pass with the great masses of India, content that they have done their duty and been faithful to their salt'.

This book gives substance to the belief that Indian soldiers did indeed achieve much to 'thrill the generations to come'. In 1914, the Indian Army was a colonial force of some 155,000 officers and men. The Indian Army, the 75,000-strong British garrison of India, the Imperial Service Troops supplied by the Indian Princes, and the Indian high command were collectively known as the 'Army in India', which numbered around 236,000 in all.

The Indian Army was, in peacetime, an all-volunteer force, taking in 15-20,000 recruits a year. Its ranks were filled mainly with illiterate peasants. Pay for a sepoy was a modest Rs. 11 a month (although increased during the war), but a hard-pressed peasant family, with few other sources of income, would value the remittances sent home by a relative serving in the ranks. Most men served for five to seven years, before returning to their village.

The Indian Army, however, was 'Indian' only in a nominal sense. By 1914, the vast majority of Indian troops were drawn from the north and north-west of the subcontinent - the provinces of Punjab, the North-West Frontier and UP, and the independent kingdom of Nepal. This regional bias was the result of the 'martial races' theory which had influenced British recruiting strategy since the 1880s. The martial races idea had at its core the belief that some Indians were inherently more warlike than others. Thus, many of the Indian troops who served in the war were Punjabi Muslims and Sikhs, reflecting the ethnic biases of the wider Indian Army; in 1912 just over half of all combatants were from the Punjab.

The Indian Army had three main functions: the defence of the North-West Frontier of India; the maintenance of internal security against threats to the colonial order; and the provision of a Field Force to fight an Afghan or Russian invasion, or to be sent overseas for imperial purposes. Approximately one-third of the Army was assigned to each of these three tasks. The immediately disposable elements of the Field Force normally consisted of two divisions and one cavalry brigade, with their attached British units. The foreign campaigns of the Indian Army added greatly to its credit and glory. It was, and still is, a force of admirable efficiency and assured valour.

When war threatened in the summer of 1914, Field Force units were put on standby to serve in Europe. When the Germans invaded France in August, the Lahore and the Meerut infantry divisions were dispatched quickly from Karachi and Bombay. They arrived at Marseilles in late September and early October 1914, detraining at Orleans before marching to the front. (Other, smaller, Expeditionary Forces were sent to Basra, Egypt and East Africa.)

The Indian troops arrived in France trained and equipped only for a colonial war. Little money had been spent on Field Army support units: there was no mechanical transport, and the artillery (which was all British) and could be made up only by denuding other divisions. The sepoys had to exchange their rifles for the newer (but unfamiliar) pattern carried by the British Army. There were shortages of medical supplies and signalling apparatus. The Germans had trench mortars, searchlights and hand grenades; the Indians had none of these (although they improvised grenades from jam tins). It was even some months before all Indian units had their full complement of warm clothes.

As they arrived, these under-equipped troops were fed piecemeal into the front line in an attempt to stem the German rush between Ypres and La Bassee. The 129th Baluchis were the first Indian unit to see action, near Wytschaete in Belgium, in late October. Decorations were liberally bestowed in these fierce little actions, including the first Victoria Cross to be received by an Indian. But honours alone could not sustain the sepoys' morale, which went into steep decline with the onset of colder weather. The Indian troops were withdrawn for rest after heavy losses.

During the winter of 1914-15, the Indian Corps was built up to two infantry and two cavalry divisions, with an establishment of some 16,000 British and 28,500 Indian troops. In the spring, the Corps was moved to the Neuve Chapelle-Givenchy sector of the front, where it remained for almost a year, apart from the detachment of the Lahore Division for a few days in April 1915 during the Second Battle of Ypres.

For most of 1915, the Indian Corps held a front of approximately seven miles. The ground was boggy, cut with ditches, drains and canals, and crossed here and there with bridges. Movement off-road was very difficult and visibility was poor, with morning mists lingering on to midday for months on end. The landscape was almost completely flat, dotted with farmhouses and clumps of trees. The only high ground was the Aubers Ridge, held by the Germans a few hundred yards beyond the Indian front line, an elevation which the Indian soldiers could see but were destined never to reach. Most of the sepoys to die in Europe - some 7,700 - fell in these few square miles.

For the Indians, the war was one of ambuscades - raids and counter-raids, patrols and surprise attacks - punctuated with larger-scale attacks on the German lines. The first of these offensives was at Neuve Chapelle in March 1915. The sepoys' morale was boosted by an apparent success, tempered by very heavy losses - much higher than the Indian Army was used to in the bloody but brisk fighting on the North- West Frontier. The attack commenced on 10 March with a 35-minute bombardment. A second major attack was made at the Battle of Festubert in early May; and a third at the Battle of Loos in late September.

The morale of the troops began to fail again as their

second winter in France approached. Despite a year of fighting, and heavy losses, no end to the war was in sight. Casualties had been especially severe among British officers. Some units had lost nearly all their original officers within a couple of days' fighting, and it proved difficult to find men who could speak Indian languages to replace them. All the Indian Army officers who had been on leave in Britain at the outbreak of war had been commandeered to train the British battalions of the 'New Armies' and those currently in post were unknown to their men, inexperienced, and often commanded little confidence.

At the end of 1915, the two infantry divisions were withdrawn in the belief that their morale would not survive another winter of trench warfare in France. They were sent to join Expeditionary Force 'D' in Mesopotamia, where the Imperial war effort was deteriorating badly. In early 1916, the Indian troops were thrown into the failed attempts to relieve General Townshend's mixed British and Indian force besieged by the Turks at Kut-al-Amara, on the Tigris, downstream from Baghdad.

From then on, Mesopotamia became the focus of the main Indian war effort in 1917-18; Indian troops were prominent in the capture of Baghdad in 1917, and in the destruction of the Ottoman Empire in the region. The III Corps was a formation of the Indian Army during World War I formed in Mesopotamia. Earlier it was known as the Mesopotamia Expeditionary Force / Indian Expeditionary Force "D". Prior to the reorganization of the British and Indian forces in Mesopotamia, it was designated as the Tigris Corps. Initially formed in December 1915, it was split into two in November 1916 to form the I Corps. Under Frederick Stanley Maude it took part in the Mesopotamian campaign. Among its component divisions during World War I were the Cavalry Division, 3rd (Lahore) Division, 6th (Poona) Division, 7th (Meerut) Division, 12th Indian Division, 14th Indian Division, 17th Indian Division, and 18th Indian Division.

The force fighting in Mesopotamia was principally one of the Indian Army, with only one solely British formation, the 13th (Western) Division. The Indian formations contained some British units. Conditions in Mesopotamia defy description. Extremes of temperature (120 degrees F was common); arid desert and regular flooding; flies, mosquitoes and other vermin: all led to appalling levels of sickness and death through disease. Under these incredible conditions, units fell short of officers and men, and all too often the reinforcements were half-trained and ill-equipped. Medical arrangements were quite shocking, with wounded men spending up to two weeks on boats before reaching any kind of hospital. These factors, plus of course the unexpectedly determined Turkish resistance, contributed to high casualty rates.

The two Indian cavalry divisions stayed on in France until the spring of 1918. They numbered 13-14,000 men in total, including the British units attached to each brigade. There was little need or opportunity for mounted troops on the Western Front, and they were mainly kept in reserve. The cavalry saw some action on the Somme in 1916 and, the following year, during German withdrawal to the Hindenburg Line, and at Cambrai.

In early 1918, the cavalry were also transferred to the Middle East, where they took part in General Allenby's offensive against the Turks in Palestine, helping to win a great success at the Battle of Megiddo in September. By the time of the Armistice, India had provided over 1.27 million men, including 827,000 combatants, contributing roughly one man in ten to the war effort of the British Empire. The wartime Indian Army reached a highest strength of 573,000 combatants, with a maximum of 273,000 serving outside the subcontinent at any one time (mostly in Mesopotamia). Of the 947,000 Imperial war dead, some 49,000 were sepoys.

Nobody should forget the conditions under which these soldiers fought. They crossed swords in countries where the climate, language, people, and customs were entirely different from any of which they had knowledge. They were not consoled by amenities or alleviations which they could hope for in India. Nevertheless, their cheerfulness, loyalty, discipline and intrepid courage cannot be praised enough.

It is apt to quote the poet Rabindranath Tagore who wrote:

> *Let me not pray to be sheltered from dangers but be fearless in facing them.*
>
> *Let me not beg for the stilling of my pain but for the heart to conquer it.*
>
> *Let me not look for allies in life's battlefield but to my own strength.*
>
> *Let me not crave in anxious fear to be saved but hope for the patience to win freedom.*
>
> *Grant me that I may not be a coward, feeling your mercy in my success alone;*
>
> *But let me find the grasp of your hand in my failure.*

This publication deals with the details of the contribution of India in the Great War in statistical detail and should form the basis for studying its performance during a crucial period in history.

The official Names of the Battle and other engagements fought by the Military Forces of the British Empire during the Great War, 1914-1919, and the Third Afghan War, 1919 as classified by the Battles Nomenclature Committee and approved by the Army Council.

TABULATED LIST OF ENGAGEMENTS

Notes

The "Operations" column is intended to give a general outline of the course of events and thus form a guide to the list of engagements given in the column following.

In the "Geographical Limits" column, when no road, river or other geographical feature is mentioned, the limit must be understood to be a straight line between the localities named. These latter are always "inclusive" unless the contrary is stated. An asterisk indicates that no more exact definition of the battle-area can be given than that the engagement took place "in the neighbourhood of" the place named.

FRANCE AND FLANDERS.

Operations.	Battles.		Actions, etc.	Miscellaneous incidents.	Limits.	
	Name.	Tactical incidents included.			Chronological.	Geographical.
I.—THE GERMAN INVASION, 1914.						
The Retreat from Mons. (23rd August–5th September, 1914.)	....	..	..	..	23rd August—5th September.	North of the Seine, and east of the road Paris—Roye—Péronne—Cambrai—Valenciennes—Condé.
	BATTLE OF MONS	..	..	..	23rd–24th August	The river d'Estinne to Peissant: thence a line to Rouveroy—Quévy-le-Petit—Athis—Quiévrechain—Condé (*exclusive*).
			—*with subsidiary* Action of Elouges	..	24th August	
			Rearguard Action of Solesmes	..	25th August	Between the rivers S. Georges and d'Erclin, north of the line Salesches—Solesmes—St. Vaast.
			Affair of Landrecies	..	25th August	*
	BATTLE OF LE CATEAU	..	..	..	26th August	Bazuel (*exclusive*)—St. Souplet—Walincourt—Esnes.
			Rearguard Affair of le Grand Fayt	..	26th August	Neighbourhood of the villages of Marbaix and le Grand Fayt, and the ground between them.
			Rearguard Affair of Etreux	..	27th August	Neighbourhood of the villages of Fesmy and Etreux, and the ground between them.
			Affair of Cerizy	..	28th August	*
			Affair of Néry	..	1st September	*
			Rearguard Action of Crépy-en-Valois	..	1st September	North of Crépy-en-Valois.

			Rearguard Actions of Villers Cotterets	..	1st September	(a) Near Taillefontaine. (b) In the forest north of Villers Cotterets. (c) Near Pisseleux.
The Advance to the Aisne. (6th September–1st October, 1914.)	BATTLE OF THE MARNE, 1914†	Passage of the Petit Morin Passage of the Marne	..	..	7th–10th September	Château-Thierry—la Ferté-Gaucher—the river Grand Morin to Crécy: thence a line to Dhuisy.
	BATTLE OF THE AISNE, 1914†	Passage of the Aisne and Capture of the Aisne Heights, including the Chemin des Dames.	..	..	12th–15th September	Oulches—Maizy—Blanzy—Septmonts—Soissons—Crouy—Allemant.
			—*with subsequent* (i) Actions on the Aisne Heights	..	20th September	North of the Aisne, between Paissy and Vailly (*exclusive*).
			(ii) Action of Chivy	..	26th September	North of the Aisne, between Troyon and Beaulne.
The Defence of Antwerp. (4th–10th October, 1914.)	....	..	..	..	4th–10th October	
Operations in Flanders, 1914. (10th October–22nd November.)	BATTLE OF LA BASSÉE	..	..	..	10th October–2nd November	Road Noyelles-lez-Vermelles—Beuvry—Béthune (*exclusive*)—Estaires (*exclusive*): thence a line to Fournes (*exclusive*).
	BATTLE OF MESSINES, 1914	..	..	..	12th October–2nd November	The river Douve from Warneton to Dranoutre: thence a line to Caestre Station—Abeele Station—Reninghelst—Dickebusch—Voormezeele: thence along the Canal.
	BATTLE OF ARMENTIÈRES	Capture of Meteren	..	..	13th October–2nd November	Fournes—Estaires—Hazebrouck Station—Caestre Station—Dranoutre (*exclusive*): thence the river Douve.

† The tactical incidents and limits given for these battles refer only to the operations of the British troops engaged.

FRANCE AND FLANDERS—*continued.*

Operations.	Battles.		Actions, etc.	Miscellaneous incidents.	Limits.	
	Name.	Tactical incidents included.			Chronological.	Geographical.
I.—THE GERMAN INVASION, 1914—*continued.*						
Operations in Flanders, 1914—*contd.*	THE BATTLES OF YPRES, 1914	..	..	..	19th October 22nd November.	The Comines Canal to Ypres: thence the Yser Canal to Steenstraat: from there the road to Bixschoote and thence along the southern edge of the Houthulst Forest.
	(i) BATTLE OF LANGEMARCK, 1914	..	..	..	21st–24th October	
	(ii) BATTLE OF GHELUVELT	..	..	..	29th–31st October	
	(iii) BATTLE OF NONNE BOSSCHEN	..	..	..	11th November	
II.—TRENCH WARFARE, 1914-16.						
Winter Operations, 1914–15. (November–February.)	....	..	Defence of Festubert	..	23rd–24th November	Givenchy (*exclusive*)—Gorre: thence road to le Touret—Rue de l'Epinette—la Quinque Rue.
			Attack on Wytschaete	..	14th December	Road Wytschaete—Lindenhoek—Mt. Kemmel—la Clytte—Hallebast—Vierstraat—Wytschaete.
			Defence of Givenchy, 1914	..	20th–21st December	The la Bassée Canal to Gorre: thence road to le Touret—Rue de l'Epinette—la Quinque Rue.
			First Action of Givenchy, 1915	..	25th January	Road la Bassée—Annequin—Beuvry—Gorre—Festubert (*exclusive*).
			Affairs of Cuinchy	..	29th January, 1st and 6th February.	Between the road and canal from Beuvry to la Bassée.

Summer Operations, 1915 March–October.)	BATTLE OF NEUVE CHAPELLE			..	10th–13th March	Road Richebourg-l'Avoué—Croix—Barbée—Pont du Hem—Fauquissart—Aubers.
			Action of St. Eloi	..	14th–15th March	The Comines—Ypres railway as far as Zillebeke Lake, and thence the Zillebeke—Klein Zillebeke road.
			Capture of Hill 60	..	17th–22nd April	
	THE BATTLES OF YPRES, 1915	..	..	..	22nd April—25th May.	
	(i) BATTLE OF GRAVENSTAFEL RIDGE	The Gas Attack	..	..	22nd–23rd April	The Comines — Ypres Canal as far as Voormezeele: thence road to Vlamertinghe Chateau—Elverdinghe Château—Boesinghe—Langemarck.
	(ii) BATTLE OF ST. JULIEN	..	..	..	24th April–4th May	
	(iii) BATTLE OF FREZENBERG RIDGE	..	..	..	8th–13th May	
	(iv) BATTLE OF BELLEWAERDE RIDGE	..	..	..	24th–25th May	
	BATTLE OF AUBERS RIDGE	Attack at Fromelles	..	..	9th May	Road Aubers—Fauquissart—Laventie—Rouge-de-Bout—Fleur baix (*exclusive*)—la Boutillerie—Bas Maisnil.
		Attack at Rue du Bois	..	..		Road la Quinque Rue (*exclusive*)—le Touret—Lacouture—Croix Barbée: thence a line to the Bois du Biez (*South-West Corner*).
	BATTLE OF FESTUBERT	..	....	..	15th–25th May	The la Bassée Canal to Gorre: thence road to le Touret—Lacouture—Croix Barbée: thence a line to the Bois du Biez (*South-west Corner*).
			Second Action of Givenchy, 1915	..	15th–16th June	Givenchy—Gorre: thence road to le Touret—Rue de l'Epinette—la Quinque Rue (*exclusive*).
			First Attack on Bellewaerde	..	16th June	Gheluvelt—Zillebeke: thence road to Ypres (*exclusive*)—Zonnebeke.
			Actions of Hooge	..	19th and 30th July and 9th August	Gheluvelt—Zillebeke: thence road to Ypres (*exclusive*)—Zonnebeke.

FRANCE AND FLANDERS—*continued.*

Operations.	Battles.		Actions, etc.	Miscellaneous incidents.	Limits.	
	Name.	Tactical incidents included.			Chronological.	Geographical.
II.—TRENCH WARFARE, 1914-16—*continued.*						
Summer Operations, 1915—*contd.*	THE BATTLE OF LOOS	..	..	..	25th September–8th October	Road Aix-Noulette—Noeux-les-Mines—Béthune (*exclusive*)—Gorre—Festubert (*exclusive*).
			—*with subsidiary* (i) Action of Piètre	..	25th September	Haut Pommereau—Neuve Chapelle (*exclusive*)—Rouge Croix—Pont du Hem—l'Epinette—Aubers.
			(ii) Action of Bois Grenier	..	25th September	Bas Maisnil—Croix-Maréchal—Bac-St.-Maur—Erquinghem—Bois Grenier—Bois Blancs.
			(iii) Second attack on Bellewaerde	..	25th–26th September	Gheluvelt—Zillebeke: thence road to Ypres (*exclusive*)—Zonnebeke.
			—*and subsequent* Actions of the Hohenzollern Redoubt	..	13th–19th October	Road Hulluch—Loos—Fosse No. 7—Noyelles lez-Vermelles—Cambrin.
Local Operations, 1916.†	....		Actions of The Bluff	..	14th–15th February and 2nd March	Between the Ypres—Comines Canal and the Ypres—Comines railway (Ypres *exclusive*).
			Actions of St. Eloi Craters	..	27th March–16th April	Road Wytschaete—Vierstraat—Ypres (*exclusive*): thence the Ypres-Comines railway.
			German Attack on Vimy Ridge	..	21st May	Thélus—Neuville-St. Vaast—Mont-St.-Eloy—Carency—Ablain-St. Nazaire: thence along

					the Notre-Dame-de-Lorette ridge to the river Souchez.
	BATTLE OF MOUNT SORREL	..	..	.. 2nd–13th June	Between the Ypres—Comines Canal and the Ypres—Roulers railway (*Ypres exclusive*).

III.—THE ALLIED OFFENSIVE, 1916.

Operations on the Somme. (1st July–18th November, 1916.)	THE BATTLES OF THE SOMME, 1916	..	..	..	1st July–18th November.	
	(i) BATTLE OF ALBERT, 1916	Capture of Montauban Capture of Mametz Capture of Fricourt Capture of Contalmaison Capture of la Boisselle	..	..	1st–13th July	The Combles valley to Hardecourt: thence the road to Maricourt—Suzanne—Bray—Albert—Bouzincourt—Hédauville—Forceville—Bertrancourt—Sailly-au-Bois (*exclusive*)—Hébuterne—Puisieux-au-Mont.
			—with subsidiary Attack on the Gommecourt Salient	..	1st July	Road Puisieux-au-Mont—Hébuterne—Sailly-au-Bois—Bayencourt—Souastre—Humbercamps—Pommier—Berles-au-Bois—Monchy-au-Bois.
	(ii) BATTLE OF BAZENTIN RIDGE	Capture of Longueval Capture of Trônes Wood Capture of Ovillers	..	..	14th–17th July	Road Hardecourt—Maricourt—Fricourt—Bécourt—Albert (*exclusive*): thence the river Ancre.
			—with subsidiary Attack at Fromelles ‡	..	19th July	Road Aubers—Fauquissart—Laventie—Rouge-de-Bout—Fleurbaix (*exclusive*)—la Boutillerie—Bas Maisnil.
			—and subsequent Attacks on High Wood	..	20th–25th July	Road Flers—Longueval—Bazentin-le-Grand—Bazentin-le-Petit—Martinpuich.

† Previous to the Allied Offensive. ‡ On the Aubers Ridge.

FRANCE AND FLANDERS—*continued.*

Operations.	Battles.		Actions, etc.	Miscellaneous incidents.	Limits.	
	Name.	Tactical incidents included.			Chronological.	Geographical.
III.—THE ALLIED OFFENSIVE, 1916—*continued.*						
Operations on the Somme—*contd.*	THE BATTLES OF THE SOMME, 1916 —*contd.*					
	(iii) BATTLE OF DELVILLE WOOD	..	..	..	15th July–3rd Sep tember	Delville Wood.
	(iv) BATTLE OF POZIÈRES RIDGE	Fighting for Mouquet Farm	..	..	23rd July–3rd September	Road Bazentin-le-Petit—Contalmaison—Fricourt—Bécourt—Albert (*exclusive*) thence the river Ancre.
	(v) BATTLE OF GUILLEMONT	..	..	..	3rd–6th September	The Combles valley to Hardecourt: thence road to Maricourt—Montauban—Longueval.
	(vi) BATTLE OF GINCHY	..	..	..	9th September	
	(vii) BATTLE OF FLERS—COURCELETTE	Capture of Martinpuich	..	..	15th–22nd September	The Combles valley to Hardecourt: thence road to Maricourt—Fricourt—Bécourt— Albert (*exclusive*): thence the river Ancre.
	(viii) BATTLE OF MORVAL	Capture of Combles Capture of Lesbœufs Capture of Gueudecourt	..	..	25th–28th September	The Combles valley to Hardecourt: thence road to Maricourt—Fricourt—Bécourt—la Boisselle—Bapaume.
	(ix) BATTLE OF THIEPVAL RIDGE		..	..	26th–28th September	The Bapaume road to Albert (*exclusive*): thence road to Martinsart—Engle belmer—Auchonvillers—Serre.

	(x) BATTLE OF THE TRANSLOY RIDGES	Capture of Eaucourt l'Abbaye Capture of le Sars Attacks on the Butte de Warlencourt	..	..	1st–18th October	The valley from Saily-Saillisel to Combles: thence road to Ginchy—Longueval—Martinpuich—Courcelette: thence the valley to Warlencourt.
	(xi) BATTLE OF THE ANCRE HEIGHTS	Capture of Schwaben and Stuff Redoubts and Regina Trench	..	..	1st October–11th November	Road Pys—le Sars—Martinpuich—Contalmaison—la Boisselle—Aveluy—Martinsart—Mesnil—Hamel.
	(xii) BATTLE OF THE ANCRE, 1916	Capture of Beaumont Hamel	..	..	13th–18th November	The Bapaume road to la Boisselle: thence road to Aveluy—Martinsart—Englebelmer—Mailly-Maillet—Colincamps—Hébuterne—Puisieux-au-Mont.

IV.—THE ADVANCE TO THE HINDENBURG LINE, 1917.

Operations on the Ancre. (11th January—13th March, 1917.)	....	..	Actions of Miraumont	..	17th and 18th February	Road Pys—Courcelette—Thiepval—Hamel—Beaucourt.
			Capture of the Thilloys	..	25th February–2nd March	Road Bapaume—Gueudecourt (*exclusive*)—le Sars—Pys (*exclusive*) Grevillers.
			Capture of Irles	..	10th March	Road Warlencourt—Courcelette—Miraumont: thence the railway to Achiet-le-Grand.
German Retreat to the Hindenburg Line. (14th March—5th April, 1917.)	....		Capture of Bapaume	..	17th March.	
				Occupation of Péronne	18th March.	

FRANCE AND FLANDERS—*continued.*

Operations.	Battles.		Actions, etc.	Miscellaneous incidents.	Limits.	
	Name.	Tactical incidents included.			Chronological.	Geographical.
	V.—THE ALLIED OFFENSIVES, 1917.					
The Arras Offensive (9th April—15th May, 1917.)	THE BATTLES OF ARRAS, 1917	..	..	..	9th April–4th May	
	(i) BATTLE OF VIMY RIDGE	..	..	..	9th–14th April	Willerval—Marœuil—Mont St. Eloy—Ablain-St. Nazaire—Liévin—Lens.
	(i) FIRST BATTLE OF THE SCARPE, 1917	Capture of Monchy-le-Preux Capture of Wancourt Ridge	..	..	9th–14th April	Chérisy—Hamelincourt—Marœuil (*exclusive*)—Willerval (*exclusive*).
	(ii) SECOND BATTLE OF THE SCARPE, 1917	Capture of Guémappe Capture of Gavrelle	..		23rd–24th April	The river Sensée from Vis-en-Artois to Ervillers (*exclusive*): thence a line to Dainville (*exclusive*)—Bailleul—Oppy.
			—*with subsidiary* Attack on la Coulotte	..	23rd April	Road Méricourt—Vimy—Neuville-St. Vaast—la Targette—Souchez: thence the river Souchez.
	(iii) BATTLE OF ARLEUX	..	..	..	28th–29th April	Boiry-Notre-Dame—Monchy-le-Preux—Beaurains—Roclincourt—Vimy—Acheville.
	(iv) THIRD BATTLE OF THE SCARPE, 1917	Capture of Fresnoy	..	..	3rd–4th May	The river Sensée from Vis-en-Artois to St. Léger: thence a line to Boyelles—Beaurains—Roclincourt—Vimy—Acheville.

			—with subsequent (i) Capture of Rœux	..	13th–14th May	Boiry-Notre-Dame—Monchy-le-Preux—Athies—Fresnes-lez-Montauban.
			(ii) Capture of Oppy Wood	..	28th June	*
—with flanking operations. *(a) round Bullecourt (11th April–16th June.)*	....	..	First Attack on Bullecourt	..	11th April	Road Quéant (*exclusive*)—Noreuil—Vaulx-Vraucourt—"l'Homme Mort"—Ecoust-St. Mein—Hendecourt.
			German Attack on Lagnicourt	..	15th April	The railway Havrincourt—Beugny: thence road to Vaulx—Vraucourt—Ecoust-St. Mein—Hendecourt.
	BATTLE OF BULLECOURT	..	..	..	3rd–17th May	Road Quéant (*exclusive*)—Noreuil—Vaulx-Vraucourt—"l'Homme Mort"—Ecoust-St. Mein—Hendecourt.
			Actions on the Hindenburg Line	..	20th May–16th June	Road Quéant (*exclusive*)—Noreuil—Vaulx-Vraucourt—"l'Homme Mort"—Ecoust-St. Mein—Hendecourt.
(b) towards Lens (3rd June–26th August.)	....	..	Affairs south of the Souchez River	..	3rd-25th June	Road Méricourt—Vimy—Neuville-St. Vaast—la Targette—Souchez: thence the river Souchez.
			Capture of Avion	..	26th–29th June	Road Méricourt—Vimy—Neuville-St. Vaast—la Targette—Souchez: thence the river Souchez.
	BATTLE OF HILL 70	..		..	15th–25th August	The river Souchez from Lens to Angres: thence a line to Grenay—Vermelles Station—Vendin-le-Viell.

FRANCE AND FLANDERS—*continued.*

Operations.	Battles.		Actions, etc.	Miscellaneous incidents.	Limits.	
	Name.	Tactical incidents included.			Chronological.	Geographical.
V.—THE ALLIED OFFENSIVES, 1917—*continued.*						
The Flanders Offensive. (7th June–10th November, 1917.)	THE BATTLE OF MESSINES, 1917	Capture of Wytschaete	..	..	7th–14th June	Road Frelinghien—le Bizet—Petit Pont—Neuve Eglise—Dranoutre—Locre—la Clytte—Dickebusch—Kruisstraat: thence a line to Zillebeke—Gheluvelt.
			German Attack on Nieuport	..	10th–11th July	Between the Nieuport Canal and the sea, east of the road from Wulpen to Oost-Dunkerke Bains.
	THE BATTLES OF YPRES, 1917	..	..	..	31st July–10th November	The Comines—Ypres Canal as far as Voormezeele: thence road to Vlamertinghe Château—Elverdinghe Château—Woesten—Bixschoote.
	(i) BATTLE OF PILCKEM RIDGE	..	..	..	31st July–2nd August	
			—*with subsequent* Capture of Westhoek	..	10th August	
	(ii) BATTLE OF LANGEMARCK, 1917	..	..	..	16th–18th August	
	(iii) BATTLE OF THE MENIN ROAD RIDGE	..	..	..	20th–25th September	
	(iv) BATTLE OF POLYGON WOOD	..	..	..	26th September–3rd October	
	(v) BATTLE OF BROODSEINDE	..	..	..	4th October	
	(vi) BATTLE OF POELCAPPELLE	..	..	..	9th October	
	(vii) FIRST BATTLE OF PASSCHENDAELE	..	..	..	12th October	
	(viii) SECOND BATTLE OF PASSCHENDAELE	..	..	..	26th October–10th November	

The Cambral Operations. (20th November–7th December. 1917.)	BATTLE OF CAMBRAI, 1917	..	..	..	20th November–3rd December.	
		The Tank Attack	..	..	20th–21st November	Road Honnecourt—Villers-Guislain—Gouzeaucourt—Metz—Ruyaulcourt—Beaumetz—Morchies Lagnicourt—Quéant.
		Capture of Bourlon Wood	..	..	23rd–28th November	
		The German Counter-Attacks	..	..	30th November–3rd December	Road Ronssoy—Villers-Faucon—Fins—Ruyaulcourt and thence as above.
			—*with subsequent* Action of Welch Ridge	..	30th December	Road Banteux—Gonnelieu—Gouzeaucourt Station: thence the railway to Marcoing.

VI.—THE GERMAN OFFENSIVES, 1918.

The Offensive in Picardy. (21st March–5th April, 1918.)	THE FIRST BATTLES OF THE SOMME, 1918	‡	..	..	21st March–5th April	
	(i) BATTLE OF ST. QUENTIN	‡	..	..	21st–23rd March	The river Oise to Chauny: thence road to Guiscard—Ham—Péronne—Bapaume—Boyelles: thence the river Cojeul.
			Actions at the Somme Crossings	..	24th–25th March	The line of the Somme from Ham to Hem.
	(ii) FIRST BATTLE OF BAPAUME†	‡	..	..	24th–25th March	The river Somme to Bray; thence road to Albert—Martinsart—Sailly-au-Bois—Monchy-au-Bois—Arras: thence the river Scarpe.
	(iii) BATTLE OF ROSIÈRES	‡	..	..	26th–27th March	Between the rivers Avre and Somme, east of road Pierrepont—Mézières—Demuin—Villers Bretonneux—Corbie.
	(iv) FIRST BATTLE OF ARRAS, 1918	‡	..	..	28th March	Road Authuille—Bertrancourt—Couin—Gaudiempré—Arras—Oppy.

† The name of "Bapaume" has been adopted for this battle in the German official list.
‡ Owing to the confused nature of the fighting over such a great area, the Committee consider that it is undesirable to attempt to mention tactical incidents.

FRANCE AND FLANDERS—*continued.*

Operations.	Battles.		Actions, etc.	Miscellaneous incidents.	Limits.	
	Name.	Tactical incidents included.			Chronological.	Geographical.

VI.—THE GERMAN OFFENSIVES, 1918—*continued.*

Operations.	Name.	Tactical incidents included.	Actions, etc.	Miscellaneous incidents.	Chronological.	Geographical.
The Offensive in Picardy—*contd.*	THE FIRST BATTLES OF THE SOMME, 1918—*contd.*					
	(v) BATTLE OF THE AVRE	‡	..	..	4th April	Between the rivers Avre and Somme.
	(vi) BATTLE OF THE ANCRE, 1918	‡	..	..	5th April	Road Méricourt l'Abbé—Warloy—Acheux—Souastre—Monchy-au-Bois—Ayette.
			—*with subsequent* (i) Actions of Villers Bretonneux	..	24th–25th April	Between the rivers Avre and Somme.
			(ii) Capture of Hamel	..	4th July	Between the road Lamotte—Longueau and the Somme.
The Offensive in Flanders. (19th–20th April, 1918.)	THE BATTLES OF THE LYS	..	..	..	9th–29th April	
	(i) BATTLE OF ESTAIRES	First Defence of Givenchy, 1918	..	..	9th–11th April	The la Bassée Canal to Béthune: thence road to St. Venant: thence a line to Vieux Berquin: from there the road to Bailleul—Armentières (*all exclusive*).
	(ii) BATTLE OF MESSINES, 1918	Loss of Hill 63	..	..	10th–11th April	Road Armentières—Bailleul—Locre—Dickebusch—Voormezeele: thence the Ypres—Comines Canal.
	(iii) BATTLE OF HAZEBROUCK	Defence of Hinges Ridge Defence of Nieppe Forest	..	..	12th–15th April	The river Lawe from le Casan to Béthune (*exclusive*): thence the railway by Hazebrouck.

						(*exclusive*) to Caestre: thence road to Mont des Cats—Meteren.
	(iv) BATTLE OF BAILLEUL	Defence of Neuve Eglise	..	..	13th–15th April	Road Meteren—Mont des Cats—Boeschepe—Reninghelst—Ouderdom—Vierstraat—Wytschaete.
	(v) FIRST BATTLE OF KEMMEL RIDGE	..	..	..	17th–19th April	Road Meteren—Mont des Cats—Boeschepe—Reninghelst—Ouderdom—Vierstraat—Wytschaete.
	(vi) BATTLE OF BÉTHUNE	Second Defence of Givenchy, 1918	..	..	18th April	The la Bassée Canal to Béthune (*exclusive*): thence road to Chocques—Busnes—St. Venant—Merville.
	(vii) SECOND BATTLE OF KEMMEL RIDGE	..	..	..	25th–26th April	Road Meteren—Mont des Cats—Boeschepe—Reninghelst—Vlamertinghe—Ypres (*exclusive*): thence the Comines Canal.
	(viii) BATTLE OF THE SCHERPENBERG	..	..	..	29th April	Road St. Jans Cappel—Boeschepe—Reninghelst—Vlamertinghe—Ypres (*exclusive*): thence the Comines Canal.
			—*with subsequent* (i) Action of la Becque	..	28th June	The Lys Canal to St. Venant (*exclusive*): thence the road to Morbecque: thence a line to Swartenbrouck—Vieux Berquin.
			(ii) Capture of Meteren	..	19th July	The Meteren Becque to Flêtre: thence a line to Fontaine Houck—Bailleul Station.
The Offensive in Champagne. (27th May–6th June, 1918.)	BATTLE OF THE AISNE, 1918†	‡	..	..	27th May—6th June	Between the Chemin des Dames and the Montagne de Reims, east of the line Bouconville—Fismes—Verneuil.

† The French names for these battles have been adopted, but the tactical incidents and limits refer only to the operations of the British troops which formed part of the French Armies.

‡ Owing to the confused nature of the fighting over such a great area, the Committee consider that it is undesirable to attempt to mention tactical incidents.

FRANCE AND FLANDERS—*continued*.

VII.—THE ADVANCE TO VICTORY, 1918.

Operations.	Battles. Name.	Battles. Tactical incidents included.	Actions, etc.	Miscellaneous incidents.	Limits. Chronological.	Limits. Geographical.
The Counter-Attack in Champagne. (20th July–2nd August, 1918.)	THE BATTLES OF THE MARNE, 1918†	..	..	..	20th July–2nd August.	
	(i) BATTLE OF THE SOISSONNAIS AND OF THE OURCQ†	Attack on Buzancy (28th July). Capture of the Beugneux Ridge	..	..	23rd July–2nd August	Between the rivers Ourcq and Aisne, east of the line Breny—Vierzy—Pommiers.
	(ii) BATTLE OF TARDENOIS†	The fighting for the Ardre Valley.	..	..	20th–31st July	The Valley of the Ardre above Sarcy.
The Advance in Picardy. (8th August–3rd September, 1918.)	THE BATTLE OF AMIENS	..	..	..	8th–11th August	Between the roads Amiens—Roye and Amiens—Albert (*Amiens exclusive*).
			—*with subsequent* Actions round Damery	..	15th–17th August	Road Roye—Bouchoir—Rosières: thence the railway to Puzeaux.
The Advance in Flanders. (18th August–6th September, 1918.)	....	..	Action of Outtersteene Ridge	..	18th August	The railway from Bailleul to Strazeele Station: thence road to Strazeele—Meteren.
The Advance in Picardy—(*contd.*) (21st August–3rd September.)	THE SECOND BATTLES OF THE SOMME, 1918	..	..	..	21st August–3rd September	
	(i) BATTLE OF ALBERT, 1918	Capture of Chuignes	..	..	21st–23rd August	Road Chaulnes—Lamotte—Corbie—Warloy—Acheux—Souastre—Berles-au-Bois—Brétencourt—Héninel.

	(ii) SECOND BATTLE OF BAPAUME	Capture of Mont St. Quentin		..	31st August–3rd September	Road Athies—Chalunes—Rosières—Bray—Miraumont—Hamelincourt—St. Léger: thence a line to Noreuil—Mœuvres.
				Occupation of Péronne	1st September	
The Breaking of the Hindenburg Line (26th August–12th October, 1918.)	THE SECOND BATTLES OF ARRAS, 1918	..	..	..	26th August–3rd September.	
	(i) BATTLE OF THE SCARPE, 1918	Capture of Monchy-le-Preux	..	..	26th–30th August	Noreuil (*exclusive*)—St. Léger (*exclusive*)—Boisleux-au-Mont—Roclincourt—Bailleul—Oppy.
	(ii) BATTLE OF THE DROCOURT—QUÉANT LINE		..	..	2nd–3rd September	Mœuvres (*exclusive*)—Noreuil (*exclusive*)—St. Léger (*exclusive*)—Monchy-le-Preux—Pelves: thence the river Scarpe.
	THE BATTLES OF THE HINDENBURG LINE	..	..	..	12th September–9th October.	
	(i) BATTLE OF HAVRINCOURT	..	..	..	12th September	Road Gouzeaucourt—Fins—Ytres—Beaumetz—Morchies: thence a line to Mœuvres.
	(ii) BATTLE OF EPÉHY	..	..	..	18th September	St. Quentin (*exclusive*)—Beauvois—Cartigny—Manancourt: thence by the southern edge of Havrincourt Wood to Villers Plouich.
	(iii) BATTLE OF THE CANAL DU NORD	Capture of Bourlon Wood	..	..	27th September–1st October	Road Banteux—Gouzeaucourt (*exclusive*)—Fins (*exclusive*)—Ytres—Lagnicourt—Vis-en-Artois: thence the river Sensée.
	(iv) BATTLE OF THE ST. QUENTIN CANAL	Passage at Bellenglise Capture of Bellicourt Tunnel Defences	..	..	29th September–2nd October	Road St. Quentin (*exclusive*)—Vermand—Roisel—Villers-Faucon—Fins—Gouzeaucourt—Banteux (*exclusive*).

† The French names for these battles have been adopted, but the tactical incidents and limits refer only to the operations of the British troops which formed part of the French Armies.

FRANCE AND FLANDERS—*concluded.*

Operations.	Battles.		Actions, etc.	Miscellaneous incidents.	Limits.	
	Name.	Tactical incidents included.			Chronological.	Geographical.
			VII.—THE ADVANCE TO VICTORY, 1918—*continued.*			
The Breaking of the Hindenburg Line —*contd.*	THE SECOND BATTLES OF ARRAS, 1918—*contd.*					
	(v) BATTLE OF THE BEAUREVOIR LINE.	..	..	..	3rd–5th October	Road Sequehart—Bellenglise—Pontru—Epéhy—Vendhuille—Villers-Outréaux.
	(vi) BATTLE OF CAMBRAI, 1918	Capture of Villers-Outréaux Capture of Cambrai	..	..	8th–9th October	Road Fresnoy—Sequehart—Bellenglise Bellicourt—Vendhuille—Villers-Guislain—Villers-Plouich—Graincourt—Bourlon—Oisy-le-Verger: thence the river Sensée.
—*including* *The Pursuit to the Selle* (*9th–12th October.*)	....	..	..	..	9th–12th October	
The Final Advance:— † *Flanders* . . (*28th September —11th November.*)	BATTLE OF YPRES, 1918	..	..	..	28th September–2nd October	Road Armentières—Bailleul—Locre—Reninghelst—Vlamertinghe Château—Elverdinghe Château: thence a line to Moorslede.
	BATTLE OF COURTRAI	..	..	..	14th–19th October	Dottignies—Comine—Messines: thence along the ridge to Passchendaele: thence a line to Moorslede—Lendelede.

			—*with subsequent* (i) Action of Ooteghem	..	25th October	Road Bossuyt—St. Genois—Sweveghem—Nieuwe Kappaart: thence the stream to Waereghem, and from there the road to Wortegem.
			(ii) Action of Tieghem	..	31st October	The river Escaut to Avelghem: thence road to Heestert—Kattestraat—Vichte—Heirweg—Mooregem—Wortegem. *
† *Artois* . . (*2nd October–11th November.*)	....	..	Capture of Douai	..	17th October	
† *Picardy* . . (*17th October–11th November.*)	BATTLE OF THE SELLE	..	..	..	17th–25th October	The railway Boué—Busigny—Caudry: thence the stream to its junction with the river Escaut: thence the latter.
	BATTLE OF	Capture of Mont Houy	..	..	1st–2nd November	The Bavai—Cambrai road as far as Vendegies: thence the stream to its junction with the river Escaut: thence a line to Wallers: thence along the southern edge of the forests of Vicoigne and Raismes.
	BATTLE OF THE SAMBRE	Passage of the Sambre—Oise Canal Capture of le Quesnoy	..	..	4th November	The railway Boué—le Cateau (*exclusive*): thence road to Romeries—Famars—Onnaing: thence the railway to Mons.
			—*with subsequent* (i) Passage of the Grande Honnelle	..	5th–7th November	Between the Bavai—Cambrai road and the Valenciennes—Mons railway, east of the line Wargnies—Onnaing. *
			and			
			(ii) Capture of Mons	..	11th November	

† Compare Chaucer :—

"With him ther was his sanne, a yang Sqyer
" . . . .
" Of twenty yeer he was of age, I gesse,
" And he had been some tyme in chivalrye
" In Flaundres, in Artoys, and in Picardie.'

ITALY.

Operations.	Battles.		Actions, etc.	Miscellaneous incidents.	Limits.	
	Name.*	Tactical incidents included.			Chronological.	Geographical.
The Italian Offensives, 1917.	TENTH BATTLE OF THE ISONZO	..	..	..	12th May–8th June	Between Gorizia and the sea, east of the Isonzo.
	ELEVENTH BATTLE OF THE ISONZO	..	..	..	17th August–12th September	Between Gorizia and the sea, east of the Isonzo.
The Austrian Offensive, 1917.	TWELFTH BATTLE OF THE ISONZO	The stand on the Carso	..	..	24th October–18th November	Between the Carso and the Piave.
—*including The Retreat to the Piave.*						
The Austrian Offensive, 1918.	THE BATTLE OF THE PIAVE	..	..	..	15th–24th June	From the Astico to the Sea.
		The fighting on the Asiago Plateau	..	..	15th–16th June	The Asiago Plateau, north of the line Conco—Cogollo.
The Italian Offensive, 1918.	THE BATTLE OF VITTORIO VENETO	..	..	..	24th October–4th November	
		Passage of the Piave	..	..	23rd October–4th November	Between the railways Treviso—Conegliano and Treviso—Oderzo.
		The fighting in the Val d'Assa		..	1st–4th November	The Val d'Assa, north of Asiago.

MACEDONIA.

Retreat from Serbia on Salonika. (December, 1915.)	....	..	Actions of Kosturino	..	7th–8th December	North of the Serbo-Greek frontier.
Doiran Operations, 1916. (August–September.)	....	..	Affairs of Horseshoe Hill	..	10th–18th August	Between the Göl Ayak and the Selimli Dere.
			Action of Machukovo	..	13th–14th September	Between the Selimli Dere and the river Vardar.
Operations in the Struma Valley. (1916–1918.)	....	..	Action of the Karajaköi's —*including* *Capture of Yeniköi*	..	30th September—4th October, 1916	The Struma Valley above Lake Takhinos.
			Affair of Barakli Juma'a		31st October, 1916	
1917 Offensive (April–May.)	BATTLE OF DOIRAN, 1917 †	..	..	..	24th–25th April and 8th–9th May	Between the Doiran—Karasuli railway and the river Vardar.
1918 Offensive (1st–30th September.)	....	..	Capture of the Roche Noir Salient	..	1st–2nd September	Between the Vardar and the line Mayadag—Pardovitsa.
	BATTLE OF DOIRAN, 1918 ‡	..	..	..	18th–19th September	Between the Dova Tepe—Doiran—Karasuli railway and the river Vardar.
—*including* *The Pursuit to the Strumitsa Valley (22nd–30th September.)*	....	..	..	..	22nd–30th September	Dova Tepe—Doiran—Karasuli: thence the river Vardar to the confluence of the Koja Dere: thence the latter.

* The Italian names for these battles have been adopted, but the tactical incidents and limits refer only to the operations of the British troops which formed part of the Italian Armies. In 1917 these consisted of brigades of heavy artillery; in 1918 of complete British formations.

† This battle forms part of the "Battle of the Vardar." (*French official title.*)

‡ This battle forms part of the "Battle of Monastir—Doiran." (*French official title.*)

DARDANELLES.

Operations.	Battles.		Actions, etc.	Miscellaneous incidents.	Limits.	
	Name.	Tactical incidents included.			Chronological.	Geographical.
Helles Operations . (25th April, 1915–8th January, 1916.)	THE BATTLES OF HELLES	..	..	..	25th April—6th June.	
	(i) THE LANDING AT CAPE HELLES	Capture of Sedd el Bahr	..	..	25th–26th April	All landings on the southern end of the Gallipoli Peninsula.
			—*with subsidiary* Landing at Kum Kale			Landing by French force on the Asiatic shore.
	(ii) FIRST BATTLE OF KRITHIA	..	..	..	28th April	
			Actions of Eski Hissarlik †	..	1st–2nd May	From the Straits on the right to the sea on the left.
	(iii) SECOND BATTLE OF KRITHIA	First Action of Kereves Dere †	..	..	6th–8th May	
			Affair of Gurkha Bluff	..	12th May	From Gully Ravine on the right to the sea on the left.
	(iv) THIRD BATTLE OF KRITHIA	Second Action of Kereves Dere †	..	..	4th June	From the Straits on the right to the sea on the left.
			Third Action of Kereves Dere †	..	21st June	From the Straits on the right to Achi Baba Nullah on the left
			Action of Gully Ravine	..	28th June–2nd July	From East Krithia Nullah (*exclusive*) on the right to the sea on the left.
			Fourth Action of Kereves Dere †	..	30th June	From the Straits on the right to Achi Baba Nullah on the left.
			Action of Achi Baba Nullah ‡	..	12th–13th July	From the Straits on the right to the Sedd el Bahr—Krithia road on the left.
			Actions of Krithia Vineyard ‡ §	..	6th–13th August	From Achi Baba Nullah on the right to Gully Ravine (*exclusive*) on the left.

‡			Affair of the Krithia Nullahs	..	29th December	From the Achi Baba Nullah on the right to West Krithia Nullah on the left
—*including The Evacuation of Helles (7th–8th January, 1916.)*	....	..	The last Turkish Attacks	..	7th January	From the Achi Baba Nullah on the right to the sea on the left.
Anzac and Suvla Operations (25th April–20th December, 1915.)	THE BATTLES OF ANZAC	..	..	..	25th April–30th June.	
	(i) THE LANDING AT ANZAC	..	..	.. —*with subsidiary* Demonstration in the Gulf of Xeros	25th–26th April	From Gaba Tepe (*exclusive*) to Fisherman's Hut (*exclusive*). *
			Attack on The Chessboard	..	2nd May	*
			Affair of Quinn's Post	..	10th May	*
	(ii) THE DEFENCE OF ANZAC	..	..	..	19th–21st May	From Gaba Tepe (*exclusive*) to Fisherman's Hut (*exclusive*).
			Affair of Holly Ridge ‖	..	28th June	*
			Defence of Walker's Ridge	..	30th June	*
	THE BATTLES OF SUVLA	..	..	..	6th–21st August	
	(i) BATTLE OF SARI BAIR	Capture of Lone Pine	..	..	6th–10th August	South of the Azmak Dere.
		Attack at Russell's Top				
	(ii) THE LANDING AT SUVLA	Capture of Karakol Dagh	..	..	6th–15th August	North of the Azmak Dere.
		Capture of Chocolate Hill				
				—*with subsidiary* Demonstration in the Gulf of Xeros	6th–7th August	*

* French official titles. ‡ The French titles for these actions are Fifth and Sixth Actions of Kereves Dere. § Subsidiary to the Battles of Suvla. ‖ Subsidiary to the Action of Gully Ravine.

DARDANELLES—*continued.*

Operations.	Battles.		Actions, etc.	Miscellaneous incidents.	Limits.	
	Name.	Tactical incidents included.			Chronological.	Geographical.
Anzac and Suvla Operations—*contd.*	THE BATTLES OF SUVLA—*contd.*					
	(iii) BATTLE OF SCIMITAR HILL	Attack on "W" Hill	..	..	21st August	North of the Azmak Dere.
			—*with subsidiary* Actions of Hill 60 (Anzac)	..	21st and 27th August	Between the Azmak Dere and the Aghil Dere.
—*including* *The Evacuation of Suvla and Anzac (19th–20th December, 1915.)*	....	..	..	..	19th–20th December.	

EGYPT AND PALESTINE.

SUDAN.

Operations.	Name.	Tactical incidents included.	Actions, etc.	Miscellaneous incidents.	Chronological.	Geographical.
Operations against the Sultan of Darfur. (1st March–31st December, 1916.)	....	..	Affair of Beringiya	..	22nd May	
				—*with subsequent* Occupation of El Fasher	23rd May	
			Affair of Gyuba	..	6th November	

WESTERN FRONTIER.

Operations against the Senussi. (23rd November, 1915–8th February, 1917.)	....	..	Affair of the Wadi Senab	..	11th–13th December, 1915	Area covered by the force under Lieut.-Colonel of L. R. Gordon.
			Affair of the Wadi Majid	..	25th December, 1915	Area covered by the two columns under Major-General A. Wallace.
			Affair of Halazin	..	23rd January, 1916	
			Action of Agagiya	..	26th February, 1916	Area covered by the force under Brigadier-General H. T. Lukin.
			Affairs in the Dakhla Oasis	..	17th–22nd October, 1916	
			Affairs near the Siwa Oasis	..	3rd–5th February, 1917	Siwa Oasis to Munasib.

EASTERN FRONTIER AND PALESTINE.

I.—The Defence of Egypt.

Defence of the Suez Canal. (26th January, 1915–12th August, 1916.)	....	..	Actions on the Suez Canal	..	3rd–4th February, 1915	East of the Suez—Qantara Railway.
			Affair of Qatia	..	23rd April, 1916	East of the Canal and north of El Ferdan Station.
	BATTLE OF RUMANI	..	..	..	4th–5th August, 1916	East of the Canal and north of Ismailia.
Operations in the Sinai Peninsula. (15th November, 1916–9th January, 1917.)	....	..	Affair of Magdhaba	..	23rd December, 1916	South and east of Bir Lahfan.
			Action of Rafah	..	9th January, 1917	North and east of Sheikh Zowa'id.

EGYPT AND PALESTINE—*continued.*

Operations.	Battles.		Actions, etc.	Miscellaneous incidents.	Limits.	
	Name.	Tactical incidents included.			Chronological.	Geographical.
			EASTERN FRONTIER AND PALESTINE—*continued.* **II.—The Invasion of Palestine.**			
The First Offensive (24th March–19th April, 1917.)	FIRST BATTLE OF GAZA	..	..	..	26th–27th March	North of the line Beersheba—Bela'.
	SECOND BATTLE OF GAZA	..	..	..	17th–19th April	
The Second Offensive (27th October–16th November, 1917.)	THIRD BATTLE OF GAZA	Capture of Beersheba. Capture of the Sheria Position	..	..	27th October–7th November	North of the Wadi Ghuzze.
			Affair of Huj	..	8th November	North of the line Beersheba—Gaza and west of the Beersheba—Jerusalem road.
			Action of El Mughar	..	13th November	
				—*with subsequent* Occupation of Junction Station	14th November	
Jerusalem Operations (17th November—30th December, 1917.)	BATTLE OF NEBI SAMWIL	..	..	..	17th–24th November	North and east of the line Hebron—Junction Station.
			Capture of Jerusalem	..	7th–9th December	
	DEFENCE OF JERUSALEM	..	..	..	26th–30th December	
	—*with subsidiary*— BATTLE OF JAFFA	..	..	..	21st–22nd December	Between the Tul Keram—Junction Station—Jaffa railway and the sea.

Operations in and beyond the Jordan Valley. (19th February–4th May, 1918.)	....	..	Capture of Jericho	..	19th–21st February	Between the Bethlehem—Nablus road and the Jordan, north of the line Jerusalem—Dead Sea.
			Passage of the Jordan	..	21st–23rd March	East of the Jordan.
			First Action of Es Salt	..	24th–25th March	East of the Jordan.
			First Attack on Amman	..	27th–30th March	East of the Jordan.
			Turkish Attack on the Jordan Bridge heads	..	11th April	East of the Jordan.
			Second Action of Es Salt	..	30th April–4th May	East of the Jordan.
—*with subsidiary Arab Operations in the Mountains of Moab. (March and April, 1918.)*	....	..	..	..	March and April	East of the Jordan.
Local Operations, 1918.	....	..	Actions of Tel Asur	..	8th–12th March	West of the Jordan, and north of the line Jericho—Ram Allah—Jaffa.
			Affair of Abu Telul	..	14th July	
The Final Offensive (18th September–31st October, 1918.)	THE BATTLES OF MEGIDDO	..	..	..	19th–25th September.	
	(i) BATTLE OF SHARON	..	..	..	19th–25th September	Between the Hejaz Railway and the sea, north of the line Dhaba Station—mouth of Jordan—Arsuf.
	(ii) BATTLE OF NABLUS	..	..	..	19th–25th September	Between the Hejaz Railway and the sea, north of the line Dhaba Station—mouth of Jordan—Arsuf.
			Actions beyond Jordan	..	23rd–30th September	Between the Hejaz Railway and the sea, north of the line Dhaba Station—mouth of Jordan—Arsuf.
			Capture of Amman	..	25th September	Between the Hejaz Railway and the sea, north of the line Dhaba Station—mouth of Jordan—Arsuf.
			Capture of Dera'a†	..	27th September	Between the Hejaz Railway and the sea, north of the line Dhaba Station—mouth of Jordan—Arsuf.
—*including The Pursuit through Syria. (26th September–31st October.)*	....	..	Capture of Damascus	..	1st October	North of the Haifa—Dera'a railway.
			Affair of Haritan	..	26th October	North of the Haifa—Dera'a railway.
				—*with subsequent* Occupation of Aleppo	26th October	North of the Haifa—Dera'a railway.

† Arab forces.

ARABIA.

Operations.	Battles.		Actions, etc.	Miscellaneous incidents.	Limits.	
	Name.	Tactical incidents included.			Chronological.	Geographical.
HEJAZ.						
The Arab Revolt (June–December, 1916.)	....	..	Attack on Medina	..	6th June	*
			Capture of Jidda	..	9th June	*
			Capture of Mecca	..	10th June	*
			Capture of Yenbo	..	27th July	
			Capture of Taif	..	22nd September	*
Operations against the Hejaz Railway. (October, 1916–November, 1918.)	....	..	..	..	October, 1916–November, 1918	From Ma'an to Medina.
Wejh Operations (January, 1917.)	....	..	Capture of Wejh	..	24th January	North of Yenbo.
Aqaba Operations (6th May–21st October, 1917.)	....	..	Affair of Aba el Lissan	..	3rd July	*
				Occupation of Aqaba	6th July	
			Turkish Attack on Petra	..	21st October	Between the Hejaz Railway and the Wadi Araba.

Tafile Operations (January–March, 1918.)	....	..	Actions for El Tafile	..	1st–28th January	Between the Hejaz Railway and the Wadi Araba.
				Seizure of the Turkish Dead Sea Flotilla	27th January	El Mezra'a.
Ma'an Operations (April–September, 1918.)	....	..	Affair of Shahim Station	..	20th April	*
			Affair of Mudawara Station	..	6th August	*
				Evacuation of Ma'an	23rd September	*

Note.—The operations of the Arab forces which co-operated with the British Army in their operations beyond Jordan and in the final offensive in Syria have been included under EGYPT AND PALESTINE.

SOUTHERN ARABIA.

Operations in the Bab el Mandeb. (1914–15.)	....	..	Capture of Sheikh Sa'id	..	10th November, 1914	Sheikh Sa'id Peninsula.
			Turkish Attack on Perim	..	14th–15th June, 1915	Perim Island (*Troops under the command of Captain H. A. C. Hutchinson*).
Defence of Aden (3rd July, 1915—31st October, 1918.)	....	..	Action of Lahej	..	4th–5th July, 1915	*
			Affair of Sheikh 'Othman	..	20th July, 1915	*
			Affair of Jabir	..	7th December, 1916	
			Affair of Imad	..	22nd October, 1918	*

MESOPOTAMIA.

Operations.	Battles.		Actions, etc.	Miscellaneous incidents.	Limits.	
	Name.	Tactical incidents included.			Chronological.	Geographical.
I.—THE CAMPAIGN IN LOWER MESOPOTAMIA.						
Basra Operations (6th November, 1914–14th April, 1915.)	....	..	..	Landing at Fao	6th November	Delta of the Shatt al 'Arab up to Basra.
			Affair of Saihan	..	15th November	
			Affair of Sahil	..	17th November	
				—*with subsequent* Occupation of Basra	22nd November	*
			First Action of Qurna	..	4th–8th December	The Tigris above Basra.
			Affair of Ahwaz	..	3rd March	North-west of Ahwaz (*exclusive*).
			Affair of Shaiba	..	3rd March	West of Shaiba (*exclusive*).
	BATTLE OF SHAIBA	..	..	..	12th–14th April	The inundation west of Basra and to the west of it.
Advance up the Tigris, 1915. (31st May–5th October.)	....	..	Second Action of Qurna	..	31st May	The Tigris above Qurna.
				—*with subsequent* Occupation of Amara	3rd June	*
	BATTLE OF KUT, 1915	..	..	..	28th September	The Tigris above Sanna-i-Yat.
—*with subsidiary Operations on the Karkha River. (7th May–3rd June.)*	....	..	Affair of Khafajiya	..	14th–16th May	*
Advance up the Euphrates, 1915. (27th June–25th July.)	....	..	Actions for Nasiriya	..	5th, 13th–14th, and 24th July	The Euphrates west of Khor al Hammar.

II.—THE FIRST CAMPAIGN FOR BAGHDAD.

Advance on Baghdad, 1915. (11th November–6th December, 1915.)	BATTLE OF CTESIPHON	..	..	..	22nd–24th November	The Tigris above Lajj.
			Affair of Umm al Tubul	..	1st December	The Tigris above Kut.
	—*with subsequent* DEFENCE OF KUT	The Christmas Eve Attack	..	..	7th December 1915–28th April, 1916	
Attempts to relieve Kut. (4th January–24th April, 1916.)	....	..	..	..	4th January–24th April.	
First Attempt (*4th–23rd January.*)	....	..	Action of Shaikh Sa'ad	..	6th–8th January	The Tigris above 'Ali Gharbi.
			Action of the Wadi	..	13th–14th January	The Tigris above Shaikh Sa'ad.
			First Attack on Hanna	..	21st January	The Tigris above the Wadi.
Second Attempt (*7th–10th March.*)	....	..	Attack on the Dujaila Redoubt	..	8th March	The Tigris above the Wadi.
Third Attempt (*1st–24th April.*)	....	..	Action of Falahiya, —*including Capture of Hanna*	..	5th April	The Tigris above the Wadi.
			First Attack on Sanna-i-Yat	..	6th April	
			Second Attack on Sanna-i-Yat	..	9th April	
			Action of Bait Aissa	..	17th–18th April	
			Third Attack on Sanna-i-Yat	..	22nd April	
				Capitulation of Kut	29th April	
Euphrates Operations, 1916. (January–September.)	....	..	Affair of Butaniya	..	14th January	North of Nasiriya.
			Action of As Sahilan	..	11th September	

MESOPOTAMIA—*continued.*

Operations.	Battles.		Actions, etc.	Miscellaneous incidents.	Limits.	
	Name.	Tactical incidents included.			Chronological.	Geographical.
III.—THE CAPTURE AND CONSOLIDATION OF BAGHDAD.						
Operations for the Capture of Kut, 1917. (13th December, 1916–25th February, 1917.)	BATTLE OF KUT, 1917	..	..	..	9th January–24th February	The Tigris above Shaikh Sa'ad.
		Capture of the Khadairi Bend	..	..	9th–19th January	
		Capture of the Hai Sailent	..	..	25th January–5th February	
		Capture of the Dahra Bend	..	..	9th–16th February	
		Capture of Sanna-i-Yat	..	..	17th–24th February	
		Passage at the Shumran Bend	..	..	23rd–24th February	
—*with subsequent Pursuit to Baghdad (25th February–10th March, 1917.)*	....	..	Passage of the Diyala	..	7th–10th March	The Tigris above Kut.
				—*with subsequent* Occupation of Baghdad	11th March	*
Operations for the consolidation of the position at Baghdad. (14th March–30th April, 1917.)	....	..	Action of Mushaidiya	..	14th March	The Tigris above Kadhimain.
			First Action of the Jabal Hamrin	..	25th March	Near Shahraban.
			Affair of Dali-'Abbas	..	27th–28th March	The Right bank of the River Diyala above Ba'quba.
			Affair of Dogame	..	29th March	The Tigris above Mushaidiya.
			Affairs on the Nahr Khalis	..	**9th–15th April**	**The Nahr Khalis Canal above Daltawa.**

			Passage of the 'Adhaim		18th April	The Tigris above Dogame.
			Action of Istabulat	..	21st–22nd April	The Tigris above the Shatt al 'Adhaim.
				—*with subsequent* Occupation of Samarra	23rd–24th April	*
			Affairs on the Shatt al 'Adhaim	..	30th April	The Shatt al 'Adhaim above its junction with the Tigris.

IV.—THE CAMPAIGN IN UPPER MESOPOTAMIA.

Euphrates Operations, 1917-18. (8th July–13th April.)	....	..	Attack on Ramadi	..	11th–14th July	The Euphrates above Dhibban.
			Capture of Ramadi	..	28th–29th September	The Euphrates above Dhibban.
			Action of Khan Baghdadi	..	26th–27th March	The Euphrates above Hit.
				—*with subsequent* Occupation of Ana	28th March	*
				Blockade of Najaf	1st–13th April	*
Tigris Operations, 1917 (1st October–6th December.)	....	..	Second Action of the Jabal Hamrin	..	18th–20th October	North of Shahraban.
			Actions for Tikrit	..	24th October, 2nd and 5th November	The Tigris above Al Ajik.
			Third Action of the Jabal Hamrin	..	3rd–6th December	North of Shahraban.
Kirkuk Operations. (25th April–24th May, 1918.)	....	..	Action of Tuz Khurmatli	..	29th April	North of Kifri.
Advance on Mosul. (23rd October–5th November, 1918.)	....	..	Action of Fatha Gorge	..	23rd-24th October	The Tigris above Tikrit.
			Actions on the Lesser Zab	..	25th October	The Tigris above Fatha Gorge.
	BATTLE OF SHARQAT	..	..	..	28th–30th October	The Tigris above Fatha Gorge.
			Affair of Qaiyara	..	30th October	The Tigris above Fatha Gorge.
				—*with subsequent* Occupation of Mosul	3rd November	*

PERSIA AND CENTRAL ASIA.

Operations.	Battles.		Actions, etc.	Miscellaneous incidents.	Limits.	
	Name.	Tactical incidents included.			Chronological.	Geographical.
SOUTH PERSIA AND THE PERSIAN GULF.						
Defence of the Gulf Ports, 1915.	....	..	Defence of Muscat	..	10th–11th January	*
			Defence of Jask	..	16th–17th April	*
			Defence of Chahbar	..	2nd–3rd May	*
			Destruction of Dilbar	..	12th–16th August	*
			Defence of Bushire	..	9th September	*
—*with subsequent Operations of the Makran Mission. (11th April, 1916–2nd February, 1917.)*	....	..	..	..	..	Persian Makran.
Establishment of order, 1916.	....	..	Capture of Saidabad	..	28th September	*
				Occupation of Shiraz and formation of the South Persia Rifles	12th November	Fars.
			Affair of Dasht-i-Arjan	..	25th December	*
Opening of the trade routes. (1st January–30th November, 1917.)	....	..	Affair of Kafta	..	5th July	*
			Affairs in the Lashani country	..	19th–30th September	The valley on the north side of Lake Niriz
			Affairs in the Chahar Rah country	..	1st–21st October	Northern Fars

Recrudescence of disorders. (14th December, 1917–31st January, 1918.)	....	..	Affairs of Gumun	..	24th–27th January	Arsinjan district, east of the Shiraz—Deh Bid road.
Operations in Northern Fars. (3rd–23rd May, 1918.)	....	..	Affair of Ziarat	..	13th–14th May	*
			Affair of Kuh-i-Khan	..	16th May	*
Qashqai Operations, 1918.	....	..	Action of Deh Shaikh	..	25th–26th May	*
				Persian Mutiny at Khan-i-Zinian	25th May	*
			Action of Ahmadabad	..	16th June	*
			Affair of Chanar Rahdar	..	7th–8th July	*
			Defence and Relief of Abadeh	Persian Mutiny	28th June-17th July	*
			Defence and Relief of Firuzabad	..	16th–24th October	Firuzabad and the Khajai valley
Persian Operations, round Ispahan and in Fars, 1919.	....	..	Capture of Kadarjan	..	10th June	*
			Capture of Feragheh	..	8th August	*
Establishment of line of communication between Bushire and Shiraz. (29th September, 1918–10th March 1919.)	....	..	..	Consolidation of the coastal belt and occupation of Borazjun	29th September–23rd October	Between Bushire and Borazjun.
			Affair of Lardeh	..	31st October	*
				Seizure of the Kamarij Pass	20th December	*
				Occupation of Kazarun	27th January	*
				Junction between the Bushire and Shiraz Columns	28th January	Mian Kotal.
				Punitive measures in Southern Fars	11th December-10th March	Area Bushire—Kazarun—Shiraz—Firuzabad.

PERSIA AND CENTRAL ASIA—*continued.*

Operations.	Battles.		Actions, etc.	Miscellaneous incidents.	Limits.	
	Name.	Tactical incidents included.			Chronological.	Geographical.
EAST PERSIA AND TRANS-CASPIA.						
Establishment of the East Persia Cordon. (29th July, 1915–31st January, 1918.)	....	..	..	Occupation of Birjand and junction with Russian Cordon	7th October, 1915	The Nushki—Kacha—Birjand road.
				Captures of German agents	17th January and 8th August, 1916	Deh Salm and Sehdeh.
			Affair of Lirudik	..	13th–14th April, 1916	*
			Affair of Kundi	..	17th–18th April, 1916	*
				Occupation of Kwash (*Vasht*)	11th May 1916	*
			Affair of the Gusht Defile	..	19th–21st July, 1916	*
			Affair of Kalmas	..	26th September, 1916	*
Extension of the Cordon into Khorasan. (1st February–18th July, 1918.)	....	..	..	Occupation of Meshed	3rd March	*

Operations in Trans-Caspia against the Bolsheviks. (19th July, 1918-15th March, 1919.)	....	..	Affairs near Kaakhka	..	28th August, 11th and 18th September.	
			Action of Dushak	..	12th October	
				—*with subsequent* Occupation of Merv	1st November	
			Action of Annen kovo	..	16th January	

NORTH-WEST PERSIA AND THE CASPIAN, 1918.

Establishment of line of communication between Baghdad and the Caspian. (27th January-29th July.)	....	..	Affair near Zuhab	..	25th April	*
			Defence of Resht	..	20th July	*
Caspian Operations (August—September.)	....	..	..	Occupation of Baku	4th August	*
				Occupation of Krasnovodsk	27th August	*
			Defence of Baku	..	26th August—15th September.	*
Azerbaijan Operations. (September.)	....	..	Rearguard Actions from Mianeh	..	5th–14th September.	North-West of Nikpai.

INDIA.†

Operations.	Battles.		Actions, etc.	Miscellaneous incidents.	Limits.	
	Name.	Tactical incidents included.			Chronological.	Geographical.
NORTH-WEST FRONTIER AND BALUCHISTAN, 1914-1918.						
North-West Frontier.						
Operations in the Tochi. (28th November, 1914–27th March, 1915.)	....	..	Affair of Miran Shah	..	28th–29th November.	*
			Affair of Spina Khaisora	..	7th January	*
			Action of Dardoni	..	25th–26th March	*
Operations against the Mohmands. (14th–19th April, 1915.)	....	..	First Affair of Hafiz Kor	..	18th April	North-west of road Abazai—Shabkadr—Michni.
Operations against the Mohmands, Bunerwals and Swatis. (17th August-28th October, 1915.)	....	..	Affair near Rustam	..	17th August	*
			Affair of Surkhawi	..	26th August	*
			Affairs of Landakai and Kak Fort	..	27th–29th August	Swat Valley above Thana.
			Affairs near Malandri	..	28th–31st August	*
			Action of Hafiz Kor	..	5th September	North-west of road Abazai—Shabkadr—Michni.
			Second Affair of Hafiz Kor	..	9th October	North-west of road Abazai—Shabkadr—Michni.
			Affair near Wuch	..	27th October	Wuch Valley north of Chakdarra (*exclusive*).

The Mohmand Blockade. (30th September, 1916–19th July, 1917.)	....	..	Third Affair of Hafiz Kor	..	15th November	North-west of road Abazai—Shabkadr—Michni.
Operations against the Mahsuds. (2nd March–10th August 1917.)	....	..	Defence of Sarwekai	..	2nd-8th March	*
			Affairs of the Gwalerai Pass	..	9th April–1st and 16th May	The Gumal between Nili Kach and Kajuri Kach (*both exclusive*).
			Action of Kharkhwasta	..	9th–10th May	The route between the Khuzma Post and Sarwekai.
			Actions in the Shahur Valley	..	19th–24th June	The Shahur Valley above Haidari Kach, Nanu and the Khaisora.

Baluchistan.

Kalat Operations (i) 1st June–10th July, 1915.	....	..	..	..	..	South of Mastung.
(ii) 5th June–18th August, 1916.	....	..	Affair of Wadh	..	25th June	South of Mastung.
Operations against the Marri and Khetran tribes. (18th February–8th April, 1918.)	....	..	Defence of Gumbaz Post	..	19th–20th February	*
			Affair of Fort Munro	..	15th March	*
			Capture of the Hadb Position	..	6th April	*

† Up to the end of the Third Afghan War (*8th August 1919*).

INDIA—*continued.*

Operations.	Battles.		Actions, etc.	Miscellaneous incidents.	Limits.	
	Name.	Tactical incidents included.			Chronological.	Geographical.
THE THIRD AFGHAN WAR (6th May-8th August, 1919).						
Chitral Operations†	.. .	..	Capture of Arnawai	..	23rd–24th May	Kala Drosh (*exclusive*) Narai.
			Affair in the Bumboret Valley	..	17th July	The Bumboret Valley.
Khyber Operations†	....	..	Action of Bagh Springs	..	9th–11th May	The Khyber, north-west of Landi Kotal.
				—*with subsequent* Occupation of Dakka	13th May	*
			Affairs near Ali Masjid	..	15th and 16th May	The Khyber, between Fort Maude and Gurgura Post
			Action of Dakka	..	16th and 17th May	North-west of Paindi. Khakh.
			Affairs near Fort Maude	..	18th and 19th July	*
Kurram Operations†	....	..	Afghan Attack on Thal	..	26th–31st May	*
			Relief of Thal	..	30th May–3rd June	West of Doaba (*exclusive*).
			Affairs in the Upper Kurram	..	27th May–2nd June	The Kurram above Alizai.
Waziristan and Derajat Operations.†	....	.	..	Evacuation of Militia Posts	25th–30th May	The Tochi Posts above Miran Shah and Spinwam line, and the South Waziristan Posts.
			Affair near Miran Shah	..	1st June	*
			Affair near Draband	..	3rd June	*
			Defence and Relief of Jandola.	..	28th May–9th June	The route from Khirgi (*exclusive*) to Jandola.

Zhob Operations†	....	..	Withdrawal from Wana	..	25th–31st May	The route between Wana and Fort Sandeman.
			Affairs round Fort Sandeman	..	3rd June–14th July	The Lower Zhob.
			Affair near Kapip	..	15th–17th July	The road between Babar and Kapip.
			Affair of Hindu Bagh	..	22nd July	*
Chaman Operations†	....	..	Capture of Spin Baldak Fort	..	27th May	*

NORTH-EAST FRONTIER AND BURMA.

Punitive measures in the Kachin Hills. (31st December, 1914–28th February, 1915.)	....	..	..	..	..	The area bounded *on the north* by latitude 26°30. *On the east* by the River Mali · Kha from where it cuts 26°30 to the confluence, and thence the Irrawaddy until it cuts 25°15. *On the west* longitude 96°. *On the south* latitude 25°.
Punitive measures in the Chin Hills. (1st December, 1917–1st June, 1918.)	....	..	..	..	..	*Eastern Boundary.*—Left bank of Chindwin River. *Southern Boundary.*—Bargelai 23° 45″, west to longitude 93°. *Western Boundary.*—Longitude 93° to Lakhipur; thence adjoining Lakhipur to Manipur Road Station.
Operations in the Kuki Hills (1st November, 1918–15th May, 1919.)	....	.	..	..	..	*Northern Boundary.*—A line joining Manipur Road Station east to Tuzu River at point of junction 42 miles east by north from Kohima; thence follow river to junction with Chindwin. Troops at Kindat, Mawlaik and Monywa are also included.

† The period for all these operations is 6th May–8th August, 1919.

RUSSIA.

Operations.	Battles.		Actions, etc.	Miscellaneous incidents.	Limits.	
	Name.	Tactical incidents included.			Chronological.	Geographical.
			MURMAN.			
Seizure of the Railway, 1918.	....	..	..	Disarmament of the Bolsheviks as far as Soroki.	29th and 30th June.	Kandalaksha and Kem.
Operations in Karelia, 1918.	....	..	Capture of Ukhtinskaya	..	11th September	
			Capture of Voknavolotskaya	..	21st September	*
			Action near Pyavozero Lake	..	3rd October	*
Winter Operations, 1918–19.	....	..	..	Occupation of Rugozerski	16th January, 1919	West of the railway and south of Soroki.
			Capture of Segeja	..	18th February	South of the line, Rugozerski—Kem—Sumski Posad.
			..	Transfer of troops to the Archangel front	February to April	The Soroki—Onega road beyond Sumski Posad.
Advance to Lake Onega, 1919.	....	..	Capture of Urosozero	..	11th April	South of the line Rugozerski—Kem—Sumski Posad.
			Capture of Maselskaya	..	3rd May	
				Occupation of Povyenets	18th May	South of the line Olimpi Sumski Posad—Nyukhhotskoe.
			Capture of Medvyejya Gora	..	21st May	South of Maselskaya.

Lake Onega Operations, 1919.	....	..	Capture of Kyapeselga ..	5th July	South of Maselskaya.
			Flotilla Actions ..	5th June, 3rd July, 2nd and 28th August.	Lake Onega.
Operations to cover withdrawal, 1919.	....	..	Action of Svyatnavolotski ..	27th August	South of Maselskaya.
			Capture of Lijma ..	14th–16th September	
			The Evacuation	1st–12th October	Murmansk and Kem.

ARCHANGEL.

Seizure of the White Sea ports and Initial Advances. (July–October, 1918.)	....	..	Capture of Archangel ..	1st and 2nd August	Mudyug Island to Archangel.
			Affair of Chunovskaya ..	3rd August	The Onega—Obozerskaya road.
			Affair of Puchuga ..	24th August	The Dvina above Seletski.
			Affairs about Obozerskaya ..	31st August and 4th September	The Vologda railway south of the Kenza river.
			Actions of Chamova ..	12th-14th September	The Dvina above Bereznik (*exclusive*).
			Affairs on the Yemtsa River ..	16th and 28th–29th September	The Yemtsa above the confluence of the Tyugra.
			Affair of Seletski ..	11th October	The Dvina above Tulgas (*exclusive*).
			Affairs near Chekuevo ..	12th–17th October	The Onega above Chekuevo.
Defensive Operations, 1918-19. (October–August.)	....	..	Affair of Kleshevo ..	27th December	The Onega above Chekuevo.
(a) *On the Onega River and the Vologda Railway.*	....	..	Affairs near Bolshi Ozerki ..	17th March—18th April	*
			Defence of Bolshi Ozerki ..	22nd–23rd July	*
(b) *Between the Vologda Railway and the Dvina River.*	....	..	Affairs at Tarasovo ..	25th and 29th January	*
			Attack on Kadish ..	7th February	Between Kadish and Avdinskaya.
			Defence of Sredmekhrenga ..	8th–11th February	*

RUSSIA—*continued.*

Operations.	Battles.		Actions, etc.	Miscellaneous incidents.	Limits.	
	Name.	Tactical incidents included.			Chronological.	Geographical.
ARCHANGEL—*continued.*						
Defence Operations, 1918-19—*contd.*						
(c) *On the Dvina and Vaga Rivers.*	....	..	Affair of Tulga	..	11th–13th November	The Dvina above Chamova.
			Defence of Shenkursk	..	16th–25th January	The Vaga above Bereznik (*exclusive*).
			Affairs round Vistavka	..	1st–4th and 8th–10th March	The Vaga above Bereznik (*exclusive*).
			Affair of Ignatyevskoe	..	26th June	The Vaga above Bereznik.
(d) *On the Pinega River.*	....	..	First Affair of Ust-Pocha	..	1st-3rd June	The Pinega above Pinega.
Operations to cover withdrawal. (August–September, 1919.)	BATTLE OF TROITSA	..		..	10th August	The Dvina above Troitsa.
			Affair of Yemtsa	..	29th–31st August	The Vologda Railway south of Obozerskaya.
			Second Affair of Ust-Pocha	..	4th September	The Pinega above Pinega.
				The Evacuation	27th September	Archangel.
SIBERIA.†						
Ussuri Operations (8th–28th August, 1918.)	BATTLE OF DUKHOVSKAYA	..	..	..	23rd–24th August	Between the lesser Ussuri River and Lake Khanka, north of Dukhovskaya.
fa Operations (October, 1918–June 1919.)	....	..	....	..	October, 1918–June, 1919	*

FAR EAST AND PACIFIC.

CHINA.

Siege of Tsing-Tau . (23rd September–7th November, 1914.)	....	..	..	..	23rd September–7th November	*

AUSTRALASIA.

(Conquest of the German Pacific Possessions.)

Operations of the New Zealand Expeditionary Force. (14th–30th August, 1914.)	....	..	..	Occupation of Samoa	29th August	*
Operations of the Australian Naval and Military Expeditionary Force. (11th September–6th November, 1914.)	....	..	Affair of Herbertshöhe	..	12th September	*
				Surrender of the German Forces.	21st September	Herbertshöhe.

† Including the operations of Siberian forces in European Russia.

EAST AFRICA.

Operations.	Battles.		Actions, etc.	Miscellaneous incidents.	Limits.	
	Name.	Tactical incidents included.			Chronological.	Geographical.
I.—THE CAMPAIGNS OF 1914-16.						
Northern and Eastern Areas.						
Defence of the Uganda Railway. (August–October, 1914.)	....	..	..	German Occupation of Taveta	15th August	
			Affair of Tsavo	..	6th September	*
			Affair of Majareni	..	23rd September	*
			Affair of Gazi	..	8th October	*
First Invasion of German East Africa. (2nd–6th November, 1914.)	....	..	Attack on Tanga	..	2nd–5th November	The port of Tanga.
			Affair of Longido	..	3rd November	Neighbourhood of Mt. Longido, south of Manga (*exclusive*).
Umba Valley Operations. (10th December, 1914–8th February, 1915.)	....	..	Affair of Jasin	..	18th–19th January.	The Umba Valley.
Victoria Nyanza Operations (August, 1914–July, 1916.)	....	..	Affairs on the Kagera River	..	August, 1914–July, 1916	South of the line Mbarara—Kanyanga.
			Capture of Bukoba	..	22nd–23rd June, 1915	*
				Occupation of Mwanza	14th July, 1916	*

Operations covering the construction of the Voi—Taveta Railway. (May, 1915–February, 1916.)	....	..	Affair of Mbuyuni		14th July	West of Kampi ya Bibi (*exclusive*).
			Attack on Salaita Hill	..	12th February	West of Mbuyuni (*exclusive*).
Kilimanjaro Operations. (5th–21st March, 1916.)	....	..	Action of Latema Nek	..	11th–12th March	West of Serengeti Camp (*exclusive*) on the Taveta line of advance, and south of Longido (*exclusive*) on that line.
			Action of Kahe	..	21st March	
Kondoa Irangi Operations (3rd April–10th May, 1916.)	....	..	Capture of Kondoa Irangi	..	17th–19th April	South-west of Arusha.
			German Attack on Kondoa Irangi	..	9th–10th May	
Operations for the Northern Railway, and Pursuit to the Nguru Hills. (18th May–24th June, 1916.)	....	..	Affair of German Bridge	..	30th May	South of the Ruvu (*Pangani*) River.
			Action of Mkaramo	..	9th June	
				Occupation of Handeni	19th June	
Operations for the Central Railway—						
(a) *Seizure of the Railway from Kilimatinde to Kilosa.* (*24th June–22nd August, 1916.*)	....	..	..	..	24th June–22nd August	South of Kondoa Irangi (*exclusive*).
(b) *Advance through the Nguru Hills to Morogoro.* (*5th–26th August, 1916.*)	....	..	Affair of Matamondo	..	10th–11th August	South of Msiha Camp (*exclusive*).
			Affairs on the Wami River	..	13th–17th August	
Clearing of the Uluguru Mountains. (27th August–15th September, 1916.)	....	..	Affair of Kisaki	..	7th September	South of Central Railway (*exclusive*).
			Affair of Dutumi	..	11th–13th September	
			—*with subsequent* Affair of Kisangire	..	9th October	

EAST AFRICA—*continued.*

Operations.	Battles.		Actions, etc.	Miscellaneous incidents.	Limits.	
	Name.	Tactical incidents included.			Chronological.	Geographical.

I.—THE CAMPAIGNS OF 1914-16—*continued.*

Northern and Eastern Areas—*continued.*

Operations.	Name.	Tactical incidents included.	Actions, etc.	Miscellaneous incidents.	Chronological.	Geographical.
Coast Operations . (January, 1915–December, 1916.)	....	..	..	Seizure of Mafia Island	10th–12th January, 1915	*
				Destruction of the "Königsberg"	11th July, 1915	River Rufiji.
				Landing at Manza Bay	4th July, 1916	*
				Landing at Pangani	23rd July, 1916	
				Landing at Sadani	1st August, 1916	
				Landing at Bagamoyo	15th August, 1916	*
				Landings at Konduchi and Msasani Bay	2nd September, 1916	
				Occupation of Dar es Salaam	4th September, 1916	*
				Landings at Kilwa Kivinje and Kilwa Kisiwani	7th September, 1916	*
				Landings at Lindi, Sudi Bay, and Mikindani	13th–16th September, 1916	*

Southern and Western Areas.

Defence of the Nyasaland—Rhodesia Border. (August, 1914–24th May, 1916.)	....	..	Affairs near Karonga	..	9th September, 1914	*
			Defence of Abercorn	..	5th–9th September, 1914	*
			Defence of Fife	..	6th–27th December, 1914	
			Affair of Sphinxhaven	Destruction of the "Hermann von Wissmann"	30th May, 1915	*
			Defence of Saisi	..	28th–29th June and 26th July–2nd August, 1915	*
Operations on Lake Tanganyika. (23rd December, 1915–March, 1916.)	....	..	Capture of the "Kingani"	..	26th December	Lake Tanganyika.
			Sinking of the "Hedwig von Wissmann"	..	9th February	
Advance from the Nyasa—Tanganyika line. (25th May–23rd June, 1916.)	....	..	..	Occupation of Neu Langenburg	27th May	*
				Occupation of Bismarckburg	8th June	*
				Occupation of Ubena	23rd June	*
Advance on Iringa. (23rd June–10th September, 1916.)	....	..	First Affair of Malangali	..	24th July	*
				Occupation of Iringa	29th August	*
Operations on the Ruhuje. (18th August–31st October, 1916.)	....	..	Affairs near Mkapire	..	28th September and 30th October.	
Operations against the Tabora Force. (8th October–26th November, 1916.)	....	..	Second Affair of Malangali	..	8th–12th October	*
			Defence of Lupembe	..	12th–14th November	*
			Affairs about Ngominyi and Muhanga	..	19th–29th October	*
			Capture of Ilembule	..	24th–26th November	*
Operations in the Songea District. (10th September–31st December, 1916.)	....	..	Defence of Songea	..	14th November	*

EAST AFRICA—*continued.*

Operations.	Battles.		Actions, etc.	Miscellaneous incidents.	Limits.	
	Name.	Tactical incidents included.			Chronological.	Geographical.
II.—THE CAMPAIGNS OF 1917.						
Advance to the Rufiji. (December, 1916–January, 1917.)	....	..	Affairs about Kibata	..	6th–16th December, 1916.	*
			Affair of Wiransi	..	1st January	*
			Action of Beho Beho	..	3rd–4th January	*
			Affair of Kibambawe	..	6th–7th January	*
			Capture of Mkindu	..	18th January	*
			Affair of Nyandete	..	24th January	*
Operations in the Kilwa and Lindi Areas, and advance to the Portuguese Frontier. (April–November, 1917.)	....	..	Affair of Ngaura	..	18th April	*
			Affair of Lutende	..	30th June	*
			Affair of Mnindi	..	6th July	*
			Action of Narungombe	..	19th July	*
			Affair of Tandamuti	..	3rd August	*
			Affair of Narunyu	..	18th August	*
			Affair of Bweho Chini	..	22nd September	*
			Action of Nyangao†	..	16th–19th October	*
			Affair of Lukuledi	..	21st October	*
			Affairs round Chiwata	..	6th–18th November	*
				Surrender of Tafel's Force	28th November	The Mwiti Valley.

Operations in the Songea District and advance on Liwalo and Mahenge (1st January–13th November, 1917.)	....	..	Capture of Likuyu	..	24th January	*
			Affairs near Kitanda	..	22nd–30th January	*
			Affairs on the Likuyu-Mponda Road	..	6th July–1st October.	
				Occupation of Tunduru	23rd August	*
			Affair of Likasa	..	30th August	†*
			Affairs of Kalimoto‡ and Mtrika‡	..	11th and 22nd September	*
				Occupation of Mahenge‡	9th October	*
				Occupation of Liwale	29th October	*
			Affair at Liganduka's	..	1st–2nd November	*
Pursuit and capture of Wintgens and Naumann 10th February —1st October, 1917	....	..	Affair of Tandala	..	19th–21st February	*
			Affair of St. Moritz	..	21st March	*

III.—THE CAMPAIGN IN PORTUGUESE EAST AFRICA, 1918.

Operations in Portuguese Nyasa. (11th January–23rd May, 1918.)	....	..	Affair of Nakote	..	5th May	*
			Affair of Korewa	..	22nd May	*
Operations in the Mozambique District (24th May–6th September, 1918.)	....	..	Affair of Nyamakura	..	1st–3rd July	*
			Affair of Nyamirue	..	21st–23rd July	*
			Affair of Nyamaroi	..	24th August	*
			Affair of Lioma	..	30th–31st August	*
Pursuit into Rhodesia (7th September–25th November 1918.)	....	..	Affair of Mpwera	.	6th September	*
			Affair at Kayambi	..	6th November	*
				Surrender of the German Forces	25th November	Abercorn.

† Called in German accounts "Mahiwa." ‡ Belgian forces.

SOUTH-WEST AFRICA.

Operations.	Battles.		Actions, etc.	Miscellaneous incidents.	Limits.	
	Name.	Tactical incidents included.			Chronological.	Geographical.
Orange River Operations (20th August–10th November, 1914.)	....	..	Affairs near Raman's Drift	..	14th–27th September	North-east of Steinkopf (*exclusive*).
			Affair of Keimoes	..	22nd October	The Orange river between Upington and Schuit Drift.
			Affair of Kakamas	..	24th October	
			—*with subsequent* Defence of Upington	..	23rd–24th January	*
Southern Operations (15th September, 1914–30th April, 1915.)	....	..	..	Landing at Lüderitz Bay	19th September	*
				Occupation of Aus	30th March	East of Chaukalb.
			Action of Gibeon	..	25th–26th April	North of Beersheba (*exclusive*).
Northern Operations (21st December, 1914–9th July, 1915.)	....	..	..	Occupation of Swakopmund	14th January	*
(i) *Advance on Windhuk* (*22nd February–20th May.*)	....	..	Actions of Jakalswater	..	20th March	East of Swakopmund.
			Affair of Trekkopjes	..	26th April	
				Occupation of Windhuk	13th May	
(ii) *Advance on Otavifontein* (*19th June–9th July.*)	....	..	Capture of Otavifontein	..	1st July	North of the Elefantsberg.
				Surrender of the German Forces	9th July	

WEST AFRICA.

TOGO.

Advance to Kamina (8th–26th August, 1914.)	....	..	Affair of Agbeluvoe	..	15th–16th August	North of Lome (*exclusive*).
			Affair of Khra	..	22nd–23rd August	
				Surrender of the German Forces	26th August	Amuchu.

FRENCH WEST AFRICA.*

Tuareg Operations (5th January–15th May, 1917.)	....	..	..	..	..	Beyond the Nigerian Frontier.

CAMEROONS.

Northern Operations (August-September 1914.)	....	..	Affair of Tepe	..	25th August	On the Benue river in German territory.
			First Attack on Garua	..	30th–31st August	
			Affairs at Kuseri†	..	25th August and 20th September	*
			First Attack on Mora	..	27th August	*
			Affair of Nsanakang	..	6th September	On the Cross river in German territory.
Duala Operations (September–November, 1914.)	....	..	Capture of Duala	..	26th–27th September	*
			Capture of Yabasi	..	14th October	North and east of Duala (*exclusive*).
including *The first advances up the Northern and Midland Railways. (29th September–15th November.)*	....	..	..	Occupation of Edea†	26th October	
				Occupation of Muyuka	13th November	
			Capture of Buea and of the Cameroon Mountain	..	14th–15th November	

* Operations of Nigerian forces in French territory.

† French forces.

WEST AFRICA—*continued.*

Operations.	Battles.		Actions, etc.	Miscellaneous incidents.	Limits.	
	Name.	Tactical incidents included.			Chronological.	Geographical.
			CAMEROONS—*continued.*			
Operations up the Northern Railway (3rd December, 1914–4th March, 1915.)	....	..	Capture of Chang Affair of Mbureku Affair of Harmann's Farm	.. .. ..	3rd February 3rd February 4th March	North of Mujuka (*exclusive*).
The German Counter-Offensive (January, 1915.)	..	..	Defence of Edea †	..	5th January, 1915	*
Coast Operations, 1914–15.	....	..	..	At Kribi At Kampo At Nyong	19th December 8th July 13th July	* *
First Advance on Yaunde (12th April 28th June, 1915.)	....	..	Affair of Ngwe Affair of Sende † First Affair of Wum Biagas	.. ..	14th April 3rd–4th May 3rd–4th May	East of Edea (*exclusive*).
Operations for the Central Plateau (26th May–31st December, 1915.)	....	..	Capture of Garua Capture of Ngaundere Capture of Bamenda Capture of Banyo Capture of Fumban	.. ..	31st May–10th June 28th June 22nd October 4th–6th November 2nd Decembe	South-east of the Nigerian frontier.
Blockade of Mora (8th September, 1915–18th February, 1916.)	....	..	Second Attack on Mora Third Attack on Mora	.. .. Capitulation of Mora	8th–9th September 30th October–4th November 18th February	*

Second Advance on Yaunde. **(22nd September–31st December, 1915.)**	....	..	Second Affair of Wum Biagas	..	9th October	South of the **Sanaga** River (*exclusive*).
			Affair at Lesog's	..	**27th November**	
			Affair of Chang Mangas	..	**17th December**	
			Affair of Mangele †	..	**21st December**	
				Occupation of Yaundee†	**1st January**	
—with subsequent Pursuit to the Spanish frontier. *(1st January–17th February, 1916.)*	....	..	..	..	**1st January–17th February**	

† French Forces.

CHAPTER I

How India Received the News of Britain's Declaration of War

The hot weather of 1914 opened in the ordinary way, so far as the Army in India was concerned at any rate, and the usual proportion of officers and men proceeded on leave and furlough.

The events of June and July excited considerable detached interest, but it was commonly felt that even if hostilities did eventuate in Europe there was but little prospect of any one getting to the front, exempt perhaps the lucky few on leave in England, and that the complicated system of international trade and credit and the perfection of modern arms would undoubtedly result in a short war of possibly a few months' duration.

On the 28th June 1914 Archduke Franz Ferdinand, Heir-Apparent to the throne of Austria-Hungary, and his Royal Consort were assassinated at Sarajevo. At a War Council held at Potsdam on the 5th of July it was decided to hold Serbia responsible for the murders and further that Germany should support to the uttermost whatever claims Austria might think fit to make on Serbia for redress.

Germany encouraged Austria to put these claims so high as either to ensure the domination of the Balkans by the Central Empires through Serbian submission, or to provoke a war by which alone the German militarists thought that German aims could be achieved.

The demands were not presented to Serbia until the 23rd July, thereby giving the Central Powers time to complete the preparations for war which rejection would provoke.

On the 24th July the British Secretary of State for Foreign Affairs suggested an international conference, with a view to the preservation of peace.

On the 28th July Germany notified her rejection of the British peace proposals and the same day Austria declared war on Serbia.

On the 29th July Belgrade was bombarded by the Austrians, and Germany made infamous proposals to Great Britain in the hope of securing her neutrality, which were rejected.

On the 1st August Germany declared war on Russia. The following day she sent an ultimatum to Belgium, demanding right of way for her Armies to France, and also invaded Poland.

On the 3rd August Germany declared war on

France. The next day she invaded Belgium and Great Britain took up arms on the side of Belgium and France. The effect of this momentous news on India was immediate. The whole country rallied to the King-Emperor. Germany for various reasons had expected England to stand aloof. In the alternative she had counted on the strain of a great war dissolving the British Empire. Prussian mentality could not grasp the essential principles underlying British administration in India and elsewhere.

Having endeavoured to foment agitation in India they relied on the opinions of agitators. They were completely out of touch with the sentiments of the people from Prince to peasant and had no conception of the abiding staunchness and loyalty of the Army.

On the 25th August the first division of the Indian Corps sailed for France, and Germany's hope of disintegration and revolt was reflected by the stern and willing unity of purpose disclosed in Lord Hardinge's famous telegram to the Secretary of State on September 7th, 1914:

> "Following is a summary of offers of service, money, etc., made in India to the Viceroy. The Rulers of the Native States in India, who number nearly seven hundred in all, have with one accord rallied to the defence of the Empire and offered their personal services and the resources of their States for the war. From among the many Princes and Nobles who have volunteered for active service, the Viceroy has selected the Chiefs of Jodhpur, Bikaner, Kishengarh, Rutlam, Sachin, Patiala, Sir Pertab Singh,

Regent of Jodhpur, the Heir-Apparent of Bhopal, and a brother of the Maharaja of Cooch Behar, together with other cadets of noble families. The veteran Sir Pertab would not be denied his right to serve the King-Emperor in spite of his seventy years, and his nephew, the Maharaja of Jodhpur, who is but sixteen years old, goes with him.

"All these have, with the Commander-in-Chief's approval, already joined the Expeditionary Forces. The Maharaja of Gwalior and the Chiefs of Jaora and Dholpur, together with the Heir-Apparent of Palanpur, were, to their great regret, prevented from leaving their States. Twenty-seven of the larger States in India maintain Imperial Service Troops, and the services of every corps were immediately placed at the disposal of the Government of India on the outbreak of war. The Viceroy has accepted from twelve States contingents of cavalry, Infantry, sappers and transport, besides a camel corps from Bikaner, and most of them have already embarked.

"As particular instances of generosity and eager loyalty of the Chiefs the following may be quoted :—Various Durbars have combined together to provide a hospital ship to be called 'The Loyalty' for the use of the Expeditionary Forces. The Maharaja of Mysore has placed Rs. 50 lakhs at the disposal of the Government of India for expenditure in connexion with the Expeditionary Force. The Chief of Gwalior, in addition to sharing in the expenses of the hospital ship, the idea of which originated with himself and the Begum of Bhopal, has offered to place large sums of money at the disposal of the Government of India and to provide thousands of horses as remounts. From Loharu in the Punjab and Las Bela and Kalat in Baluchistan come offers of camels with drivers, to be supplied and maintained by the Chiefs and Sardars. Several chiefs have offered to raise additional troops for military service should they be required, and donations to the Indian

Relief Fund have poured in from all States. The Maharaja of Rewa has offered his troops, his treasury, and even his private jewellery for the service of the King-Emperor. In addition to contributions to the Indian Fund, some Chiefs—namely, those of Kashmir, Bundi, Orchha, Gwalior and Indore—have also given large sums to the Prince of Wales' Fund. The Maharaja of Kashmir, not content with subscribing himself to the Indian Fund, presided at a meeting of 20,000 people held recently at Srinagar and delivered a stirring speech, in response to which large subscriptions were collected.

"Maharaja Holkar offers, free of charge, all horses in his State Army which may be suitable for Government purposes. Horses have also been offered by Nizam's Government, by Jamnagar, and other Bombay States. Every Chief in the Bombay Presidency has placed the resources of his State at the disposal of Government, and all have made contributions to the Relief Fund. Loyal messages and offers have also been received from the Mehtar of Chitral and tribes of the Khyber Agency as well as the Khyber Rifles. Letters have been received from the most remote States in India, all marked by deep sincerity of desire to render some assistance, however humble, to the British Government in its hour of need.

"Last, but not least, from beyond the borders of India have been received generous offers of assistance from the Nepal Durbar; the military resources of the State have been placed at the disposal of the British Government and the Prime Minister has offered a sum of three lakhs of rupees to the Viceroy for the purchase of machine guns or field equipment for British Gurkha Regiments proceeding overseas, in addition to large donations from his private purse to the Prince of Wales' Fund and the Imperial Indian Relief Fund. To the 4th Gurkha Rifles, of which the Prime Minister is Honorary Colonel, the Prime Minister has offered Rs. 30,000 for the purchase of machine guns in the event of their going on service.

The Dalai Lama of Tibet has offered 1,000 Tibetan troops for service under the British Government. His Holiness also states that Lamas innumerable throughout the length and breadth of Tibet are offering prayers for success of British Army and for happiness of souls of all victims of war.

"The same spirit has prevailed throughout British India. Hundreds of telegrams and letters have been received by Viceroy expressing loyalty and desire to serve Government either in the field or by co-operation in India. Many hundreds have also been received by local administrations. They come from communities and associations, religious, political, and social, of all classes and creeds, also from individuals offering their resources or asking for opportunity to prove loyalty by personal service. The following may be mentioned as typical examples:—The All India Moslem League, the Bengal Presidency Moslem League, the Moslem Association of Rangoon, the Trustees of the Aligarh College, the Behar Provincial Moslem League, the Central National Mahomedan Association of Calcutta, the Khoja Community and other followers of Aga Khan, the Punjab Moslem League, the Mahomedans of Eastern Bengal, the Citizens of Calcutta, Madras, Rangoon and many other cities, the Behar Landholders' Association, the Madras Provincial Congress Committee, the Taluqdars of Oudh, the Punjab Chiefs' Association, the United Provinces Provincial Congress Committee, the Hindus of the Punjab, the Khalsa Diwan representing orthodox Sikhs, the Bohra Community, and the Parsee Community of Bombay.

"The Delhi Medical Association offer the field hospital that was sent to Turkey during the Balkan War; Bengalee students offer enthusiastic services for an ambulance corps, and there were many other offers of medical aid. The Zemindars of Madras have offered 500 horses, and among other practical steps taken to assist

Government may be noted the holding oi meetings to allay panic, keep down prices, and maintain public confidence and credit. Generous contributions have poured in from all quarters to Imperial Indian Relief Fund."

In presenting the above statement to Parliament Lord Crewe said that similar offers had reached the Secretary of State from Chiefs who happened to be in Europe. The Gaekwar of Baroda and the Maharaja of Bharatpur, to mention two only, had placed the whole resources of their States at the disposal of His Majesty's Government. The Indian community in England, including the Indian students, had made loyal offers of services. He felt confident that the House and the country would feel deep appreciation of this magnificent demonstration of the loyalty with which the Princes and peoples of India had identified themselves with the cause of the Empire.

The Aga Khan also offered all his resources and to serve in the ranks of any Indian regiment.

At the opening of the Legislative Council Session on the 8th September 1914, the Viceroy, Lord Hardinge, made a speech on the war from which the following is an extract:—

"Before we pass to the ordinary business of Council, I will ask Hon'ble Members to stand up while I read to Council a gracious message addressed to the Princes and Peoples of India by His Majesty the King-Emperor :—

'During the past few weeks the peoples of my whole

Empire at home and overseas have moved with one mind and purpose to confront and overthrow an unparalleled assault upon the continuity, civilisation and peace of mankind.

'The calamitous conflict is not of my seeking. My voice has been cast throughout on the side of peace. My Ministers earnestly strove to allay the causes of strife and to appease differences with which my Empire was not concerned. Had I stood aside when, in defiance of pledges to which my Kingdom was a party, the soil of Belgium was violated and her cities laid desolate, when the very life of the French nation was threatened with extinction, I should have sacrificed my honour and given to destruction the liberties of my Empire and of mankind. I rejoice that every part of the Empire is with me in this decision.

'Paramount regard for treaty faith and pledged word of Rulers and peoples is the common heritage of England and India.

'Amongst the many incidents that have marked the unanimous uprising of the populations of my Empire in defence of its unity and integrity, nothing has moved me more than the passionate devotion to my Throne expressed both by my Indian subjects and by Feudatory Princes and Ruling Chiefs of India and their prodigal offers of their lives and their resources in the cause of the realm. Their one-voiced demand to be foremost in conflict has touched my heart and has inspired to highest issues the love and devotion which, as I well know, have ever linked my Indian subjects and myself. I recall to mind India's gracious message to the British nation of good-will and fellowship which greeted my return in February 1912, after the solemn ceremony of my Coronation Durbar at Delhi, and

I find in this hour of trial a full harvest and a noble fulfilment of the assurance given by you that the destinies of Great Britain and India are indissolubly linked.'

"I think that I am voicing the views of my Council and of the whole of India when I say that we are profoundly grateful to His Majesty for his gracious and stirring message, and that we can only assure His Majesty of our unflinching loyalty and devotion in this time of crisis and emergency.

"I propose now to add a few words explaining in greater detail the situation described by His Majesty in the first few sentences of his message.

"It is now five weeks ago that the British Empire was plunged into war with the two great military nations, Germany and Austria. As has been said by His Majesty the war was none of our seeking, but it has been thrust on us in what one can only describe as a wicked and wanton manner. Although we all deeply deplored the horrible assassination at Sarajevo of the Austrian heir to the throne and his consort, we cannot but feel regret that this was made the pretext for a conflict in which it was well known that there was every probability that most of the great Powers of Europe would be involved. It was not however until Germany, with a callous disregard for international obligations to which she herself was a party, refused to respect the neutrality of Belgium guaranteed in the Treaties of 1831 and 1839 by Austria, Russia, Great Britain and Prussia, that the intervention of Great Britain became inevitable. It is hardly necessary for me to describe the steps taken by the King-Emperor to ensure peace, and the patient, genuine and whole-hearted efforts of that great statesman, Sir Edward Grey to induce Germany to take a reasonable attitude, nor need I relate in detail what Mr. Asquith has described as the infamous proposals of Germany to buy our neutrality while giving her a free hand to destroy the independence of Belgium and the integrity of France and her possessions. All these details have been given by Sir E. Grey and Mr. Asquith in the House of Commons on the 3rd and 4th August.

"It suffices for me to say here that Great Britain having with other great Powers guaranteed the neutrality of Belgium, the vital interests of England being concerned in the independence and integrity of that State, it was her duty to keep her word and to maintain that neutrality with all the forces and resources at her disposal. It was in accordance with this stern sense of duty and with the conviction that her cause was just and righteous that Great Britain, in her accustomed role of protector of the smaller independent States, took up the sword to maintain the independence and integrity of Belgium and declared war on Germany. We have only to refer to the words of the German Chancellor in the Reichstag when he admitted that Germany had done a grievous wrong to Belgium to find more than ample justification for the action of our statesmen. The excuse then given that France meditated an attack on Germany through Belgium is one that can deceive no one, for it is notorious that France, who desires peace as much as we do, had already promised to respect the neutrality of Belgium. No Government and no people in Europe had less desire for war than the French, but their engagements by treaty and of honour compelled them to recognise their obligation to Russia. It is common knowledge that Germany for the last ten or fifteen years has been carefully planning and preparing for a campaign of aggression and self-aggrandisement, and in spite of all the denials of the German Government of any hostile intentions those who, like myself, have been engaged in watching over the foreign interests of Great Britain during the past few years, correctly gauged the intentions of Germany to force war upon England, France and

Russia as soon as she was ready for it and at the most favourable moment. We are now face to face with a possibly long and exhausting war, which, however just and righteous on our side, must be a terrible ordeal through which we should pass with firm confidence in the justice of our cause, and with strong determination to spare no effort to bring it to a successful conclusion. When this result has been achieved, as I have no doubt it will, let us not boast, but thank Him who has given us the victory. War is a terrible and horrible thing, but there is a worse thing than war, and that is national dishonour and failure of a nation to keep its engagements. This we have been happily spared by the firm and straightforward attitude of our statesmen in England. In this great crisis it has been a source of profound satisfaction to me that the attitude of the British Government has been so thoroughly appreciated in India and has met with such warm support. I have no hesitation in saying that the valuable offers of military assistance that I have received from the Ruling Chiefs of India and the countless offers of personal service and of material help made to me by both rich and poor in the provinces of British India have touched me deeply, and have given me one more proof, which I never needed, of what I have long known, and never for an instant doubted, namely, the deep loyalty and attachment of the Indian people to the King-Emperor and the Throne, and their readiness to make any sacrifice on their part to further and strengthen the interests of the Empire. The fact that the Government of India are in a position to help the mother country by the despatch of such a large proportion of our armed forces is a supreme mark of my absolute confidence in the fidelity of our troops and in the loyalty of the Indian people. I trust that this may be fully recognised in England and abroad.

"That, owing to the war, sacrifices will have to be made

is inevitable, and that suffering will be entailed is unhappily certain, but I am confident that the people of India, standing shoulder to shoulder, will shrink from no sacrifice, and will loyally co-operate with Government in maintaining internal order and in doing all in their power to secure the triumph of the arms of our King-Emperor. The countless meetings to express loyalty held throughout India and the warm response of the people to my appeal for funds for the relief of distress in India during the war have filled me with satisfaction, and have confirmed my first impression that in this war the Government would be supported by the determination, courage and endurance of the whole country.

"It was moreover with confidence and pride that I was able to offer to His Majesty the finest and largest military force of British and Indian troops for service in Europe that has ever left the shores of India. I am confident that the honour of this land and of the British Empire may be safely entrusted to our brave soldiers, and that they will acquit themselves nobly and ever maintain their high traditions of military chivalry and courage. To the people of India I would say at this time. 'Let us display to the world an attitude of unity, of self-sacrifice and of unswerving confidence under all circumstances in the justice of our cause and in the assurance that God will defend the right.'

At the same Council Meeting, the Hon'ble Sir Gangadhar Chitnavis moved the following Resolution, which was seconded by the Raja of Mahmudabad :—

"That in view of the great war involving most momentous issues now in progress in Europe, into which our August Sovereign has been forced to enter by obligations of honour and duty to preserve the neutrality guaranteed by treaty and the liberties of a friendly State, the

> Members of this Council, as voicing the feeling that animates the whole of the people of India, desire to give expression to their feelings of unswerving loyalty and enthusiastic devotion to their King-Emperor, and an assurance of their unflinching support to the British Government.
>
> "They desire at the same time to express the opinion that the people of India, in addition to the military assistance now being afforded by India to the Empire, would wish to share in the heavy financial burden now imposed by the War on the United Kingdom, and request the Government of India to take this view into consideration and thus to demonstrate the unity of India with the Empire.
>
> "They request His Excellency the President to be so good as to convey the substance of this Resolution to His Majesty the King-Emperor and His Majesty's Government."

This Resolution received the ungrudging and enthusiastic support of the entire Legislative Council, the speeches of the non-official members being marked by sentiments expressing the most whole-hearted loyalty and co-operation.

CHAPTER II

India's Contribution in Men

To view in its proper perspective the extent of India's effort and to arrive at the reasons why the full volume of assistance eventually rendered was long in maturing, it is necessary to bear in mind the policy which governed the scale of India's preparation for war.

The primary functions of the pre-war Army in India were two-fold, namely, the maintenance of order within and on the borders of British India, and, secondly, the provision of a field army capable, should the necessity arise, of undertaking a campaign beyond the border. The Army in India was in no sense maintained for meeting external obligations of an Imperial character. This policy was stated by the Army in India Committee to be as follows:—

> "While India should provide for her own defence against local aggression and, if necessary, for an attack on the Indian Empire by a great Power until reinforcements can come from home, she is not called upon to maintain troops for the specific purpose of placing them at the disposal of the Home Government for wars outside the

Indian sphere, although—as has happened in the past—she may lend such troops if they are otherwise available."

Having regard to these considerations, the Government of India accepted in 1913 the estimate, arrived at in the Majority Report of the Army in India Committee, of the strength and organization requisite for these two main objects; and the Secretary of State, in a despatch dated 20th March 1914 endorsed the view that the needs of external defence and the maintenance of internal order could be met from the armed forces at present maintained in India without increasing their numbers or materially altering their constitution. He added that he was glad to learn that the Government of India had decided to maintain the existing divisional organization of the Army both in peace and war, since this might prove especially valuable in the event of India being called upon in the future, as in the past, to supply troops for Imperial purposes outside India, when her own circumstances permitted her to spare them. "I do not, of course, suggest," he wrote, "that any additional expenditure should be thrown on Indian finances in anticipation of such a call, but I consider that your organization, where this can be done without such expenditure, should take into account the possibility of such a call."

In the year preceding the outbreak of war the Secretary of State had invited the Government of India to consider the extent to which India, on any occasion when in their opinion troops could be spared from that country, would be prepared to cooperate with the Imperial forces by the despatch and maintenance of reinforcements in the event of a serious war breaking out in Europe in which Great Britain was involved. In their reply dated July 30th, 1914, the Government of India intimated that if the situation were quiet in India and on her frontiers, the Army Council could usually rely on getting two divisions and one cavalry brigade, which in circumstances of special urgency might be increased to three divisions and one cavalry brigade, but that this increase could not be counted on with any degree of certainty.

Such, then, was the position on the outbreak of war. India proceeded to provide at once for France an expeditionary force of a strength of two infantry and two cavalry divisions. The two infantry divisions were accompanied by four field artillery brigades in excess of the normal allotment of artillery to divisions on the Indian establishment. The despatch of this force represented a greater sacrifice on the part of India than the mere numbers imply, for the troops—with the exception of the formations retained on the North-West Frontier—were those most ready for war.

Concurrently with the despatch of the Indian Expeditionary Force to France, a mixed force was despatched to East Africa for the protection of Zanzibar and the Mombassa-Nairobi railway, and an infantry brigade to the head of the Persian Gulf, increased to a complete division after the declaration of war with Turkey, for the protection of the Abadan pipe-line. In addition, a force of approximately six infantry brigades (one of which was composed of Imperial Service troops) and one Imperial Service Cavalry Brigade was sent to Egypt. The total strength of the troops sent abroad amounted to 23,500 British and 78,000 Indian ranks, *i.e.*, a contribution considerably in excess of the maximum which, as explained above, the Government of India had suggested as possible, even in circumstances of special urgency.

But in addition to the above all but nine of the regular British infantry battalions in India, and the bulk of the regular horse, field and heavy batteries were sent to England to facilitate the expansion of the Army at home. To replace them, 29 Territorial field batteries and 35 Territorial battalions were sent from England. The exchange was an unprofitable one for India and involved considerable risk; for the Territorial units were inadequately equipped, they were armed with an old pattern of rifle and no maxim guns, their batteries consisted of four instead of six guns each, and the guns themselves were of an obsolescent pattern. During the first four months of war the Army in India was reduced by 21 regiments of cavalry, 204 mobile guns and 69 battalions of infantry, leaving a force which in certain contingencies would have been altogether inadequate, both in numbers and training, to fulfil the dual role for which it existed. Events justified the risk, for no serious disorder occurred either within or beyond the borders; but the risk was nevertheless a big one, and must be taken into account in assessing India's contribution in the early stages of the war.

In other words, India's conditional promise of military assistance for Imperial purposes overseas had envisaged the despatch of two divisions and a cavalry brigade, or at the most of three divisions and a cavalry brigade.

In actual performance her initial effort was as follows. By the end of 1914 six Expeditionary Forces had been despatched overseas (excluding the operations against German Tsingtao in North China), comprising the following formations :—

3 infantry divisions,

8 infantry brigades,

1 mixed force including 3 infantry battalions,

2 cavalry divisions,

1 cavalry brigade,

with their full complement of attached troops, administrative services, and reinforcements, as well as four field artillery brigades in excess of the normal Indian allotment.

In addition, 32 regular British infantry battalions and the bulk of the regular horse, field and heavy batteries were sent to England.

By the early spring of 1915 two more infantry brigades were despatched from India to form, with a brigade already overseas, a new division, and also another cavalry brigade, thus bringing India's total initial effort up to :—

2 Indian Army Corps,
7 infantry brigades,
1 mixed force including 3 infantry battalions,
2 cavalry divisions,
2 cavalry brigades,

plus corps, divisional, attached troops, administrative services and reinforcements.

It is not the intention of this record to describe the gradual enlargement of India's overseas commitments or to trace the course of events which led to the full development of her military effort. It is proposed rather to take these commitments for granted and to treat of her effort without reference to the strategical and political considerations which directed it. But before proceeding to describe in detail the nature and extent of India's contribution, it may not be out of place to mention here that during the course of the war her soldiers have fought in such widely separated theatres as France and Belgium, Gallipoli, Salonika, Palestine, Egypt and the Soudan, Mesopotamia, Aden and the Red Sea littoral, Somaliland, the Cameroons, East Africa, North-West Persia and Kurdistan, South Persia; the Gulf of Oman, the whole length of East Persia from Mekran to Khorasan, Trans-Caspia, North China, and the North-West and North-East Frontiers of India. The mere enumeration of these theatres, covering as they do so wide a range of climatic and other conditions, will of itself convey some idea of the extent and diversity of the obligations undertaken by the Government of India.

The total numbers of men, animals and stores despatched from Indian Ports from the outbreak of war up to November 1918 were:—

Personnel		1,302,394
Animals		172,815
Supplies and Stores	tons	3,691,836

The heavy work imposed by these despatches on the railways and ports of India will be realised from the above figures. As regards supplies, India has been responsible throughout the war for the provision, either from India itself or from overseas, of everything required for the troops in Mesopotamia, both British and Indian, though the assistance of the War Office had to be obtained in procuring certain special items. India has also provided all foodstuffs demanded for the Indian troops serving in East Africa, Egypt, France and Salonica. Before the war, the only troops in India rationed by the State were the British garrison of 75,000 men,—(for the Indian soldier was fed at his own expense under regimental arrangements); towards the close of the war, India was rationing about 1,000,000 men, besides making large shipments of foodstuffs to assist allied troops and civilians in the Eastern Mediterranean.

At the outbreak of war the strength of the Army in India was :—

British, officers	4,744	
British other ranks	72,209	
TOTAL BRITISH		76,953
Indians serving	159,134	
Indian reservists	34,767	
Total Indian combatants		193,901
Indian non-combatants		45,660
GRAND TOTAL		239,561

Up to the 31st December 1919 the following Indian ranks, etc., were recruited in India, namely 877,068 combatants and 563,369 non-combatants, making a total of 1,440,437; and up to the same period the grand total of British and Indian officers, other ranks, and non-combatants sent on service overseas from India amounted to 285,037 British and 1,096,013 Indian or to 1,381,050 all told, including 42,430 British ranks despatched to England whence they subsequently proceeded on service. These latter, however, were replaced on the Indian establishment by Territorial units from the United Kingdom.

During the same period the total number of animals sent overseas amounted to 184,350.

The provision of British officers for Indian units has been one of the most difficult problems of the war. In the first place, the small British community in India, being engaged for the most part in Government service or in industries of national importance, offers a very limited scope as a source of recruitment; and, secondly, the pre-war organisation of the Army in India having been based on the requirements of a frontier campaign only, had made no provision, even within the limits available, for a reserve of officers to replace casualties on a large scale or to fill the junior commissioned ranks of newly raised units. Moreover, coming in the middle of the furlough season, the outbreak of war found a large proportion of British officers of the Indian Army on leave in England, and 253 of these, out of a total establishment of 2,586, were detained for employment under the War Office. To meet this initial loss, there were only 40 officers on the strength of the Indian Army Reserve on the outbreak of war.

The first step, therefore, was to increase the Indian Army Reserve, and this source of recruitment gradually developed until, by the end of October 1918, over 5,300 commissions had been given. Measures were also taken to increase the quota of young regular officers for the Indian Army, hitherto derived almost entirely from the Royal Military Colleges at home and in Canada, by opening Cadet Colleges on the same lines at Quetta and Wellington; and, by arrangement with the War Office, a large number of officers were transferred to the Indian Army on probation from the Special Reserve and Territorial Force or granted temporary commissions from the ranks of British units. The number of British officers added to the Indian Army and Indian Army Reserve between the 1st August 1914 and the 31st October 1918 was nearly four times the number on the strength of the Indian Army at the outbreak of war. The source from which they were obtained are tabulated below :—

	Source from which obtained	Number of Commissions granted
(*i*)	Permanent Commissions :—	
	(*a*) From R.M.C. Sandhurst	221
	(*b*) From R.M.C. Kingston, Canada	6
	(*c*) From Universities	15
	(*d*) From Cadet Colleges, Quetta and Wellington	944
	(*e*) From Special Reserve and Territorial Force (on probation)	2,050

Source from which obtained	Number of Commissions granted
(*ii*) Temporary Commissions :—	
(*f*) From ranks of British units	940
(*iii*) Commissions in Indian Army Reserve :—	
(*g*) From Indian Civil Service	200
(*h*) From Public Works Department	144
(*i*) From Indian Police Service	122
(*j*) From other sources	4,841
TOTAL	9,583

We have seen that the pre-war establishment of British officers of the Indian Army (as opposed to the total number of British officers of the Army in India) amounted to 2,586. Up to the 31st October 1918 the total casualties amounted to 2,702, since when there have been heavy casualties in Mesopotamia, Kurdistan and on the Indian frontiers, the figures for the North-West Frontier alone shewing an increase up to September 1920 of 91 killed, or died, and 74 wounded.

With regard to officers of the British Service the replacement of wastage was primarily the concern of the War Office, but a contribution made by India in this connection was the creation of an Officer Cadet Unit at Sialkot and Campbellpore on the lines of the Officer Cadet Battalions at Home. The object of this institution was to train specially selected Warrant officers, non-commissioned officers and men of the British Service in the duties of platoon commander, with a view to their receiving commissions, and so to make India self-supporting in respect of the Eastern theatres of war.

For the training of newly commissioned officers, both of the British and Indian Services, Officers' Schools of Instruction were also established at Ambala (and Sabathu), Bangalore and Nasik.

The numbers actually trained were as follows :—

School, etc.	Place	Nos.
Officers' School of Instruction	Ambala (and Sabathu)	1,570
Officers' School of Instruction	Bangalore	1,392
Officers' School of Instruction	Nasik	658
Cadet College	Quetta	710
Cadet College	Wellington	602
Officer Cadet Unit	Sialkot (and Campbellpore)	721
	TOTAL	6,653

The total number of British officers, of both British and Indian Services, sent overseas from India up to 31st October 1918 amounted to 23,040 and up to 31st December 1919 to 27,251.

With regard to medical personnel the sources ordinarily available in India are confined to the following categories :—

(*a*) The Indian Medical Service, a corps of officers more than half of whom are in civil employ.

(b) The Indian Medical Department, consisting of military assistant and sub-assistant surgeons, whose functions are supplementary to those of the Indian Medical Service in military hospitals, etc.

(*c*) The civil assistant and sub-assistant surgeons, whose functions are supplementary to those of the Indian Medical Service in civil hospitals, etc.

(d) Private practitioners.

(*e*) Queen Alexandra's Military Nursing Service for India.

(*f*) The Medical Follower establishments, who provide the menial and other lower grade categories in military hospitals, field medical units, etc., and who are represented chiefly by the Army Bearer and Army Hospital Corps.

As regards (*a*), there were 261 officers of the Indian Medical Service in military employ who were immediately available on the outbreak of war. The balance required to meet the great expansion of the army during the course of the war was obtained from the following sources :—

By surrender of officers from civil employ	380
By ordinary recruitment	37
By special recruitment by Secretary of State	21
By grant of temporary commissions—	
To private practitioners in India	486

To private practitioners at Home	91
To civil assistant and sub-assistant surgeons	352
By grant of honorary commissions to private practitioners	23
By re-employment of retired officers	4
TOTAL	1,394

27 Lady Doctors were also employed.

(b) The increase during the war to the Indian Medical Departments are as follows :—

	Assistant Surgeons	Sub-Assistant Surgeons
Establishment at outbreak of war	433	796
Increase during war	213	503
TOTAL	646	1,299

(*c*) The number of civil sub-assistant surgeons liable to surrender to military duty on mobilization was 482. The actual number obtained from this source was, however, 989.

(d) Private practitioners in India furnished 486 temporary officers to the Indian Medical Service.

(e) The only nurses serving in military hospitals in India at the outbreak of war were ladies of Queen. Alexandra's Military Nursing Service for India, numbering about 90, of whom 17 were despatched at once with the Indian Contingent to France. The local

recruitment of nurses for temporary duty was undertaken on a large scale,—mainly from civil hospitals and through the St. John's Ambulance Association,—and about 900 were obtained. Of these, rather more than 400 were for duty with Indian troops, and about 220 were sent overseas, either for duty in theatres of war or on hospital ships. The employment of lady nurses in Indian hospitals was an innovation and met with marked success.

(*f*) The strength of the Army Bearer Corps at the outbreak of war was 3,258 including 108 reservists; during the war it expanded to a strength of 22,750. Over 1,700 ward orderlies *i.e.,* specially enlisted soldiers trained as medical attendants, were also sent overseas, after being attached to one of the various war hospitals in India for a period of instruction.

Altogether 1,069 officers of the Indian Medical Service and 360 of the Royal Army Medical Corps, 1,200 Nursing Sisters, 2,142 Assistant and Sub-Assistant Surgeons, 979 British other ranks, 2,674 Indian other ranks and 26,179 followers were sent overseas to the various war theatres up to 31st October 1918.

The expansion of medical units has also been most marked during the same period as will be seen from the following statement:—

	Existing before the war	Raised during the war	Despatched overseas
Field Ambulances	$65\frac{3}{4}$	$40\frac{1}{4}$	64
Sanitary Sections	8	$24\frac{1}{2}$	$13\frac{1}{2}$
Clearing Hospitals	$15\frac{1}{2}$	$17\frac{3}{4}$	15
Stationary Hospitals	80	94	49
General Hospitals	12	41	32
X-Ray Stations	15	13	10
Advanced Depots, Medical Stores	8	11	11
Hospital ships	...	6	6

plus General and Base Depots for Medical Stores.

The drain on India's resources in respect of the provision of skilled technical personnel in particular, for service overseas, created a most difficult problem at a time when the domestic demand for these classes was severe; but all difficulties were successfully overcome by the Railway Board and subsequently by the Technical Recruiting Directorate at Army Headquarters.

Personnel for the various technical directorates overseas was originally recruited through the agency of the Railway Board. The classes then required were mainly for railways. Later, when operations developed, skilled staff was required for Military Works Services, Inland Water Transport, Irrigation, Ordnance Labour

Corps and various other directorates. When the War Branch of the Railway Board was broken up on the constitution of the Munitions Board the technical recruiting organization was placed under the control of the Adjutant-General in India. The technical staff recruited included skilled and unskilled classes.

The recruitment of technical staff commenced early in May 1916. From that time to the end of October 1918 a total of nearly 150,000 of all classes were sent overseas, representing an average of 5,000 a month. Of this staff the skilled classes may be taken, roughly, as equal in number to the unskilled. Railways, Inland Water Transport, and Works have absorbed the largest numbers, the proportion being:—

Railways	67,000
Inland Water Transport	56,000
Works	11,000
All others	16,000
TOTAL	150,000

Before recruiting had proceeded for any length of time, it was recognised that good results could not be obtained without the formation of training camps and schools for various classes of technical labour. The railways in the country originally provided the principal field for recruitment of technical staff, but owing to the rapid drain on their resources they soon became unable to meet the increasing demands for staff from the various technical directorates. Steps were accordingly taken to form training camps for training permanent-way men at the stations of Saharanpur, Gaya, Tirupattur (North Arcot), Puri and Jubbulpore. These camps were designed to accommodate between 500 and 1,000 men, and the following statement shows the number of men passed through the various training camps and schools:—

Training Camp or School	Situation	Number of men passed through up to 31st December 1918
Military Railway Labour Training Camp		
Ditto	Saharanpore	21,964
Ditto	Tirupattur	79,638
Ditto	Gaya	3,553
Ditto	Puri	9,618
Ditto	Jubbulpore	304
Signallers and Assistant Station masters' School	Lucknow	73
Signallers' School	Calcutta	37
Motor Tractor Drivers' School	Lahore	270
Oil Engine Driver and Ice Mechanics' School	Bombay	95
Motor Boat Drivers' School	Bombay	54
Sodawater Mechanics' School	Bombay	134
Clerks' School	Guindy	502

The personnel released from Indian railways or specially recruited in India for military duty or military railway work overseas was as follows:—

Class	Staff sent to Mesopotamia for workshops	Military duty	Railways under military control	TOTAL
Officers	4	301	181	486
Subordinates	20	300	2,235	2,555
Artisans, Menials and labourers	780	100	12,320	13,200
TOTAL	804	701	14,736	16,241

Various Mechanical Transport units were raised in India during the war, as shewn below, the Ford Van Companies consisting of 128 vans; and the Mechanical Transport Companies of 72 supply lorries, (including reserves, as well as stores and workshop lorries, etc.), or else of motor ambulances:—

Theatre in which employed	Officers	British ranks	Indian ranks	REMARKS
Mesopotamia	30	56	1,125	Five Ford Van Companies
Aden	2	33	53	One Mechanical Transport Section
South Persia Rifles	3	13	39	One Mechanical Transport Section

Theatre in which employed	Officers	British ranks	Indian ranks	REMARKS
East Persia	8	140	198	One Ford Van Company, one Lorry Section and one Section, Motor Ambulance Convoy
Bushire	2	7	37	One Mechanical Transport Section
India	28	605	515	Five Mechanical Transport Companies, one Advanced Repair Workshop, and other details.
TOTAL	73	854	1,967	

A Mechanical Transport Training School was established at Rawalpindi, from which 2,113 trained drivers were despatched overseas. Another school was established at Meerut for training drivers for service in India.

An important contribution made by India was the provision of labour for various theatres of war, especially France and Mesopotamia. A wide variety of classes were enlisted for this purpose, many of whom had never before been used in the army, either as combatants or non-combatants. The number of corps raised during the war was as follows:—

Theatre in which employed	Labour Corps Strength 1,150	Porter Corps Strength 576	Syce Companies Strength 210
France	54	...	6
Mesopotamia	19	12	6
Salonika	2	...	...
Egypt	...	...	1/2
East Africa	...	1	...
South Persia	8	...	1
East Persia	1	...	...
India	20	...	1 1/2
TOTAL	104	13	15

As the majority of these corps were formed of men on limited engagements of 6, 9 or 12 months, their maintenance in the field involved the replacement of practically the whole of the personnel.

The demand from overseas for miscellaneous followers became so heavy that five Central Depots and one Syce Corps Depot were established to regulate the recruitment and distribution of this class of personnel, which included bakers, blacksmiths, butchers, carpenters, cooks, hammermen, gardeners, herdsmen, shoemakers, shoeing smiths, packers, sweepers, tailors, washermen, weighmen, etc., etc. The number enrolled and supplied at each of these depots is given below :—

Depot	Number enrolled	Number supplied
Followers Central Depôt, Amritsar	9,610	5,576
Followers Central Depôt, Kirkee	11,636	5,313
Followers Central Depôt, Lucknow	14,792	8,730
Followers Central Depôt, Meerut	25,918	20,727
Followers Central Depôt, Rawalpindi	946	759
Syce Corps Depôt, Sehore	928	2,632
GRAND TOTAL	63,830	43,737

The following Supply and Transport Personnel were sent overseas from India during the war :—

British officers	717
British other ranks	1,602
Indian supply personnel	14,125
Indian transport personnel	61,000

Veterinary personnel sent overseas, amounted to eighteen Field Veterinary Sections, four Mobile Veterinary Sections, three Base Depôts of Veterinary stores, and :—

British officers	68
British subordinates	45
Veterinary assistants	52

During the war 4,000 men were deputed from Indian Post Offices for duty in the field or for censorship purposes. Base Postal Depots were also established at Bombay and Karachi. 8,300 men, including 1,200 trained telegraphists, were also sent overseas for duty with field telegraphs.

The Ordnance Services, Arsenals, Inspection and Ordnance Factories were all administered by the Director-General of Ordnance in India during the first three years of the war and the small staff of Factory Officers and Inspectors was depleted at an early stage by the despatch of several officers to England at the request of the War Office. On the 1st January 1918 the control of the Ordnance Factories was transferred to the Indian Munitions Board. To conform with the War Office Organization the administration of the Stores Section (Arsenals) of the Ordnance Department was transferred to the Quartermaster General in India on 1st April 1918. The normal establishment of British Ordnance personnel in the arsenals was 54 officers and 332 other ranks; of these 19 officers and 168 other ranks were despatched overseas. At the same time the work in arsenals increased three-fold. The difficulty was met by employing temporary additional personnel from the Royal Army Ordnance Corps, from Territorial and Garrison Battalions and general re-organisation.

With regard to animals the total number sent overseas up to the date of the Armistice was :—

Theatre	Horses	Ponies and Mules	Camels	Draught Bullocks	Dairy cattle	TOTAL
France	31,075	8,970	...	...	...	40,045
East Africa	536	793	172	...	...	1,501
Egypt	7,208	4,553	6,393	...	...	18,154
Mesopotamia	44,288	45,577	3,026	4,649	4,986	102,526
Other theatres	2,846	5,505	1,190	412	636	10,589
TOTAL	85,953	65,398	10,781	5,061	5,622	172,815

The above figures include horses and mules obtained from abroad and reshipped to overseas theatres after being trained in India.

In this connection it may be of interest briefly to mention the steps that are being taken to improve indigenous stock.

To the extent that Army funds will admit every endeavour is being made to stimulate the production of equine stock in the country. A large addition is being made to the number of free grants of land to peasants in the Canal Colonies on horse-breeding conditions; the Imperial stallion breeding stud is being enlarged by an increase in the number of brood mares; the price paid for thoroughbred English stallions has been greatly augmented; the price allowed for country-bred cavalry remounts has just been liberally increased; the Royal Calcutta Turf Club and the Western India Turf Club have placed at the disposal of Government a generous yearly donation for the improvement of country-breds for cavalry by the grant of premiums to the owners and breeders of the best brood mares and as prizes for good fillies and remounts; Zemindars are being judiciously guided and assisted in purchasing suitable brood mares for breeding cavalry remounts; excellent donkey stallions in sufficient numbers have recently been imported from America for the improvement of mule and donkey breeding; and lastly, efforts are being made to interest the Rulers of Indian States in reviving horse-breeding in their States.

Having outlined in figures India's gross contributions to the war with respect to personnel, we now turn to a more detailed account of its employment.

Up to the 31st October 1918 the following number of purely Indian combatant and non-combatant personnel had been despatched to the various expeditionary forces overseas :—

	Combatants			
	Indian officers and Warrant Officers	Indian other ranks	Non-combatants	Total
To France	1,911	82,974	47,611	132,496
To East Africa	826	33,633	12,477	46,906
To Mesopotamia	7,812	287,753	293,152	588,717
To Egypt	1,889	94,396	19,674	116,159
To Gallipoli .	30	3,003	1,335	4,428
To Salonika	31	3,643	1,264	4,938

	Combatants			
	Indian officers and Warrant Officers	Indian other ranks	Non-combatants	Total
To Aden	343	15,655	4,245	20,243
To Persian Gulf	615	17,537	11,305	29,457
Total	13,517	538,794	391,033	943,344

From the outbreak of war up to 31st December 1919 the following British and Indian personnel was sent from India on service overseas direct to the theatres enumerated :—

Theatre	Combatants					Totals		Grand total of all ranks British and Indian
	B.O.'s	B.O.R.	I.O. and Warrant officers	I.O.R.	Non-combatant Indians	British	Indian	
France	2,395	18,353	1,923	87,412	49,273	20,748	138,608	
East Africa	928	4,681	848	33,835	13,021	5,609	47,704	
Mesopotamia	18,669	166,822	9,514	317,142	348,735	185,491	675,391	
Egypt	3,188	17,071	2,208	107,743	34,075	20,259	144,026	
Gallipoli	42	18	90	3,041	1,819	60	4,950	
Salonika	86	85	132	6,545	3,254	171	9,931	
Aden	952	7,267	480	19,936	5,786	8,219	26,205	
Persian Gulf	991	1,059	967	29,408	18,823	2,050	49,198	
TOTAL	27,251	215,356	16,162	605,062	474,789	242,607	1,096,013	1,338,620
The above figures exclude 42,430 British ranks sent from India to England, all, or nearly all of whom proceeded on service from the United Kingdom								42,430
							TOTAL	1,381,050

The above figures include personnel sent overseas to the various theatres direct, and do not shew transfers as, for instance, the advance into Palestine of a portion of the force from Egypt; nor do they include Indian troops engaged in hostilities who were already overseas, such as the 36th Sikhs in China who furnished half a battalion towards the British Contingent in the operations round Kiau-Chau.

During the one hundred and fifty years of its existence the Indian Army had taken no part in a European War with the exception of some few troops that were engaged against the French in Southern India, and in Java and the Spice Islands. In 1878 some troops had been sent as far as Malta with a view to their employment in case of a war with Russia, and in the South African War detachments drawn mostly from Indian Regular and Imperial Service Troops cavalry had been utilised for remount and escort work in that country.

The Indian Army had been organised and trained mainly for warfare on or beyond the frontiers of India, (including the possibility of war with Russia), and the experience of the rank and file had been limited for the most part to frontier operations.

In July 1917, Lord Hardinge (ex-Viceroy of India) made the following statement in the House of Lords showing the extent of India's initial help in the early days of the war :—

"In August and the early part of September 1914 an Indian Expeditionary Force of an Indian army corps of two divisions, under the command of General Sir James Willcocks, and one-cavalry division was sent to France, and a second cavalry division was sent to join this force in the following November. It may be of interest to remark here that the theatre of action of these splendid Indian divisions was, in the first instance, restricted to the Mediterranean garrisons and the Sudan, and it was due to the insistence of the Government of India that they were sent to France, where they arrived in time to fill a gap that could not otherwise have been filled, and there consecrated with their blood the unity of India with the British Empire and their loyalty to the King-Emperor. There are very few survivors of those two splendid divisions of infantry. But India has a land frontier, needing at all times a watchful eye, and at times such as those giving cause for special care. To guard that frontier three divisions were immediately mobilised. In September 1914, by the order of His Majesty's Government, a mixed division of troops was sent to East Africa, the co-operation of India with this force being limited to the supply of personnel, transport, equipment and ships. In October and November 1914, two divisions of Indian infantry and one brigade of cavalry were sent to Egypt. It was not till September 26th, 1914, by which time eight divisions had already been mobilised and sent either abroad or to the frontier, that the possibility of action at the head of the Persian Gulf was foreshadowed by the Secretary of State, and it was on October 31st that Turkey having entered the war against us, hostilities commenced with the seizure by an Indian brigade of the mouth of the Shatt-el-Arab. This brigade was re-inforced to the strength of a division before the capture of Basra on November 23rd and in three months' time increased to an army corps of two divisions. Of these 10 divisions of infantry and two divisions and two brigades of cavalry, enumerated above, seven divisions and all the cavalry were sent overseas. But in addition to these organised forces 20 batteries of artillery, and 32 battalions of British infantry, the flower of the British Army, many of them 1,000 strong and more, were sent to England. A battalion of Indian Infantry was sent to Mauritius, another to the Cameroons, and two battalions to the Persian Gulf, while Indian troops also co-operated with the Japanese at the capture of Tsingtao. Approximately 80,000 British officers and men and 210,000 Indian officers and men, all fully trained and equipped were despatched overseas. I would here remark that the largest Indian expedition ever previously sent overseas amounted to 18,000 men.

"A comparison between the ordinary establishment of the Army in India and of the units sent overseas in connection with various expeditions shows in a striking manner the military effort made by India to assist the Empire. Of the British establishment in India, seven regiments of British cavalry out of nine, were sent overseas : 44 British battalions of infantry out of 52, and 43 batteries of Royal Artillery out of 56; while of the Indian establishment, 20 regiments of Indian cavalry out of 39 and 98 battalions of Indian infantry out of 138 were sent abroad. In return for these troops, India received many months after the outbreak of war and the despatch of Indian divisions overseas, 29 Territorial batteries and 35 Territorial battalions, but these were unfit for immediate employment on the frontier or in Mesopotamia until they had been entirely re-armed and equipped and their training completed. Many of them were sent later to Mesopotamia, whether as units or drafts for Regular regiments, and all did splendid service.

"It is, however, a fact that for the space of some weeks before the arrival of the Territorials the British garrison in India was reduced to about 15,000 men. The safety of India was thus imperilled in the interests of the Empire as a whole. In such a cause I was naturally prepared to take risks, and I took them confidently because I trusted the people of India, and I am proud to say they fully justified my confidence in them. From the moment of the outbreak of war, and after, it was the steady policy of the Government of India to give readily to the home Government of everything it possessed, whether troops or war material. In the summer of 1914 India was absolutely ready for war in the light of what was then accepted as the requisite standard of preparation of her military forces and equipment. The Army was at war strength, the magazines were full, and the equipment was complete. Thanks to these facts, India was able, not merely to send her divisions to France and elsewhere, but also to supply to England within the first few weeks of the war 70,000,000 rounds of small-arm ammunition, 60,000 rifles and more than 550 guns of the latest pattern and type. In the first week of the war some 530 officers of the Army, who could ill be spared, were handed over to the War Office, and nearly 3,000 additional combatant officers have been sent overseas since the war began."

CHAPTER III

INDIA'S CONTRIBUTION IN MATERIAL

We have seen in a previous chapter that on the outbreak of war the Indian Princes placed the entire resources of their States at the disposal of the King-Emperor and both they and the peoples of India, throughout the whole period of the war, continued to contribute gifts in kind and money in lavish quantities for the purchase of comforts for the British and Indian troops employed in the various war theatres. And with regard to the provision of munitions, which term includes clothing, railway plant and every variety of material required for the maintenance and movement of armies in the field and on lines of communication, India has played a worthy part.

The normal output of the Indian arsenals and military clothing factories was designed to meet peace requirements and the necessities of a war of limited magnitude. The expansion incidental to the needs of the great war presented immense difficulty owing to the meagre resources possessed by this country in essential machinery and in technically trained men, and India has sound reason to be proud of the way she surmounted inherent obstacles and attained such a marvellous result. Early in 1915 the Railway workshops as well as the principal engineering firms in Calcutta and Rangoon undertook to supply shell cases to supplement the inadequate output of the United Kingdom, until the Ministry of Munitions at home became independent of such assistance. This was in addition to equipping her own expanding armies in Mesopotamia, Egypt and elsewhere and in furnishing the Allies with many urgent requisites. As the war progressed it became imperative in the interests of general economy for the Allies to review their industrial position and to render themselves, in so far as might be possible independent of many articles which they had imported hitherto.

With regard to India it was felt that if the various purchasing departments were brought under the control of one organisation for regulating contracts and amalgamating demands, buying could be undertaken on a large scale and competition avoided. Further, that by revising official indents on the India Office and by curtailing certain imports many of India's local resources would be developed and new industries created.

On the 1st March 1917 the Indian Munitions Board was formed, with Sir Thomas Holland as President. Its functions were threefold :—

(*a*) to restrict demands on the United Kingdom and later, on the United States of America, for articles which would cause interference with war work in those countries and which could be dispensed with or obtained in India or from elsewhere,

(*b*) the supply of large quantities of plant and materials to Mesopotamia, East Africa, Egypt and other theatres of war, as well as to the Army and Civil departments in India,

(*c*) the development of local industries and manufactures.

Despite the difficulty of developing industries under war conditions and of securing the necessary staff the Board got to work with astounding promptitude. It eventually took over the organisation in its entirety of all Government ordnance, clothing, hide and leather factories and created subsidiary ones; it worked up the production of woollen and worsted goods in the existing mills to meet Army requirements; it assumed responsibility for the shipment of raw and tanned hides for army purposes; it provided vast quantities of railway track, rolling stock and plant to overseas theatres; it established a government tent factory and furnished materials to new factories started by private agency; it centralised the purchases of jute goods, thereby effecting enormous savings; it constituted a rivercraft branch to take over the work of constructing or re-erecting vessels for water transport; it formed a timber branch which collected for shipment nearly a quarter of a million tons of various kinds of timber for structural work, in addition to lighter wood suitable for other forms of construction and repairs, and conducted an exhaustive search for timber suitable for aircraft with good results; it controlled the products of the Tata Iron and Steel Works at Jamshedpur in steel and pig-iron; it controlled the entire manufacture of cement in India, of ship repairs, and of certain engineering materials, and provided enormous quantities of miscellaneous plant and stores including machinery of all kinds and various equipment for the docks and workshops in Mesopotamia and East Africa.

In addition to the above, use was made of the Board's organisation in furthering war interests by the scrutiny of priority applications for assistance in obtaining goods from the United Kingdom and the United States of America; by the scrutiny of Government indents on the India Office; and by the curtailed export of certain materials. From this terse catalogue some conception may be gained of the immense variety of the Board's activities and of the complex organisation required to control them.

At the time of the Armistice it was controlling expenditure upon war material amounting to two millions sterling a month.

By utilising to the full her local resources India was enabled to provide the greater portion of the supplies required by the troops in Mesopotamia and other theatres, thereby lessening demands on Great Britain and America.

By the end of September 1918 the value of equipment and stores despatched to the various fronts amounted to about £80,000,000 sterling.

In addition, she supplied vast quantities of raw materials and partly manufactured articles to the Allies such as raw and rough-tanned hides, wolfram, manganese, mica, saltpetre, timber and bamboos, raw silk, hemp, coir, tea, rubber, petroleum, various oils and certain foodstuffs.

In this connection it should be mentioned that during the war the output of wolfram was increased from a negligible figure to a third of the world's production. In manganese ore, too, India has been practically the only source, and in mica the main source of supply to the Allies in Europe.

In textiles India had a monopoly of jute and during the war exported for all purposes some £137,000,000 worth of raw jute, sacks and cloth, whilst her output of cotton and woollen goods was enormously expanded. Though India in the past has suffered severely from wars within her frontiers it is through wars beyond her borders that much of her material progress has been attained.

In this one aspect alone the effects of the Great War are bound to be far-reaching, and the growing demand for State assistance in industrial undertakings must eventually result in India becoming to a very large extent economically self-sufficing.

We have seen that the munition-making resources of the country were first co-ordinated in July 1915, by the Railway Board, which employed a special staff to supervise and develop output. In this way it was possible to make the best use of existing railway workshops, in which a considerable quantity of shell cases were manufactured, as well as a variety of other articles which could not be produced by the Ordnance and other Government factories. Much assistance was also rendered by the Indian Rivercraft Board, a voluntary organisation developed under the direction of the Railway Board and consisting of representatives of the principal engineering firms at Calcutta, with affiliated committees at Karachi, Bombay and other ports.

Through their Mining Engineer and coal inspecting organization, the Railway Board undertook supplies of coal to all Railways, Military Services, Overseas Forces, Marine and Royal Navy. It was soon found that supply was likely to be in defect of demand, and that powers must be taken by Statute to requisition coal for purposes of the war and to control the distribution of coal for public consumption after the demand for immediate war and quasi-war services had been met. These increased rapidly, and it was necessary, therefore, to set up a close control over output as well as consumption. One of the Members of the Railway Board accordingly was appointed Coal Controller and a system of requisitioning and rationing was introduced, by which works of national or military importance had first lien on available coal supplies. At the same time, the withdrawal, on account of rising prices, of essential labour from 1st class to 2nd class collieries was regulated by the closing down, where necessary, of mines producing low grade coal. Latterly, the whole output of first class coal and coke in India was under requisition and was distributed by the Coal Controller, his activities extending to the regulation of bunker supplies to all shipping.

With regard to the work of the Munitions Board it is only with respect to certain subjects that complete figures are available. These are the subjects, the organizations of which were taken over in their entirety by the Board after its formation and comprise :—

(1) Ordnance factories.
(2) Hides and leather.
(3) Railway track, rolling stock and plant.
(4) Clothing.

As regards other services, the information available is limited to the work done directly under the control of the Munitions Board; the heads regarding which such information can be given are :—

(5) Textiles.
(6) Boots.
(7) Tents.
(8) Jute goods.
(9) Rivercraft.
(10) Timber.
(11) Miscellaneous engineering plant and stores. To these particulars may be added an indication of other ways in which use was made of the Board's organization, *viz.*:—
(12) Scrutiny of priority applications for assistance in obtaining goods from the United Kingdom and the United States of America.

(13) Scrutiny of Government indents on the India Office.

(14) Control of export of certain materials.

(15) Control of the distribution of the products of the Indian iron and steel works.

(16) Control of the distribution of the products of the Indian cement works.

(17) Control of public dealings in certain engineering materials.

(18) Control of ship repairs.

The following paragraphs deal briefly with each of these heads as numbered above. Care has been taken to distinguish between the information which relates to the entire duration of the war, and that which, for the reasons given above, refers only to the period of the Munitions Board's own activities. An abstract of the cash expenditure of the Board, which amounted to more than $38^1/_2$ crores of rupees at the end of October 1918, is also given.

(1) *Ordnance Factories.*—Shows the output of some of the more important war stores by the Indian Ordnance Factories, or by other establishments under the supervision of the Director of Ordnance Factories :—

—	8 Months 1st August to 31st March 1915	12 Months 1st April to 31st March 1916	12 Months 1st April 1916 to 31st March 1917	12 Months 1st April 1917 to 31st March 1918	7 Months 1st April 1918 to 31st October 1918
Cartridges, S.A.—					
Ball-303 millions	101	141	147	*(a)* 76	84
Revolver millions	1.8	1.1	3.5	4.3	3.2
Other kinds millions	3.6	4.6	2.9	5.6	3.4
Cordite (all descriptions) tons	365	844	999	934	461
Guncotton—					
Dry primers	93,120	84,630	28,616	109,152	27,400
Wet slabs	32,038	47,380	18,242	69,390	36,546
Rifles (new and converted)	13,862	25,481	36,791	42,362	27,262
Bayonets (new and converted)	35,224	59,809	60,327	27,400	8,896
Cartridges—					
Q.F. 13 and 18-pr.	100,208	170,681	204,035	227,939	183,130
Other kinds	17,562	6,821	24,501	69,052	34,505
Empty cases	67,925	233J18	270,560	331,339	154,781
Guns (all natures)	27	23	22	60	44
Steel (in hundreds of tons)—					
Ingot	40	69	62	94	46
Rolled bars and rods	30	64	81	108	52
Shell (all natures)	114,655	277,400	366,945	399,713	202,255
Filled fuzes	*(b)* 132,840	216,233	215,086	459,035	249,900
Filled tubes—					
Vent sealing	*(c)* 86,800	212,600	130,000	150,000	248,000
Other types	52,200	52,500	81,500	10,000	97,500
Heliographs	...	1,345	700	...	...
Bandolier equipment (sets)	32,471	67,763	101,902	96,664	22,835
Harness, transport—					
Pack (sets)	301	5,300	2,000	...	...
Draught	674	8,006	4,000	...	...

(a) Manufacture changed from Mark VI to Mark VII.

(b) In addition 431,750 empty fuzes were sent home to England.

(c) In addition 536,000 empty T. Tubes were sent to England.

—	8 Months 1st August 1914 to 31st March 1915	12 Months 1st April 1915 to 31st March 1916	12 Months 1st April 1916 to 31st March 1917	12 Months 1st April 1917 to 31st March 1918	7 Months 1st April 1918 to 31st October 1918
Slings, rifle (a)	35,977	96,762	94,296	46,508	143,207
Gun carriages	15	5	46	66	19
F.A. wagons	...	139	75	...	9
F.A. limbers	...	202	59	...	30
Wagons, G.S.	21	18	61	48	52
Transport carts	527	1,195	1,506	400	...
Mountain artillery saddles			534	467	...
Wheels (all kinds)	2,204	6,478	11,289	18,801	3,003
Leather, buffalo (In thousands of lbs.)	505	1,163	1,304	1,594	1,126

(a) In 1917 two sources of manufacture of a satisfactory substitute for the imported webbing had been developed; one in Calcutta and one in Madras. The combined capacity was over 60,000 yards monthly. From this material complete slings were made up in Calcutta, Madras, and Cawnpore.

Throughout the war the policy was followed of developing as far as possible the outside manufacture of war stores. Early in the war, such manufacture had to be confined to the near neighbourhood of Ordnance Factories, but in 1916 a beginning was made to extend it systematically. The Ordnance Department supplied patterns, drawings and specifications. Instructions to guide manufacture were drawn up, and, as far as possible, tuition was given in methods of manufacture. In many cases Ordnance Factories had to make up and supply jigs, special tools and fittings and provide the raw materials. This policy, of course, involved the surrender of the bulk of the large and recurring orders and all the simpler manufactures, but it set free the Ordnance Factories plant to meet rush orders and the more specialised demands.

(2) *Hides and Leather.*—The Indian tanning industry made an important contribution towards the war by the supply of rough tanned cow hides—known as East India kips—from Madras and Bombay. East India kips have been very largely utilised in the manufacture of upper leather for army boots, and from August 1916 all available supplies were purchased in India for the War Office and shipped direct to London. Between 60 and 65 per cent of the hides shipped were suitable for army work and of the balance a large proportion was utilised in the manufacture of war-time standard boots in England. The growth of the trade during the war and the value of the contribution made can be seen from the following figures of shipments.

Shipments of tanned hides and calf to the United Kingdom

Year	Quantity in cwts.				Value in thousands of Rs.			
	Cow	Buffalo	Calf	Total	Cow	Buffalo	Calf	Total
1914-15	189,551	24,371	10,114	224,036	21,525	2,280	1,202	25,007
1915-16	246,366	23,894	7,173	277,433	28,299	2,143	801	31,243
1316-17	286,109	31,910	12,801	330,820	40,363	3,569	1,988	45,920
1917-18	346,044	18,073	6,095	370,212	47,084	1,838	816	49,738
1918-19*	272,614	3,917	3,824	280,355	39,093	327	535	39,956
Total	1,340,684	102,165	40,007	1,482,856	176,364	10,157	5,342	191,863

* 7 months, April to October.

The total value of this contribution up to the end of October 1918 was £12,791,000.

In addition to supplies of tanned hides India furnished large quantities of raw hides to the British War Office and to the Italian Government. From June 1917, these supplies were purchased by the Indian Munitions Board and shipped to London and Italy.

Shipments of raw hides (including calf) from British India to the United Kingdom and Italy

—	To United Kingdom		To Italy	
	Quantity in cwts.	Value in thousands of rupees	Quantity in cwts.	Value in thousands of rupees
1914-15	139,029	8,535	72,199	5,763
1915-16	99,166	6,537	383,360	32,919
1916-17	144,789	11,910	172,871	15,128
1917-18	176,847	12,853	156,231	11,652
1918-19*	133,000	7,966	92,671	6,499
Total	692,831	47,801	877,332	71,961

* 7 months, April to October.

The value of these raw hide shipments during the war was, therefore, approximately £7,984,000; and, taking tanned hides and raw hides together, India's contribution in export of hides, during the war exceeds £20,750,000.

(3) *Railway track, rolling stock and plant.*—Railway track, rolling stock and plant supplied by India up to the 30th October 1918 :—

—	Mesopotamia	Egypt	East Africa	Aden	Bushire	Total
Railway track (miles)	1,031	555	200	18	51	1,855
Locomotives	164	...	55	3	7	229
Vehicles	5,017	...	740	85	144	5,986
Bridging material (in ft.)	8,783	...	3,700	50	540	13,073

(4) and (5) *Clothing and Textiles.*—As the army requirements of woollen and worsted goods under war conditions exceeded the maximum capacity of the five existing woollen mills in India, it was necessary to import a certain proportion of these materials from home. But the mills in India were utilised to their utmost, all five having been under engagement to supply the whole of their output to the Board and to work both day and night. In addition, arrangements were made to develop the supply of blankets from jails and from groups of hand weavers, while Kashmir and other centres of woollen hand-weaving were exploited to provide puttoo for use as warm linings to followers' garments. The following woollen goods of Indian manufacture were provided from the time when the duty of supply was undertaken by the Board :—

Serge and greatcoat cloth	1,600,000 yards
Puttoo and linings	2,000,000 yards
Flannels	1,500,000 yards

Putties	1,500,000 pairs
Socks and mittens	2,000,000 pairs
Jerseys, comforters, etc.	600,000 pairs
Blankets	1,900,000 pairs

The whole of Government's requirements of cotton goods, with the exception of mosquito netting and cotton sewing thread, were supplied from the products of Indian manufactures; the following figures of purchases from July 1917 to October 1918 show the extent of these supplies :—

Dyed drills, turban cloths, etc.	67,500,000	yards
Grey and bleached cloths	15,000,000	yards
Towelling	3,000,000	yards
Flannelette	2,250,000	yards
Webbing and tape	43,000,000	yards
Sheets, mattress cases, pillow covers, etc.	1,600,000	numbers
Kit-bags (cotton canvas)	2,500,000	numbers
Kullahs (for turbans)	1,500,000	numbers
Cotton Blankets	1,000,000	numbers
Rezais (quilts)	600,000	numbers
Durries and Rugs	200,000	numbers
Cotton rope	10,000,000	fathoms
Yarn and thread	1,000,000	lbs.

As regards manufactured articles of clothing, the output of the Army Clothing Department for the pre-war years 1912-13 and 1913-14 was 551,847 and 477,821 garments, respectively. During the period August 1914 to March 1915, the number was 1,269,393. In 1915-16, India began to provide clothing for various

Expeditionary Forces and that year the output rose to over 3 million garments. During the following year, it continued to increase and reached its maximum in June 1917, when the Department turned out about 2,000,000 garments, *i.e.,* about 45 times the average monthly supply before the war. From that date, the rate of output settled down to approximately $1^1/_4$ millions of garments monthly. The actual figures for the whole period for the war were :—

August 1914 to March 1915	1,269,393
April 1915 to March 1916	3,181,298
April 1916 to March 1917	12,084,736
April 1917 to March 1918	16,944,398
April 1918 to October 1918	8,440,408
TOTAL OUTPUT OF GARMENTS	41,920,233

It may be added that 775,000 gross of buttons and 700,000 sets of shoulder titles, badges, etc., all of Indian manufacture, were also supplied.

(6) *Boots.*—It was barely possible to meet the greatly increased demands for army boots, pending the completion of arrangements which were being made for the extension of manufacture in India. From July 1917 to October 1918, the Board supplied a total of 2,200,000 pairs of boots against army demands.

(7) *Tents.*—The Board supplied tents of all descriptions to the Ordnance Branch from the beginning of 1918. To meet the very great increase in military requirements, it became necessary to supplement existing sources of supply. A Government Tent Factory was established at Fatehgarh in April 1918, and a second Government Tent Factory, under private management, commenced work in Madras in October 1918. New tent factories were started by private agency in other centres and were supplied by the Board with the necessary materials. The total number of tents of all descriptions delivered up to the end of October 1918 amounted to 148,000, representing approximately thirty million yards of dosuti, the cloth of which they are made.

(8) *Jute goods.*—Large savings were secured to Government by centralising the purchase of jute goods in a branch directed by a Comptroller who was an expert in the jute trade. His operations comprised the supply of army requirements in India and Mesopotamia as well as arranging for purchases on account of Australia and other British possessions overseas. It is estimated that during the first six months after the formation of this Branch, in February 1918, savings of more than Rs. 2 crores were made; this was rendered possible by the consolidation and forecasting of demands and by taking expert advantage of favourable market conditions.

The statement below shows the principal supplies made up to the 31st October 1918 :—

Articles	Quantity	
Atta bags	6,302,845	
Barley bags	3,549,140	
Dhal bags	1,401,100	
Sugar bags	300,000	
Sand bags	8,074,500	
Heavy "C" cloth	1,711,233	yards
Heavy "C" packets	539,000	
Heavy "C" bags	4,673,708	
Hessian cloth	13,634,335	yards
Gunny cloth	1,521,700	
Twine	7,304	maunds
Paulins	83,773	
Bags, coffee	64,362	
Bags, feeding and watering	63,720	
Bags, ration	286,860	
Bags, charcoal	20,000	
Bags, pin (tent)	37,486	
Bags, pole (tent)	22,052	
Sheets, ground	32,636	
Sheets, others	1,038	
Jute waste	196	tons
Jute rope	48,673,785	yards
Hemp rope	737,270	yards
Saddlery nets	6,000	yards
Canvas	1,046,281	yards
Tanks	502	yards
Jhools	26,414	
Chaguls	185,358	
Gunny double narrow	103,525	yards
Rick covers	1,589	
Covers, I.P. harness	30,000	

Rucksacks	1,000
Logline	13,847 skeins
Chut for palans	8,000 yards
Camel hair belting	2,200 feet
Cordage hemp hawser	37,270 fms

Owing to scarcity of flax canvas the manufacture of 5,000,000 yards of jute canvas was also arranged to meet all demands particularly during the rainy season of 1918.

(9) *Rivercraft.*—The demand for water transport in the Eastern theatres of war became so heavy that, in 1916, the Government of India found it necessary to form a special agency to organise the work of construction, as the resources of the existing dockyards under the control of the Director of the Royal Indian Marine were already fully taxed in other directions. The Rivercraft Branch of the Railway Board's establishment was accordingly formed and, shortly after its formation, transferred to the administrative control of the Indian Munitions Board. A Board, styled the Indian Rivercraft Board, was constituted at Calcutta with sub-committees at Bombay, Karachi, Rangoon, Colombo and Singapore. In June 1918, as the programme of work was completed for which the Indian Rivercraft Board had assumed responsibility, this agency was dissolved.

After the arrival of the Controller of Shipbuilding and his staff from the Admiralty in December 1917, all demands for craft were met by the Shipbuilding Branch of the Indian Munitions Board.

The following craft were supplied for war purposes up to 31st October 1918 :—

For Mesopotamia

Sternwheel tugs, 150'	5
Hospital sternwheelers, 174' 6" ...	2
Barges, 125'	70
Barges, 125' (steel)	49
Barges, 125' (composite)	11
Barges, 50' (port)	90
Motor launches	20
Motor launch hulls	14
Marine motors	22
Driving boats, 42'	4
Mooring boat, 28'	1
Diving boat, 36'	1
Light steel pontoons	110
Steel decked pontoons, 35'	2
Pontoons, 50'	2
Steam launches, 46' 6"	2
Anchor pick-up boats, 45'	2
Anchor boats, 25'	40
Anchor boats, 19'	46
Anchor boats, 18'	130
Anchor boats, 17'	70
Anchor boats, 15'	65
Dinghies, 12'	174

For East Africa.

Hospital motor launch, 35'	1
Steam launch, 72'	1
Steel lighters, 45'	2
Steel canoes, 30'	4
Motor launch, 25'	1

For Bandar Abbas

Dinghy, 12'	1

For Sistan

Pontoon, punts, 17' 6"	8

For Bombay Motor Boat Instruction School

Motor launches	2
Marine motor engines	2

A considerable number of mooring buoys and spare parts, such as rudders, propellers and shafting, were also supplied to forces overseas.

(10) *Timber.*—The statement below summarises the operations of the Timber Branch of the Indian Munitions Board from its organization in April 1917 to the end of October 1918. The figures include bamboos, but not wooden railway sleepers (which have been included under the head railway track), or wood fuel, the supply of which was not made by the Board. The quantity of timber and bamboos is expressed in tons of 50 cubic feet:—

Destination	Indents received	Amount shipped or despatched	Balance to be supplied
	Tons	Tons	Tons
Egypt	64,116	56,904	7,212
Mesopotamia	131,406	121,386	10,020
Salonika	19,624	15,647	3,977
Other Theatres	10,106	3,744	6,362
TOTAL SENT OVERSEAS	225,252	197,681	27,571
India	46,052	30,395	15,667
GRAND TOTAL	271,304	228,076	43,228*

*Of this amount 19,395 tons was ready for shipment or despatch on 31st October 1918.

In order to enable indents to be met without undue delay (the extraction of timber from the forest being possible as a rule only during certain seasons of the year) and to season the timber before despatch as far as time allowed, the Board established large depots in Bombay, Rangoon and Karachi. The total balance of stock in hand in the three depots at the end of October 1918 was 42,624 tons, *viz.*, 22,693 tons (including 347,849 bamboos) in Bombay, 13,720 tons in Rangoon and 6,211 tons in Karachi.

Every effort was made to substitute indigenous timber for foreign supplies, in order to reduce the demands on shipping to a minimum and to encourage as far as possible the use of the locally-grown article.

It may be mentioned that the great majority of the timber supplied was in the form of sawn beams, planks and scantlings, and the conversion of this presented great difficulty (elsewhere than in Burma) owing to the very limited number of saw mills existing and the impossibility of importing additional plant.

Apart from supplying timber and bamboos for structural work, *e.g.,* the construction of bridges, piers, wharves, buildings and temporary huts and lines, the Board provided wood of suitable species for the construction and repair of craft, telegraph poles, bamboos for river training works, tent poles and mosquito poles. In addition, it engaged on an exhaustive search for timber suitable for use in aircraft. Numerous promising species were tested.

(11) *Miscellaneous Engineering Plant and Stores.*—It is impracticable within the limits of this record to give details of the enormous quantities of miscellaneous engineering plant and stores provided through the agency of the Indian Munitions Board. These included considerable supplies of all kinds of machinery and engineering equipment required for the docks and workshops which were constructed in

Mesopotamia and East Africa. An idea of the magnitude of the supplies may be gauged from the figures contained in the summary of expenditure on page 132.

(12) *Scrutiny of Priority applications.*—The institution of a methodical scrutiny of priority applications on behalf of the British Ministry of Munitions synchronised with the creation of the Indian Munitions Board in March 1917. The Priority Branch at headquarters working in cooperation with Provincial Priority authorities, carefully examined all applications in accordance with the principles laid down by the Priority Branch of the Ministry of Munitions and only forwarded such applications as appeared to be justifiable in each particular instance. Substantial assistance was thus rendered to the Home authorities in ensuring that Indian trade demands made upon the United Kingdom during the latter period of the war were rigidly limited to essential cases.

After the introduction of a similar priority control in the United States of America to that already in force in the United Kingdom, the Board acted in a similar capacity as the Indian representative of the American priority authorities.

Up to the 30th October 1918 over 15,000 priority applications were examined at the Board's headquarters, and the list of articles for which priority recommendation was refused comprised more than 2,000 headings.

(13) *Scrutiny of Government Indents.*—A Home Indents Branch of the Munitions Board, which worked in close co-operation with the Priority Branch, was constituted to exercise a careful scrutiny over all indents made by Government Departments on England, and substantial reductions were secured in many cases. This branch scrutinized 1,046 indents during the period under review.

(14) *Control of exports of certain materials.*—In co-operation with the Department of Commerce and Industry, the Board undertook the control of export from India of certain articles required for war use or essential national purposes, the stocks of which it was desirable to conserve, in view of internal demands. From June 1917 to 31st October 1918, 1,737 export applications were dealt with.

(15) *Control of Steel and Pig-iron.*—The only works producing steel in India were the Tata Iron and Steel Works at Sakchi. With the ready consent of the management of that company, Government exercised complete control over the distribution of the output of steel, and obtained favourable rates for supplies on Government account, without having recourse to compulsion under the Defence of India Rules. The principal portion of the steel output took the form of

rails and fastenings for railway work, the Tata works having provided 985 track miles of the supplies detailed in paragraph (3) above. In addition to railway material, large quantities of rolled steel sections were procured for war purposes under similar arrangements.

Towards the end of 1917 difficulty was experienced with regard to supplies of pig-iron. In December 1917 it became clear that action must be taken to conserve the pig-iron being manufactured in India for India's own needs, both military and civil, and some form of control exercised in order that supplies could be distributed in accordance with national needs. Exports were prohibited except under certificates, and after consultation with the two producing firms the Board took complete control of its distribution. This was effected by priority grading.

(16) *Control of cement.*—In 1914 only an insignificant quantity of Portland cement was being manufactured in India, and war demands were met from stocks of imported cement, most of which was of English origin. In the following year two firms in India began to manufacture in appreciable quantities, and in 1916 a third commenced production. Early in 1917, owing to the depletion of stocks of imported cement, it became clear that Government would be compelled to draw much more largely upon Indian cement works to

meet its requirements, and therefore entered into an agreement with the three cement companies, by virtue of which Government obtained an option on three quarters of their output. In March 1918 it became necessary to control the whole output of the cement works, and from that date all supplies of cement from these firms, whether for Government or private use were regulated by the Indian Munitions Board. During the nine months, March to November 1918, a total of 59,000 tons of cement were dealt with in this way, the material being distributed in the following proportions:—

	per cent
Overseas Forces	30
Military in India	23
Public Works	20
Railways	9
Public bodies	4
General public	14

(17) *Control of dealings in certain engineering materials.*—Advantage was taken by the Munitions Board of the provisions of one of the Defence of India Rules to introduce a necessary measure of control over public dealings in the following articles:—

Steel plates;

Galvanised and black iron sheets;

Steel or iron beams, girders, bars, channel angles, and other rolled sections;

Steel wire ropes;

Steel scrap;

Tin plates;

Copper tubing.

The regulation of trade in these materials was necessitated by the fact that stocks in India had become greatly depleted by the unusually large demands made and the almost insuperable difficulty of replenishing them by import from home for war and other purposes. Evidence had also accumulated that speculative dealings were taking place with the result that prices had been advanced in an unjustifiable manner.

(18) *Control of ship repairs.*—The first measure of control assumed by the Board over the execution of ship repairs in India was adopted with the object of restricting the use of structural materials to really essential requirements, for while it might be justifiable in normal times to make repairs such as may be expected to last for many years, it was proper in existing circumstances to permit only so much material to be used as was reasonably necessary to maintain ships in service for a comparatively limited period. Subsequently, at the instance of the Admiralty, a more general measure of control over ship repairs was introduced.

Abstract of expenditure by Munitions Board

The following table, which shows the cash expenditure in thousands of rupees incurred in India by the Munitions Board from the 1st April 1917 to the 31st October 1918, may be of interest:—

Head of expenditure	1st April 1917 to 31st March 1918	1st April 1918 to 31st October 1918
	Thousands of rupees	Thousands of rupees
I. Salaries, Establishments, etc.—		
(a) Headquarters—		
(i) Supply Branches	6,45	8,83
(ii) Industrial Development Branches	1,34	85
(b) Provincial	9,85	22,46
TOTAL I	17,64	32,14
II. Supplies—		
(a) Rivercraft and Inland Water Transport stores.	1,50,97	82,79
(b) Tata's rails and fishplates	1,05,16	28,98
(c) Other railway materials	1,46,82	1,56,80
(d) Timber	86,36	1,43,68
(e) Textiles and Jute	85,50	80,51
(f) Ordnance and miscellaneous stores	2,63,83	9,10,81
TOTAL II	8,38,64	14,03,57
III. Factories, etc.—		
(a) Army Clothing Factories	3,87,67	7,03,70
(b) Ordnance Factories	67,74	2,71,00
(c) Acetone Factory	1,09	52
(d) Albion Shell Factory	6,69	6,71
(e) Tanneries and Tanstuff	15,35	9,36
(f) Kutra Iron Works	1,37	58
(g) Tent making Factory	...	48
TOTAL III	4,79,91	9,92,35
GRAND TOTAL	13,36,19	24,28,06

The above figures do not include the value of the bulk of the hides supplied to the War Office and Italian Government which were paid for by demand draft, and amounted to the following sums :—

	To 31st March 1918	From 1st April 1918 to 31st October 1918
	£	£
For tanned hides (Madras)	5,908,528	2,638,656
For tanned hides (Bombay)	520,174	339,407
For raw hides (Calcutta, Karachi and Rangoon)	382,775	469,191
TOTAL	6,811,477	3,447,254

As explained above, the Rivercraft Board consisted of representatives of the principal engineering firms at Calcutta, and to it were affiliated Rivercraft Committees, similarly constituted at Karachi, Bombay, Rangoon, Colombo and Singapore. The first item undertaken by the Board was the fitting out of the steamship Abydos as a floating workshop for use at Basra, which left Calcutta with 300 skilled Chinese artizans and 150 unskilled Indian labourers on the 7th November 1916.

In accordance with the programme laid down by the British War Office, arrangements were made for the construction of a large number of rivercraft in India, and for the re-erection at Karachi and Bombay of craft of various kinds sent out from Home in plates and angles. The main portion of this work was done at Karachi, where a very large yard was laid down capable of building at one time 20 large rivercraft.

In Calcutta the work consisted principally in the construction of 125' steel and composite barges and of 50' steel barges; also pontoons for two large floating bridges. A number of spare parts, such as rudders, propellers and shafting, were manufactured and despatched for the use of the oversea forces; and a large number of anchor boats, cutters and dinghies were also supplied.

Bombay constructed barges of the 125' type both in steel and wood, and also undertook the smaller type of 50' barges for use in port work at Basra. The re-erection of two sternwheel tugs and of three sternwheel hospitalships was also undertaken, the sternwheel hospitalships being large and very complicated vessels.

The building of the Karachi yard and the expeditious way in which work was carried on in it is a record most creditable to the organisers and to the executive who carried it through. The yard launched its first 125' barge on the 29th March 1917, and the launchings thereafter, month by month, were as follows :—

1917—	
April	3
May	3
June	9
July	18
August	14
September	15
October	22
November	20
December	16
1918—	
January	15
February	4
March	2

In addition to the above a large number of pontoons for floating bridges were despatched from Calcutta to Karachi in plates and angles for re-erection and completion at Basra. Three sternwheel tugs sent out from Home were also erected.

In Rangoon, the Committee built a composite barge and a large number of wooden anchor boats, cutters and dinghies, and gave much assistance in plant and skilled labour.

The Singapore Committee helped the Board very considerably not only in meeting large indents for plant of all kinds but also in obtaining a large number of highly skilled Chinese labourers.

The Colombo Committee had very few calls made on them but they gave considerable assistance in the provision of labour and in the examination of existing launches and cargo boats.

The Rivercraft Board was dissolved in August 1918 on the completion of the programme of work entrusted to it.

Medical equipment and material

The statement below shows the quantities of vaccines and sera in cubic centimetres issued by the Central Research Institute, Kasauli, during the period of the war, excluding those manufactured for Indian civilian needs. The yearly issue averaged 1,514,551 cubic centimetres as against 18,423 the average of the two years prior to the war.

Some thousands of cubic centimetres of other miscellaneous vaccines were also manufactured and issued. Issues of anti-diptheritic, anti-tetanic, anti-streptococcic, and other anti-toxic, sera obtained from England and stored in India, totalled nearly a million cubic centimetres; and issues of anti-venin and other sera manufactured in India, over 185,250 cubic centimetres.

Contributions from the Bombay Bacteriological Laboratory, Parel, included:—sera to the value of Rs. 1,335; vaccines, other than plague vaccine 515,354 cubic centimetres; plague vaccine 2,500,500 cubic centimetres; iodine for antiseptic solution 14,108 phials;

tincture of iodine for shell dressings 48,000 phials; instruments, apparatus, etc., to the value of Rs. 11,937.

—	Aug.-Dec. 1914	1915	1916	1917	1918	TOTAL
Central Research Institute, Kasauli.						
Typhoid vaccine	46,269	147,371	82,945	12	20	276,617
T.A.B. vaccine	...	...	408,831	1,155,415	807,341	2,371,587
Cholera vaccine	...	50,670	629,426	1,225,222	1,883,744	3,789,062
Bombay Bacteriological Laboratory, Parel.						
Pague vaccine	..	..	..	..	..	2,500,500
Other vaccines	..	..	..	..	..	515,354
TOTALS	46,269	198,041	1,121,202	2,380,649	2,691,105	9,453,120

Other contributions included seven Bacteriological Laboratories, one Malaria Laboratory, forty-three sets of X-Ray apparatus, and six hospital river boats. Six hospitalships were equipped and manned in India, *viz.*, the Madras, Loyalty, Takada, Varela, Ellora and Erinpura, of which the Loyalty was equipped and maintained by certain Ruling Chiefs.

The maximum hospital accommodation provided in India is shown in the following table :—

—	British Officers' beds	British rank and file beds	Indian rank and file beds	TOTAL
War hospitals	540	10,100	12,630	23,270
Convalescent Homes	120	...	...	120
Convalescent Sections	...	8,250	15,750	24,000
Convalescent Hospital Camps	...	...	2,250	2,250
Enteric Convalescent Depot	...	2,440	...	2,440
War beds in civil hospitals	...	...	1,190	1,190
TOTAL	660	20,790	31,820	53,270

Mechanical Transport Material

A Central Mechanical Transport Stores Depot was formed at Rawalpindi for all mechanical transport units in India. To this organisation were affiliated the purchasing agencies for procuring available mechanical transport stores in India; through these agencies large quantities of spare parts, tyres and mechanical transport material generally were purchased from markets in India and despatched to the various overseas forces. From the date of the outbreak of war, the number of mechanical transport vehicles sent overseas from India was :—

Motor lorries	72
Motor cars	102
Motor cycles	117
Motor vans	675
Motor ambulances	72
Workshop lorries	2
Store lorries	2
Armoured lorries	3
Armoured cars	8
Motor M.G. Armoured side-car combinations	12
Rail tractors	60
Mobile kitchens	4

In addition to the above, the monetary contributions made by Ruling Chiefs and others towards the provision of motor vehicles for service in India amounted to Rs. 40,74,333-5-4, and a further contribution of Rs. 1,200,000 was offered by His Highness the Maharaja Scindia.

Supplies

The approximate value of the supplies sent overseas during the war to the various forces dependent on India was :—

	£
To France	704,000
To East Africa	1,485,000
To Mesopotamia	24,842,000
To Egypt	6,554,000
To Persia	460,000
To Aden (half)	363,000
TOTAL	34,408,000

Some of the more important items which were shipped from India up to the end of March, 1919 were:—

	Tons
Rice	219,889
Flour	133,025
Atta	322,587
Grain for animals (*i.e.*, Barley, Gram, Oats and Bran)	545,788
Hay and Bhoosa	771,737
Dhall	48,650
Ghi	26,214
Sugar	35,602
Tea	6,502
Tinned meat (*i.e.*, tinned and preserved meat, mutton and beef and essence of beef and of mutton)	10,763
Jam	5,977
Biscuits	7,905
Firewood	603,223
TOTAL	2,737,862

The greater portion of the sugar, tinned meat, jam, and biscuits was first imported to India, sugar from Mauritius and Java, and the remainder from Australia.

In addition large quantities of oils and lubricants, equipment and various supplies were shipped from India.

The table below shows the rise in the yearly shipments of hay and bhoosa to overseas forces.

—	1914-15	1915-16	1916-17	1917-18	1918 to January 1919	TOTAL
	Tons	Tons	Tons	Tons	Tons	Tons
Bhoosa	52,883	71,692	67,213	179,583	62,946	434,317
Hay	50,553	36,509	88,184	82,190	14,124	271,560
TOTAL	103,436	108,201	155,397	261,773	77,070	705,877

For duty with Farms, 35 Europeans and 454 Indians, 3,513 head of dairy cattle, and 2,139 bullocks were sent overseas. In connection with the agricultural development of Mesopotamia, 200 pumping sets, 40 hand and 24 power baling presses, 1 cotton press, some thousands of tons of seed, threshers, winnowers, ploughs, etc., were provided.

Military Works

Prior to the creation of the Indian Munitions Board in 1917, the Military Works Branch of the Army in India were responsible for the supply of Engineer stores to overseas theatres. Some of the items sent from India during this period were:—

Roofing felt	1,700,000 sq. ft.
Corrugated sheets	6,000 tons.*
Screws	69,500 gross
Nails	1,000 tons

* *i.e.*, 825 miles of sheets, 32 inches wide.

Glass panes	168,000	
Water tanks, iron, total capacity	2,000,000	gallon
Canvas tanks, total capacity	50,000	gallon
Piping	234	miles
Bolts and nuts	950,000	
Timber	75,000	tons
Poles and rafters	125,000	
Bamboos	400,000	
Iron and steel work	5,700	tons
Bedsteads	11,600	
Ice-boxes	585	
Cots, iron trestle	2,360	
Sleepers (to Egypt and Salonika)	150,000	

The barrack and hospital furniture supplied against various demands was of a total value of Rs. 800,000, and iron framed buildings covering an area of $17^{1}/_{2}$ acres.

Among the electrical plant and stores provided for Mesopotamia were :—

(*a*) The greater part of the plant and all other electrical stores for Basra Central Electrical Power Station.

(*b*) All electrical stores, except plant, for Qurna and Nasiriya Electrical Installations.

(*c*) All plant and electrical stores for Sheikh Sa'ad Electrical Installation.

(*d*) Part of the plant and the greater part of stores for Baghdad Central Electrical Power Station.

(*e*) Six generating sets for cinematographs at Basra.

(*f*) Various small and miscellaneous electrical and mechanical stores.

The total generating plant supplied from India for the above installations and for water supplies amounted to over 4,000 H.P. Material for wiring some 20,000 points, together with 10,000 fans, were also supplied. The total value of the electrical stores sent to Mesopotamia prior to the creation of the Munitions Board was approximately Rs. 4,300,000. Ice plants to a value of Rs. 370,000 were also provided for Mesopotamia and the Persian Gulf.

In India itself the Military Works Branch of the Army was responsible for the provision of temporary accommodation for 28,000 British ranks, over 250,000 Indian ranks, and 25,000 animals; temporary hospitals or convalescent accommodation or 27,500 beds; and accommodation for over 20,000 men at various training schools in camps, factories, etc., etc.

Marine

Transports.—From the date of the outbreak of war some 229 vessels were chartered from time to time, 5,966 transports were dealt with at Bombay, 4,905 at Karachi, and 483 at Calcutta. The tonnage of supplies and stores despatched to the different bases represented upwards of 3,870,000 tons from Bombay and Karachi.

River Flotilla for Mesopotamia.—156 steamers, 271 launches, and 531 barges were provided or arranged from India. In addition a small number of craft were despatched to Aden and East Africa.

Dockyard work.—1,400 transports and 120 hospital-ships were fitted, refitted or repaired at Bombay.

85 British war vessels were repaired and refitted at Bombay, which formed an important depot for the ships of the Royal Navy.

The seven Royal Indian Marine vessels which were handed over to the Royal Navy on the outbreak of war for employment as auxiliary cruisers were all altered, armed and fitted out at Bombay. In addition to the above, repairs and fittings were carried out as follows:—

6 Foreign war vessels repaired.

83 Prize steamships repaired and refitted.

1,100 vessels of various classes (mainly river-craft) fitted or repaired for Mesopotamia.

About 30 vessels were taken up and fitted for patrolling in the Bay of Bengal and the Arabian Sea.

Royal Indian Marine Vessels.—The Royal Indian Marine vessels, Hardinge, Dufferin, Northbrook, Minto, Dalhousie, Lawrence, and Comet were transferred to the Royal Navy on the outbreak of war for employment as auxiliary cruisers.

The Palinurus and Investigator were on various occasions employed in towing river craft to Mesopotamia; at other times they were employed on patrolling and mine-sweeping duties.

Mine-sweeping.—Owing to the sowing of mines in Indian waters by an enemy mine-layer in the early part of 1917, it became necessary to institute measures of protection at the various defended ports. The actual direction and responsibility of mine-sweeping and patrolling originally devolved on the Royal Indian Marine, who were however able to rely on the assistance and advice of the local Royal Naval authorities. After some months the direction of mine-sweeping at Bombay was placed under Naval control owing to the importance of the port and the increasing scope of the measures necessary. Although this arrangement proved satisfactory, the Government of India considered that a central control of these operations and undivided responsibility for the requirements of Indian ports as a whole would ensure more efficient working and better results. The mine-sweeping and patrolling organization was accordingly placed under the control and direction of the Naval Commander-in-Chief, East Indies, the Royal Indian Marine remaining responsible for the provision of suitable vessels and the supply of the requisite personnel to man them.

Suitable craft were not available locally in the numbers required and, to make up the deficiency, 3 vessels were obtained from China, and 9 trawlers, the designs and specifications for which were supplied by the Admiralty, were laid down—6 in the Royal Indian Marine Dockyards and 3 by Messrs. Burn and Company, Calcutta.

Foodstuffs

Amongst the more important services rendered by India during the war must be reckoned her shipments of foodstuffs to supplement the home production of Great Britain and her Allies.

Wheat purchases came under Government control early in 1915, and during the period of these operations the Royal Commission on Wheat Supplies purchased in India nearly 5 million tons of various foodstuffs of a total value of over £40,000,000 sterling.

Miscellaneous

Mention has already been made of the development of the Burmese wolfram industry during the war and some 15,000 tons of this mineral, valued at over £2,500,000, were sent to England at fixed prices considerably below those ruling in other countries. Of manganese ore India's exports amounted to nearly 2 million tons valued at over £2$^1/_4$ millions; and of saltpetre she supplied the Allies with 90,000 tons of a value exceeding £2 millions sterling.

With regard to Indian mica its high insulating properties brought it into great demand and some 6,000 tons were shipped to the United Kingdom, valued at over £1,600,000.

Of wool, in addition to the vast quantity of manufactured articles supplied, the exportable surplus was reserved for the War Office and some £8 million pounds worth was shipped to England. Oils and oil-seeds have provided a valuable contribution, the surplus available during the war for export within the Empire and to the Allies amounting to 2$^1/_2$ million tons of a value of about £31,000,000.

India also supplied to Mesopotamia the whole of the railway transport, as well as the telegraphic and telephonic equipment employed in that country, thus making very heavy demands on the Departments concerned both in material and personnel, all of which were loyally accepted and successfully met.

It is too early yet to attempt to measure the true incidence of India's material development as a result of the war. The first post-war fiscal year witnessed an exceptional boom in trade of every description, which was followed by a period of natural depression. But of India's contribution to the war in munitions and essential material there can be no doubt that her share has not been inferior in extent to that of any portion of the Empire.

CHAPTER IV

INDIA'S CONTRIBUTION IN MONEY

THE wealth of the East Indies was handed down as a tradition from Roman times and for centuries has been an accepted belief amongst ill-informed persons in Europe.

Wealth of a kind there certainly was; but it was concentrated in a few hands and never diffused. And it was collected too in an unproductive form. The Indian Princes were compelled, by the absence of any system of national credit, to hoard great sums with a view to meeting sudden demands, such as the mutiny of their troops or the rebellion of a too powerful kinsman. These hoards they kept to a large extent in precious gems so that the national reserve fund was also a principal means of courtly display. It is said that when Nadir Shah sacked Delhi in 1739 he found $3^1/_2$ millions of specie and $28^1/_2$ millions worth of jewels, ornaments and plate in the Imperial treasury, but that only one million of the specie was in the form of gold or silver coin.

Nowadays the Government of India's cash balances are hidden away in strong rooms out of sight, but in the time of the Emperor Shah Jahan the Peacock Throne blazed with its diamonds before the eyes of every foreign ambassador. Travellers were dazzled by the magnificence of the court surroundings and made no effort to appraise the wealth or poverty of the country as a whole. Judged not by the splendour of individuals but by the prosperity of the people India was then, and still is now, a poor country.

Nearly three-quarters of her population of over 315 million souls, for the whole of India, consists of small husbandmen contending, without reserve of capital, against the chances, and misfortunes of the tropical year, their very lives depending on a few inches more or less of rainfall. In view of her poverty, therefore, the financial contributions made by India have been very considerable.

The monetary assistance which she rendered during the war may conveniently be divided into two categories:—

(a) measures taken through the instrumentality of Government,

(b) private gifts.

Dealing firstly with Government measures it may be postulated that, owing to the severe economic conditions referred to above, which govern the lives of the bulk of the population, the expansion of direct taxation has presented peculiar difficulties in this country, and thereby placed India at an initial disadvantage as compared with the fiscal resources of other countries.

In an earlier chapter we have seen what a wonderful wave of enthusiasm swept over the whole of India on the outbreak of war and how one Indian non-official member of the Imperial Legislative Council moved, and another seconded a resolution, which was passed unanimously, requesting His Excellency the President to convey to the King-Emperor and to His Majesty's Government an expression of the desire of the people of India to share in the heavy financial burden imposed by the war on the United Kingdom.

Section 22 of the Government of India Act, 1915, prescribes that except for preventing or repelling actual invasion of His Majesty's Indian possessions, or under other sudden and urgent necessity, the revenues of India shall not, without the consent of both Houses of Parliament, be applicable to defraying the expenses of any military operation carried on beyond the external frontiers of those possessions by His Majesty's forces charged upon those revenues.

In communicating the terms of this Resolution to the Secretary of State, His Excellency the Viceroy* pointed out that the desire of the Hon'ble Members to share this

* Lord Hardinge.

financial burden was a natural and legitimate aspiration with which the Government of India were in complete sympathy, so far as it was legitimately possible, having due regard to the interest of the Indian tax-payer, and to the fact that Indian revenues were bound to suffer through the falling off of customs and railway receipts.

India would have been within her legal rights in asking the Home Government to bear the whole cost of the Expeditionary Force and could thus have effected counter-savings; but such a course was not in accord with the wishes of the people, and the Government of India therefore recommended that the country should accept such portion of the costly of the Force as would have fallen upon India had the troops concerned remained there.

This proposal was accepted by His Majesty's Government and Resolutions were passed by both Houses of Parliament, firstly in September, 1914, and again in November, 1914, permitting the payment of the contribution from Indian revenues. The terms of these Resolutions are as follows:—

> "That, His Majesty's Government having directed military forces charged upon the revenues of India to be despatched out of India for service in the war in which this country is engaged, this House consents that the ordinary pay and other ordinary charges of any troops so despatched, or that may be so despatched during the continuance of the war, as well as the ordinary charges

> of any vessels belonging to the Government of India that may be employed in these expeditions which would have been charged upon the resources of India if such troops or vessels had remained in that country or seas adjacent, shall continue to be so chargeable, provided that, if it shall be necessary to replace the troops or vessels so withdrawn by other vessels or forces, then the expense of raising, maintaining, and providing such vessels and forces shall be repaid out of any moneys which may be provided by Parliament for the purposes of the said expeditions."

In other words it was decided that India should continue to pay the normal pre-war cost of maintaining those of her troops sent overseas, while the extra expenditure involved was met by the Imperial Government.

Before describing in detail the various forms in which India's monetary contributions were obtained, it may be of interest briefly to review her fiscal history.

Without making any allowance for the enormous increase in population and for the infinitely larger acreage since made available for cultivation, the average annual demand of the Moghul Empire for the period 1593 to 1761 amounted to about 60 millions sterling a year, of which the net annual land revenue averaged 25 millions for the first hundred years and 32 millions sterling during the remainder of that period. The balance was made up by not less than forty imposts of a personal character, such as taxes upon religious assemblies, upon trees, upon marriage, upon the peasant's hearth and upon his cattle. How severe some of them were may be judged from the Poll Tax, for the purposes of which the non-Muhammadan population was divided into three classes, paying respectively £4, £2, and £1 annually to the Exchequer for each adult male.

To-day a similar impost would yield an amount exceeding the total revenue of the country.

During the ten years ending 1879, the Imperial taxation of British India, with its far larger population of 190 millions, averaged £35 millions sterling, of which the net land revenue amounted to 18 millions, the balance being found from excise, customs, etc. This total of 35 millions spread over the entire population worked out to a *per caput* tax of 3*s.* 8*d.* For the last six years, with a population of some 244 millions, India's annual revenue has averaged about £106 millions, being provided by land revenue, excise and customs receipts, profits on State Railways, irrigation, forests, etc., and by a comparatively small and graduated income tax on non-agricultural incomes of Rs. 1,000 to Rs. 25,000 a year, with a super tax on incomes above Rs. 50,000. These then were among the main items from which, during the war, India raised her annual average revenue of approximately £106 millions sterling, the burden of taxation averaging 2*s.* 5*d.** per head, or, if

* Calculated on the assumption that the burden of taxation is borne by the entire population of British India.

land revenue (which is akin to rent) be added, 4*s*. 1*d*. per head per annum.

But although India is a poor country her general financial position in recent years has been extremely strong. On the 31st March 1914 her total debt amounted to £274,188,476, almost the whole of which represented productive outlay on railways and irrigation, normally yielding a return which exceeded considerably not only interest on the amount borrowed, but also interest on the small debt classified as unproductive. And throughout the whole period of the war her average revenue approximately balanced her average expenditure.

To return to India's initial contribution under the Parliamentary Resolutions of September and November 1914, the gross amount payable to the end of 1919-20 was £47.*5* millions.

But as the Imperial Government bore the cost of the Territorial and Garrison battalions, sent to India to replace British units which had proceeded overseas, the charges relating to these substituted troops must be deducted thereby bringing India's net contribution under this one heading to £29.6 millions. The arrangement under which India bore the normal cost of troops in India terminated with effect from the 1st July 1919, in respect of Indian troops, and from 1st

April 1920 in respect of British troops. In addition to above a sum of £3.5 millions was paid by India as war gratuities of British officers and men of the normal garrison of India.

In effect India's contribution under the Parliamentary Resolutions of 1914 represents the amount which she would have saved owing to the depletion of her military garrison, if she had not offered, and been permitted by Parliament, to bear the ordinary pay and other ordinary charges of troops sent out of India, and the ordinary charges of her vessels employed in connection with the war. Political and financial circumstances in India and the uncertainty of the position on the North-West Frontier precluded the Government of India from rendering at the outset more pecuniary assistance to His Majesty's Government. At the beginning of 1917 however, the position had sufficiently improved to enable the Government, with the general assent of the Imperial Legislative Council, to offer His Majesty's Government a lump sum of £100 millions as a special contribution by India towards the expenses of the war. The offer was gratefully accepted by His Majesty's Government, and a Resolution was passed by the Houses of Parliament on the 14th March, 1917, permitting the payment of the contribution from Indian revenues. Towards this contribution, nearly £75 millions were raised in India by the war loans of 1917 and 1918 and as regards the balance, the Government of India took over the liability for interest on an equivalent amount of the British Government war loan.

Small as this sum may seem in comparison with the expenditure of European countries during the war, it must be remembered that it adds over 30 per cent to India's national debt, that it was then rather more than her entire income for a whole year, and that it entails an extra annual burden of 6 per cent of that income for its maintenance. Further, it should be noted that the largest loan ever previously raised by Government in India amounted only to £3 millions distributed amongst 1,172 investors. The war loans above-mentioned were designed to attract those classes which hitherto had not been in the habit of investing their money and they were pushed by a vigorous publicity campaign, but their success exceeded all expectations. The 1917 loan realised no less than £35$^{1}/_{2}$ millions, including £6 millions realised by the issue of Post Office 5-year cash certificates; and, despite many adverse predictions, the 1918 loan yielded a further total of £38 millions, including £2 millions from cash certificates, the subscribers in this case numbering 227,706. This free gift of £100 millions sterling was fully appreciated by His Majesty's Government, who realised that India was contributing what she could to the common fund, and on the 21st March 1917 Lord Chelmsford received the following message from Mr. Lloyd George :—

> "I wish on behalf of the British Government to express to the Government and the people of India our most sincere gratitude for the magnificent contribution which India has just made to financing the War. Coming in addition to the enthusiasm and loyalty manifested throughout India on the outbreak of war and to the invaluable services since rendered by the Indian Army this gift is to us a living proof that India shares wholeheartedly with the other subjects of the Crown in the ideals for which we are fighting in this war. That India should come forward of her own accord in this crisis and render such real and opportune assistance is not only a source of sincere satisfaction to His Majesty's Government, but must produce a better mutual understanding among all the resources and peoples under the British Crown."

In September 1918 a Resolution was passed by the non-official Members of the Legislative Council of the Government of India, offering a further contribution to His Majesty's Government towards the expenses of the War. This Resolution recommended that, so long as financial conditions permitted, the following charges should be borne by the revenues of India, namely :—

(i) With effect from the 1st April 1918, the ordinary charges of 200,000 Indian troops in excess of the normal garrison, and with effect from 1st April 1919 of a further 100,000 men.

(*ii*) The cost of certain war allowances in the shape of an initial gratuity and recurring bonus, which was granted to Indian troops with effect from 1st June 1918, so far as it related to the normal garrison of Indian troops and the additional body of troops referred to in clause (*i*) above.

(*iii*) The cost from 1st April 1917 of the temporary accommodation provided for the additional Indian troops raised during the war.

(*iv*) The cost of the European section of the Indian Defence Force raised during the war.

(*v*) Certain non-effective charges in respect of (*a*) British and Indian troops despatched from India for service in connection with the war, and (*b*) British troops employed in the war who, though not despatched from India, had previously served in that country. Under the Resolutions of 1914 these charges would be borne by His Majesty's Government.

The offer was accepted by His Majesty's Government; and under the terms thereof a further contribution was paid from Indian revenues towards the expenses of the war amounting to £13.1 millions.

Thus the contributions from Indian revenues towards the cost of the war amounted to £146.2 millions to the end of 1919-20.

The above figures relate to India's direct monetary contribution towards the cost of the war. They do not, however, give a complete account of the additional charges which India has borne as a necessary result of war conditions. The war has, of course, directly and materially affected the military and political situation in India, and has rendered it necessary to take additional measures for the protection of the North-West Frontier. The actual expenditure up to the end of 1921-22 on these measures, and on the minor military operations which have taken place from time to time, amount to about £49.8 millions. Not only has expenditure been necessary on the safeguarding of the frontier, but in addition strict measures had to be taken for the protection of sea-coasts and ports from enemy attacks, and minesweeping operations had to be undertaken in Indian waters : these measures cost about £2.1 millions to the end of 1921-22. A moiety of the cost of the Aden operations which is borne by Indian revenues amounted to about £2.3 millions by the end of 1921-22. Certain measures of internal defence (other than those already referred to), including the entertainment of a censor staff and the internment of hostile aliens, involved an expenditure of £2.7 millions to the end of 1921-22. The total expenditure on these various special services thus amounted to about £57 millions up to the end of the financial year 1921-22. In addition India has been compelled to incur heavy military expenditure in other directions in consequence of the great European war. In this connection the lump figures of military expenditure, exclusive of the cost of special services and special contributions to His Majesty's Government mentioned above, speak for themselves. In the last Budget which was framed on peace conditions, *i.e.*, that for the year 1914-15, provision was made for a total net military expenditure of £20.5 millions, which was higher than the average of the preceding six years. In the five years ending with 1918-19 the total net military expenditure, exclusive of the cost of the special services and of the special contributions to His Majesty's Government mentioned above, amounted to £1215 millions, or an average of £3.8 millions in excess of the 1914-15 standard.

Free rations were granted to all Indian ranks of the Indian Army and the pay of Indian officers and non-commissioned officers was increased, with effect from 1st January 1917, the cost of the measures amounting to about £400,000 a year. The higher standards of comfort set in other parts of the Empire in the matter of accommodation for sick and wounded have also led to considerable expenditure on the improvement of hospitals for Indian troops in India, all war hospitals being fitted, with electric lights and fans; while motor ambulances have taken the place of the bullock ambulance carts which formerly sufficed for India's needs. Heavy expenditure has been and is being incurred on the provision of mechanical transport, armoured cars, armoured trains, machine guns, motor ambulances, aircraft, etc. The expenditure on these measures, which amounted to about £2¼ millions by the end of 1918-19 has been necessitated largely by the fact that India voluntarily depleted herself of a large part of her normal garrison of trained soldiers, and had therefore to adopt every possible mechanical contrivance to increase the mobility and fighting value of her remaining troops. The introduction of mechanical transport, again, has led to large expenditure on the improvement of frontier roads, which cost about £800,000 by the end of 1918-19.

It must, of course, be recognised that even had India taken no direct part in the war, she would still have been forced, in view of the uncertainty of the military position, to take special measures for the defence of her frontier and her coast; and that in respect of the hasty provision of mechanical transport, etc., she merely gave immediate effect to a policy which had been accepted to a large extent in principle before the war began and which she would probably have in any case put into operation before long, as her circumstances permitted. Nevertheless, the fact that the war has brought about this marked acceleration of India's progress towards a higher and more costly standard of military equipment, and has directly led to considerable expenditure on measures of defence against external aggression and internal disturbances, has to be taken into account in gauging India's real contribution.

Again, the political situation in Persia, aggravated by the intrigues of German and pro-German agents, necessitated vigorous counter-measures which included cash subsidies to the Persian Government and the Shah, a so-called moratorium, and the raising of an irregular Persian military force. The organisation of the South Persia Rifles has thrown a charge on Indian revenues of about £3.2 millions to the end of 1920-21; while India's share on other items of abnormal expenditure arising out of the war amounted to £674,000 up to the end of 1918-19 and involved a further outlay of over £500,000 in 1919-20.

Besides the contributions made towards the cost of the war and the additional expenditure undertaken as a direct result of it, India has also afforded material assistance to His Majesty's Government by financing Imperial expenditure to the extent of about £367 millions to the end of 1921-22. These sums have been ultimately repaid by the War Office, but their immediate provision imposed a very considerable strain on the resources of the Government of India. It was impossible to meet the large disbursements involved and at the same time to provide for the trade demand for remittance. Special arrangements were, therefore, made with the Exchange Banks by which finance was reserved for exports of national importance. In spite of these restrictions, however, the provision of funds in India by the ordinary methods was impracticable. Gold could not be imported, not earmarked in London against notes issued in India, and the extent of silver purchases was limited by the keen competition for, and the high price of, that metal. Borrowing in the form of war loans and Treasury Bills, though successful beyond the most sanguine expectations, did not suffice, and the Government of India were forced to adopt the expedient of increasing the investments held against the note circulation and issuing notes in India against British and India Treasury Bills. Thus at the end of February 1919 the amount of securities held in the Paper Currency Reserve was over £66 millions, as against £9.3 millions at the beginning of the war.

An important incidental result of these operations has been that out of the funds repaid in London against expenditure undertaken on behalf of the "War Office in India, Mesopotamia and elsewhere, a considerable portion has been re-invested in British war securities. In other words, apart from the direct financial assistance just described, India during the war not only ceased to indent on the Home market for funds but also advanced to the Home Government for the prosecution of the war no less than £75 millions, this representing investments in British war securities from the Secretary of State's balances and the Paper Currency and Gold Standard Reserves. An examination of the effects of these operations on India's internal financial position and currency arrangements would be out of place here, but the legacies which the war has left in the shape of currency difficulties and a large volume of temporary debt must not be overlooked in estimating the effort entailed by the financial assistance which India has so freely given.

It must be remembered, too, that no comparison between India's financial contribution to the war and that of the self-governing Dominions, the Crown Colonies and the Protectorates, would be fair or complete without a reference to their respective scales of pre-war expenditure on defence. Immediately prior to the war the percentage of defence expenditure to net public revenue in the United Kingdom was 43.9, in India 35.8, in the self-governing Dominions 12.7 and in the Crown Colonies and Protectorates 8.1, while for the whole Empire the percentage was 38.02. It is because India has for many years past maintained a large army, that she was able, at a critical moment, to despatch a large and fully equipped force to the Western front to help in stemming the tide of invasion of the territory of our Allies. The army in India proved itself once more to be a great Imperial asset. So, too, have been the forces hastily raised and trained in every part of the Empire, but the essential difference is that India at the outbreak of war had an army in being, which cost her annually a large sum to maintain; while the Colonies and Dominions had been exempted for all these years from a correspondingly heavy burden of military expenditure. In estimating whether there has been an equality of sacrifice between India and the rest of the overseas possessions of the Crown in respect of money contribution to this war, it is only fair to remember that before the outbreak of war India's burden of defence expenditure had been vastly greater than theirs.

The dominant consideration remains that India is a comparatively poor and backward country, which still lacks many administrative requisites which England and the Dominions have long possessed. India's money contribution towards the expenses of the war was rendered possible by Government enforcing the strictest economy, reducing the scale of much needed expenditure on administrative improvements, and rigidly vetoing all new expenditure which was not either immediately and imperatively necessary or directly remunerative. With India it has not been a case of denying herself luxuries, but of severely restricting expenditure on what may fairly be regarded as administrative necessities.

While, however, the Government of India's responsibilities to the people of this dependency precluded their proposing the imposition of a greater burden of heavy taxation for the purposes of the war, there was gratifying evidence that those of the people of India who were fortunately circumstanced were sensible of the benefits which they derive from India's membership in the Empire. Their active sympathy in the cause of the mother country and her Allies was shewn by generous donations to the numerous war relief funds, and by subscribing liberally towards the purchase of motor ambulances, hospitalships, aeroplanes, etc. Again, the Ruling Chiefs and the Rulers of Independent States, such as Nepal, displayed most conspicuous liberality in their contribution to the war and vied with one another in making gifts both in money and in kind. The bare list of these donations would fill a closely printed book of large dimensions and their total value, in money alone, can hardly be less than £5 millions sterling or $7^1/_2$ crores of rupees.

These gifts covered a wide range and were touched with an imagination and a goodwill which alone are a great Imperial asset. They included lump sums towards the general expenses of the war; money for the provision of aeroplanes, tanks, motor ambulances, mechanical transport, refrigerating plant, upkeep of war hospitals, maintenance of Convalescent Homes both in India and overseas, construction of religious edifices for troops on field service, the purchase, equipment and maintenance of the Hospital Ship "Loyalty," for the provision of motor boats and launches, and for measures to counter the German submarine campaign. Enormous sums were given to the Imperial Indian Relief Fund and to the various war and relief funds opened in this country. They also subscribed lavishly to various funds in Great Britain, including provision for the relief of British and Indian prisoners of war and monetary gifts to munition workers in England. Nor were the needs of Allied countries forgotten.

In addition they rendered numerous miscellaneous services, the money value of which it is impossible to estimate, in connection with the expansion and organisation their Imperial Service Troops so as to meet war conditions, and the grant of concessions, including pensionary privileges, similar to those granted in British India, to State subjects connected with these troops and to their dependents.

Again, they presented to Government large quantities of grain, fodder and other supplies, as well as much material in the shape of tents, blankets, railway engines and rolling stock, transport carts and harness, and various machinery and plant. Horses and other animals were also freely offered and the training of remounts for Government purposes was likewise undertaken. Their private residences in various centres were cordially lent as Hospitals and also to provide accommodation for the increased clerical establishment in Government offices incident to the war.

In addition to placing their State troops and the entire resources of their States at the disposal of Government, they provided large numbers of recruits for the regular Indian Army and themselves proceeded on field service whenever it was in their power to do so.

The spirit which inspires the generosity of great princes is the same as that which animates the humbler gifts of lessor mortals. Retired Indian officers too aged to fight begged that the incomes they derived from grants of land, bestowed on their ancestors for military service, might be utilised for the benefit of their old Regiments at the front, or for general war purposes.

Some individuals in Government service declined even to accept their pay. Other persons voluntarily doubled their income tax.

Instances such as these must fire the enthusiasm of any one conscious of the foundations of loyalty upon which the Indian Empire is based.

In each province and district War Funds were started for the collection of subscriptions towards the various Central Funds and for special purposes, such as the maintenance of Hospital ships, River Hospital ships and steamers; the purchase of horses; the equipment, training and clothing of motor cyclists; the provision of aeroplanes, motor ambulances and launches; the equipment of laboratories for the diagnosis of special diseases and the provision of special nurses and masseuses; special comforts for Hospital patients; the expenses of overseas furlough men and convalescents; the supply of enormous quantities of delicacies suitable for the various classes of soldiers at the front; and the equipment and maintenance of Gardeners' Corps for service in Mesopotamia.

Minor administrations and communities out of close touch with the mainland of India were no less generous. From the Andamans and Nicobars came a sum of no less than Rs. 28,650-2-8, together with nearly 14,000 garments, etc., for the use of Indian troops; the contributions of the Nicobarese being made in the form of monthly consignments of cocoanuts, which were sold and the proceeds included in the cash total mentioned.

Within the compass of a brief record it is not possible to give details of the varied gifts, in kind and in money, so lavishly contributed by the peoples and princes of India; but an indication of their extent may be gained from the subscriptions to the Imperial Indian Relief Fund, the largest charitable fund ever raised in this country, though but one of the many such funds subscribed to during the war.

The total amount subscribed to the Central Imperial Indian Relief Fund from the date of its inception up to the 30th June 1921, was Rs. 2,33,18,600. The interest upon the sums placed at fixed deposit amounted to Rs. 19,12,400 bringing the total income of the Central Fund up to* Rs. 2,52,31,000, or to £1,682,066 at Rs. 15 to £1 sterling. The expenditure up to the same date amounted to Rs. 2,27,68,500, the principal items being:—

	Rs.
Placed at the disposal of Brigade Area Committees during the war for the immediate relief of distress among the families of soldiers absent on field service and for the payment of donations to men permanently disabled and to the heirs of deceased soldiers and followers	79,53,700

*Rs. 2,55,01,900 or £1,700,126-13-4 up to 31st October 1921.

	Rs.
Placed at the disposal of local Governments and Administrations during the war for the relief of distress among certain classes of dependents of Indian soldiers	4,54,000
Donations to the Soldiers' and Sailors' Families Association	4,35,000
Donations to the Officers' Families Fund	2,91,000
Donations to the Indian Soldiers' Fund	1,00,000
Donations to the Indian Comforts for Troops Fund	5,34,000
Donations to the St. John's Ambulance Association	64,000
Donations to the Queen Mary's Technical School for disabled Indian Soldiers, Bombay, and to the Government Railway Technical School, Lahore	49,000
Assistance to officers and crews of vessels sunk during the war	1,09,000
Assistance to convalescent British officers during the war	8,86,000
Grant to provide extra medical comforts for the sick and wounded during the war	3,70,000
Assistance to the families of post and telegraph employees who proceeded on field service during the war	25,000
Placed at the disposal of local Governments and Political Officers for *post-bellum* relief to the dependents of deceased Indian officers and soldiers	73,77,500

	Rs.
Placed at the disposal of Controllers of Military Accounts for *post-bellum* relief to incapacitated Indian officers, soldiers and followers, admitted to wound and injury pensions of the 1st and 2nd degree	14,60,400
Placed at the disposal of the Officers' Families Fund for *post-bellum* relief to the families and dependents of deceased British officers of the Indian services and to British officers of the Indian Services incapacitated by the war	26,60,000
Placed at the disposal of the heads of departments for *post-bellum* relief to the families and dependents of deceased European and Anglo-Indian civil and military departmental employees	92,600
Placed at the disposal of local Governments and Administrations for *post-bellum* relief to the families and dependents, resident in India, of deceased British soldiers and volunteers	1,93,000

During June 1921, the subscriptions received together with amounts refunded on the closing of provincial distributing centres and the interest on sums placed at fixed deposit amounted to Rs. 51,900, while the disbursements during the same period amounted to Rs. 58,000, respectively.

The balance in hand on the 30th June 1921, amounted to Rs. 24,62,500.

In addition to the contributions in money and in kind which have been outlined above, mention must be made of the highly successful committees, organised by ladies throughout the Indian Empire, for war purposes. They collected and distributed to the troops overseas comforts of every description, including tobacco, sweetmeats, clothing, newspapers and books. They made with their own hands vast quantities of bandages and other hospital requisites. They provided cases of luxuries to troops on embarkation. They were prominent on the Reception Committees that welcomed and entertained the troops on their return. They managed Canteens for soldiers at railway and other centres. They organised the activities of women in all parts of the country and thereby prevented overlapping or neglect.

The need of funds for Red Cross work met with a generous response from public bodies and individuals, and although it required some initial supplementary grants from the Home Committee, Lord Chelmstord's appeal on behalf of the "Our Day" fund resulted in the raising of sufficient money to enable the Indian Branch of the Joint War Committee of the Order of St. John of Jerusalem and the British Red Cross Society to provide almost the whole of the supplies of comforts for the sick and wounded from the 2nd August 1916 onwards.

It is of interest to note that this Indian Branch, which was constituted as a Committee for war purposes only, has since been brought within the International League of Red Cross Societies and enjoys the same status as has been granted to British Dominions.

Provincial branches of the Indian Red Cross Society are being established throughout India and the Indian States and will cater for the needs of both military and civil hospitals. In all this work both British and Indian women have been closely associated, cheerfully giving their leisure and their means to aid in the prosecution of the war. Of the former especially, many went through the preliminary training necessary for enrolment as nurses should occasion demand. It is refreshing to feel that machinery which owed its initiation to the agency of war should have its energies diverted in peace time to the much-needed work of hospital improvement, both civil and military.

The war, too, brought into being many voluntary committees; and provincial district and women's work parties were established all over the country. From this there has arisen, amongst all classes and creeds in the community, a realisation of the need for co-operative effort for the relief of distress and suffering.

CHAPTER V

CASUALTIES

Total Indian casualties as compiled up to 31st December 1919

Theatre.	DEAD FROM ALL CAUSES.			WOUNDED.			MISSING AND PRISONERS.		
	I. O.	I. O. R.	Foll.	I. O.	I. O. R.	Foll.	I. O.	I. O. R.	Foll.
France	176	5,316	2,218	404	15,893	144	15	830	4
East Africa	67	2,405	500	59	1,927	17	..	40	3
Mesopotamia	364	17,567	11,624	828	31,330	450	15	1,510	284
Dunsterforce	..	158	23	..	15	..	..	..	..
Persia	25	1,779	670	11	454	6	..	1	..
Egypt	74	3,713	555	135	6,286	8	2	158	5
Gallipoli	33	1,591	127	72	3,578	1	..	101	..
Aden	7	500	79	16	548	4	1	21	3
Muscat	1	39	2	..	16	..	1	25	..
Frontier operations	17	2,245	1,621	65	1,759	24	16	701	26
GRAND TOTALS	764	35,313	17,419	1,590	61,806	954	50	3,387	325

Summary of Indian casualties :—

Died from all causes	53,486
Wounded	64,350
Missing and prisoners on 31st December 1919	3,762
GRAND TOTAL	121,598

NOTE.—Prisoners repatriated are not shown.

Total casualties as compiled up to 30th April 1920 for overseas forces, and up to 19th September 1920 for frontier operations, including figures for British officers of the Indian Army and British ranks on the permanent Indian Establishment.

Figures for British units serving with Indian formations are not available.

Theatre.	DEAD FROM ALL CAUSES.					WOUNDED.					MISSING AND PRISONERS.				
	B. O.	I. O.	B. R.	I. R.	Foll.	B. O.	I. O.	B. R.	I. R.	Foll.	B. O.	I. O.	B. R.	I. R.	Foll.
France	380	189	17	6,094	2,227	376	404	26	15,893	144	..	1	..	110	..
East Africa	50	67	11	2,439	504	62	59	3	1,929	17	..	..	..	2	1
Mesopotamia	730	380	905	19,186	12,261	1,000	830	540	31,376	450	..	2	30	218	61
Dunsterforco	6	..	50	158	23	9	..	10	15	..	..	..	..	..	..
Persia	14	28	..	1,875	758	13	11	..	464	6	..	..	..	..	..
Egypt	89	79	17	4,282	626	120	136	..	6,301	98	..	..	..	8	..
Gallipoli	72	33	3	1,690	128	100	72	2	3,578	111	..	..	..	..	..
Aden	14	8	2	522	86	24	16	..	548	4	..	..	..	1	1
Muscat	1	1	..	64	4	1	..	..	16	..	..	..	..	..	..
Frontier operations	111	62	190	2,439	2,166	98	90	179	2,511	129	..	19	..	791	17
GRAND TOTALS.	1,467	847	1,195	38,749	18,783	1,803	1,618	760	62,631	959	..	22	30	1,130	80

Summary of casualties :—

Died from all causes	61,041
Wounded	67,771
Missing and prisoners	1,262
GRAND TOTAL	130,074

NOTE.—Prisoners repatriated are not shown.

An approximate comparative table shewing the Empire's military casualties, as recorded at the date of compilation, excluding post war and Indian Frontier operations :—

	Dead from all causes.	Missing and prisoners.	Wounded.
British Isles	662,083	140,312	1,644,786
Canada	56,119	306	149,733
Australia	58,460	164	152,100
New Zealand	16,132	5	40,749
South Africa	6,928	33	11,444
India	47,746	871	65,126
Other Colonies	3,649	366	3,504
TOTAL	851,117	142,057	2,067,442

Summary of casualties :—

Died from all causes	851,117
Wounded	2,067,442
Missing and prisoners	142,057
GRAND TOTAL	3,060,616

NOTE.—Prisoners repatriated are not shown. Under "Other Colonies" are excluded 44,262 African native followers, *i.e.*, died and killed 42,318 ; wounded 1,322 ; missing 622. The deaths were due mainly to epidemies.

REWARDS

Statement shewing the rewards, other than mentions in Despatches, gained by British and Indian Officers and men of the Indian Army and Departments, and of the Royal Artillery and Royal Engineer Officers and men attached to Indian units.

Figures shewing the rewards gained by British Service units attached to Indian formations are not available.

"A" = Indian Expeditionary Force	"A" = France and Belgium
"B" = do.	"B" = East Africa.
"D" = do.	"D" = Mesopotamia.
"E" = do.	"E" = Egypt and Palestine.
"G" = do.	"G" = Gallipoli.'

British.

—	A.	B.	D.	E.	G.	Indian Frontier.	Indian Area.	Europe with England.	Unspecified.	India.	Black Sea.	TOTAL.
V.C.	3	..	3	..	..	1	2	..	..	..	..	9
A.D.C. Genl. to King	..	..	1	..	..	..	..	..	..	..	..	1
A.D.C. to King	..	..	..	..	..	1	..	..	..	..	..	1
G.C.B.	..	..	..	..	..	..	..	..	..	1	..	1
K.C.B.	4	..	5	1	..	1	1	4	..	1	..	17
C.B.	23	4	24	9	5	5	6	7	..	1	..	84
G.C.S.I.	..	..	..	..	..	..	1	1	2	1	..	5
K.C.S.I.	..	..	4	..	..	..	..	..	..	2	..	6
C.S.I.	..	..	37	..	..	1	10	..	..	13	..	61
G.C.M.G.	1	..	..	..	..	..	..	..	..	..	..	1
K.C.M.G.	1	2	4	4	2	..	1	2	..	..	..	16
C.M.G.	63	3	54	24	10	..	11	26	..	1	..	192
G.C.I.E.	..	..	1	..	..	..	..	..	1	..	..	2
K.C.I.E.	1	..	4	..	..	1	4	..	2	8	..	20
C.I.E.	5	4	60	2	..	9	44	5	..	70	..	199
G.B.E.	..	..	..	..	..	..	..	..	1	8	..	9
K.B.E.	..	..	..	1	..	..	..	3	..	..	..	7
C.B.E.	7	2	10	2	..	1	19	12	3	36	..	92

O.B.E.	20	9	154	25	..	1	114	22	6	140	7	498
M.B.E. . . .	1	6	97	4	..	..	37	1	4	55	1	206
D.S.O. 2nd Bar . .	..	..	..	2	..	..	..	..	..	..	..	2
D.S.O. Bar . .	8	1	9	4	..	..	6	1	..	..	..	29
D. S O. . . .	123	42	287	72	27	9	40	9	..	4	2	615
M.C. Bar . .	2	5	16	9	..	..	12	..	..	1	1	46
M.C.	154	78	362	146	21	4	109	..	8	9	3	894
D.S.C. . . .	..	..	12	..	..	..	..	..	..	..	..	12
D.F.C. . . .	1	..	..	..	..	..	..	..	..	1	..	2
A.F.C. . . .	..	..	..	..	..	..	..	..	..	1	..	1
D.C.M. . . .	4	5	24	2	4	..	..	..	2	..	..	41
M.M.	1	..	5	..	..	1	..	..	..	1	..	8
M. S. M. . . .	55	20	262	23	9	19	24	..	47	76	1	536
B.E.M. . . .	..	..	1	..	..	..	..	..	..	..	..	1
A.M. 1st class . .	1	..	..	..	..	..	..	..	..	..	..	1
R.R.C. 1st class . .	3	..	7	..	..	1	3	..	..	9	..	23
R.R.C. 2nd class . .	1	..	17	..	..	3	11	..	..	13	..	45
French Decoration .	55	12	55	7	10	7	9	7	41	4	..	207
American Decoration .	2	..	..	..	..	..	..	2	..	..	..	4
Italian Decoration. .	5	4	10	6	3	..	..	3	8	..	3	42
Belgian Decoration .	25	1	..	..	..	..	..	4	9	..	..	39
Russian Decoration .	7	6	32	1	2	..	2	12	16	..	..	78
Egyptian Decoration .	..	..	..	20	1	..	..	..	44	..	..	65

British—contd.

—	A.	B.	D.	E.	G.	Indian Frontier.	Indian Area.	Europe with England.	Unspecified.	India.	Black Sea.	TOTAL.
Greek Decoration	..	..	..	..	..	..	..	..	2	..	..	2
Serbian Decoration	..	..	69	8	9	..	..	1	4	..	..	91
Siamese Decoration	..	..	..	..	..	..	..	..	3	..	..	3
Roumanian Decoration	..	..	..	..	..	..	..	1	11	..	..	12
Persian Decoration	..	..	..	..	..	..	..	..	8	..	..	8
Japanese Decoration	..	..	..	..	..	..	..	1	11	..	..	12
Chinese Decoration	..	..	..	..	..	..	..	..	1	..	..	1
Portuguese Decoration	..	..	..	..	..	..	..	..	9	..	..	9
Nepalese Decoration	..	..	..	..	..	..	..	..	16	..	..	16
Hedjaz Decoration	..	..	..	..	..	..	..	..	6	..	..	6
Panamanian Decoration	..	..	..	..	..	..	..	..	9	..	1	10
Lieut.-Genl.	2	..	2	..	1	1	..	..	..	..	..	6
Major-Genl.	10	2	3	3	..	3	1	..	..	3	..	25
Bt. Colonel	28	7	40	5	5	5	6	8	1	11	..	116
Bt. Lieut.-Col.	44	10	130	22	4	4	16	17	..	28	1	276
Major	..	..	..	..	..	..	..	2	2	2	..	6
Brevet Major	18	5	68	12	6	1	18	11	..	13	1	153

Captain	..	..	..	..	..	..	..	..	2	2	..	4
Captain R.I.M.	..	..	..	..	..	..	..	..	..	3	..	3
Commander R.I.M.	..	..	1	..	..	..	..	..	..	1	..	2
Lt.-Commander R.I.M.	..	..	..	..	..	..	..	..	..	1	..	1
Temp. Lt.-Comdr. R.I.M.	..	..	..	..	..	..	..	..	1	..	..	1
Lieutenant	..	..	..	..	..	..	..	..	15	17	..	32
Temp. Lieut. R.I.M.	..	..	..	..	..	..	..	..	..	1	..	1
Senior Chaplain	..	..	1	..	..	..	..	..	..	..	..	1
Subordinate Promotion	52	16	58	16	7	4	7	..	131	123	..	414
Hon. Lieut.-Genl.	1	..	..	..	..	..	..	..	1	3	..	5
,, Colonel	..	..	..	..	..	..	..	..	1	2	..	3
,, Lieut.-Col.	2	..	..	..	..	..	1	..	..	7	..	10
,, Major	2	..	3	..	1	..	..	..	5	6	..	17
,, Captain	4	1	5	3	..	..	..	..	71	25	..	109
,, Lieutenant	13	5	16	2	1	2	..	2	299	33	..	373
,, 2nd-Lieut.	..	..	..	..	..	..	..	..	..	4	..	4
TOTAL	752	250	1,953	435	128	85	515	164	803	744	21	5,850

Indian.

—	A.	B.	D.	E.	G.	Indian Frontier.	Indian Area.	Europe.	Unspecified.	India.	Black Sea.	TOTAL.
V.C.	6	..	3	2	..	..	1	..	..	..	..	12
C.I.E.	1	4	2	..	1	2	..	..	..	1	..	11
C.B.E.	..	..	..	..	..	..	..	..	..	1	..	1
O.B.E.	1	..	..	..	..	..	3	..	..	..	..	4
M.B.E.	1	..	..	..	..	..	21	..	..	10	..	32
M.C. Bar	..	..	1	..	..	..	..	..	..	..	..	1
M.C.	23	1	42	32	2	1	2	..	..	..	..	103
O.B.I. (1)	3	6	16	6	2	1	8	..	..	11	1	54
O.B.I. (2)	84	31	172	53	12	10	35	..	22	78	2	499
I.O.M. (1)	4	3	11	4	..	2	1	..	..	..	..	25
I.O.M. (2)	239	71	455	138	43	44	139	..	8	..	7	1,144
I.D.S.M. Bar	4	..	15	7	..	1	7	..	1	..	..	35
I.D.S.M.	625	247	1,756	473	104	149	453	4	10	..	3	3,824
I.M.S.M. Bar	1	..	3	3	..	..	1	..	..	..	..	8
I.M.S.M.	406	300	909	2,829	56	167	334	..	629	773	37	6,440
B.E.M.	..	..	..	..	..	..	..	..	..	1	..	1
French Decoration	21	15	23	4	3	17	18	..	13	..	..	114

Italian Decoration	..	11	14	..	..	..	..	..	1	..	..	26
Belgian Decoration	15	..	..	..	..	..	..	..	..	..	..	15
Russian Decoration	47	12	73	5	..	..	..	..	..	..	..	137
Egyptian Decoration	..	..	..	3	..	..	..	..	1	..	..	4
Serbian Decoration	..	..	115	36	..	..	..	..	..	..	..	151
Roumanian Decoration	..	..	..	..	..	..	..	..	16	..	..	16
Honorary Promotion	1	1	..	2	..	..	..	..	..	24	..	28
Special Promotion	13	2	12	..	..	1	5	1	54	35	.	123
TOTAL	1,495	704	3,722	3,597	223	395	1,028	5	755	934	50	12,908

Recipients of the Victoria Cross who belonged

		Regimental No., Name, Rank and Corps
No.	4050	**Khudabad,** Sepoy, 129th Duke of Connaught's Own Baluchis.
No.	1909	**Darwan Sing Negi,** Naik, 1-39th Garhwal Rifles
		***De Pass, Lieutenant F.A.,** 34th Prince Albert Victor's Own Poona Horse.
		***Bruce, Lieutenant W.A. McC.,** 59th Scinde Rifles (Frontier Force).
No.	1685	***Gobar Sing Negi,** Rifleman, 2-39th Garhwal Rifles.
		Mir Dast, Jemadar, 53th Coke's Rifles (F.F.), attached 57th Wilde's Rifles (F.F.)
		Smyth, Lieutenant J.G., 15th Ludhiana Sikhs.
No.	2120	**Kulbir Thapa,** Riflesman, 2-3rd Queen Alexandra's Own Gurkha Rifles.
No.	2008	**Gobind Singh,** Lancer-Dafedar, 28th Light Cavalry, attached 2nd Lancers (Gardner's Horse).
		***Wheeler, Major G.G.M.,** 7th Hariana Lancers.
No.	3398	**Chatta Singh,** Sepoy, 9th Bhopal Infantry.
		Sintou, Captain, J.A., Indian Medical Service.
No.	501	**Lala,** Lance-Naik, 41st Dogras.
No.	1605	**Shahamad Khan,** Naik, 80th Punjabis.
		Wheeler, Major G.C., 2-9th Gurkha Rifles.
No.	4146	**Karanbahadur Rana,** Rifleman, 23rd Queen Alexandra's Own Gurkha Rifles.
		***Badlu Singh,** Ressaldar, 14th Murray's Jat Lancers, attached 29th Lancers (Deccan Horse).
		***Jotham, Captain E.,** 51st Sikhs (Frontier Force).
		***Andrews, Temporary Captain H.J.,** M.B.E., Indian Medical Service.
		***Kenny, Lieutenant W.D.,** 4-39th Garhwal Rifles.
No.	1012	**Ishar Singh,** Sepoy, 28th Punjabis.

*Posthumous.

to the Indian Army at the time it was won

Theatre	Place and date	Date of Gazette
Belgium	Hollebeke, 31-10-14	7-12-14
France	Festubert, 23-24-11-14	7-12-17
France	Near Festubert, 24-11-14	18-2-15
France	Near Givenchy, 19-12-14	4-9-19
France	Neuve Chapelle, 10-3-15	28-4-15
Belgium	Ypres, 26-4-15	29-6-15
France	Near Richebourg L'Avoué, 18-5-15	29-6-15
France	South of Fauquissart, 25-9-15	18-11-15
France	East of Peizières, 1-12-17	11-1-18
Mesopotamia	Shaiba, 12-4-15	1-9-15
Mesopotamia	Wadi, 13-1-16	21-6-16
Mesopotamia	Orah Ruins, 21-1-16	21-6-16
Mesopotamia	El Orah, 21-1-16	13-5-16
Mesopotamia	Near Beit Ayeesa, 12-13-4-16	26-9-16
Mesopotamia	Tigris at Shumran, 23-2-17	8-6-17
Egypt	El Kefr, 10-4-18	21-6-18
Palestine	West bank of River Jordan, 23-9-18	27-11-18
Indian Frontier	Tochi Valley, 7-1-15	24-7-15
Indian Area	Waziristan, 22-10-19	7-9-20
Indian Area	Waziristan, 2-1-20	7-9-20
Indian Area	Waziristan, 10-4-21	25-11-21

Recipients of the Victoria Cross who have

		Regimental No., Name, Rank and Corps
No.	9539	**Belcher, Lance-Sergeant D.W.,** 1-5th Battalion, The London Regiment (T.F.), now with 1st Ballation, 6th Gurkha Rifles.
No.	3902	**Barter, Company Sergeant-Major F.,** Special Reserve, attached 1st Battalion, Royal Welch Fusiliers, now with 2nd Battalion, 3rd Queen Alexandra's Own Gurkha Rifles.
		Forshaw, Lieutenant W.T., 1-9th Battalion, Manchester Regiment (T.F.) now with 76th Punjabis.
		Holland, Lietuenant J.V., 3rd Battalion, Leinster Regiment, attached 7th Battalion, now with 9th Hodson's Horse.

been subsequently appointed to the Indian Army

Theatre	Place and date	Date of Gazette
Belgium	South of Wieltje, St. Julien Road, 13-5-15	23-6-15
France	Festubert, 16-5-15	29-6-15
Dardanelles	Gallipoli Peninsula, 7-9-8-15	9-9-15
France	Guillemont, 3-9-16	26-10-16

CHAPTER VI

*The Imperial Service Troops

A perusal of the treaties formulated between the Indian States and the Paramount Power from the year 1803 onwards shows that subordinate military co-operation formed an important clause in most cases.

In almost every Indian campaign conducted in the past century a contingent from some State has served alongside British troops, and we find the Iron Duke, no liberal giver of praise, testifying in his early Indian despatches, to the courage, willingness and orderly behaviour of the Mysore troops in the Deccan fighting.

Despatches and reports relating to the Gurkha War, the first Afghan War, the first and second Sikh Wars, the Mutiny, the second Afghan War, and several Frontier Expeditions, record the good service done by various contingents of State troops long before they were selected, well-equipped and designated by an Imperial title.

* Title altered to Indian State Forces from 1st January 1922.

In 1885 when the course of affairs on the Afghan Frontier had brought about a near prospect of war between England and Russia, the Indian States came forward with enthusiasm and unanimity to place their resources at the Empire's disposal. The danger which then seemed imminent was happily averted, but the feelings which had been raised by it did not die away, and both in the Indian States arid elsewhere the idea began to gain ground that a scheme for utilizing their military resources should be initiated.

The matter was engaging attention when in the summer of 1887, the year of Her Majesty Queen Victoria's Jubilee, His Highness (now His Exalted Highness) the Nizam of Hyderabad made an offer of a considerable sum of money as a contribution towards the defence of the frontier. His Highness added an intimation that in time of war his own sword would be ready on the Empire's behalf.

The announcement of such an offer from the ruler of the greatest State in India naturally led other Chiefs to follow his example and many of them came forward, others remaining silent only because they had freely placed their resources at the disposal of the Government of India two years before. This favourable opportunity for making an attempt to settle the question of the State armies was taken and Major Melliss, of the Bombay Staff Corps, was specially selected and deputed to visit the States, and study the actual condition and probable future capabilities of their forces.

Major Melliss travelled through many of the Indian States, and, after consultation with His Excellency, the Commander-in-Chief and the Lieutenant-Governor of the Punjab, His Excellency the Viceroy, Lord Dufferin, came to the conclusion that a portion of the troops of Indian States could, with advantage to the Empire, be equipped and trained for active service.

A beginning was made with the armies of the Punjab States, because from their position near the North-West Frontier and the martial spirit of the population they seemed specially suitable for the experiment.

With this object the representatives of the Indian States of the Punjab were asked to meet the Lieutenant-Governor and to explain their views. A committee consisting of Sir Frederick Roberts, Commander-in-Chief, the Lieutenant-Governor of the Punjab, Sir James Lyall, Lieutenant-General the Hon'ble G.T. Chesney, and the Foreign Secretary, Sir Mortimer Durand, was then appointed to consider the question, and make specific proposals.

This report made certain recommendations with regard to the numbers and composition of the force to be kept up by each State, the way in which the forces should be armed, and their inspection and instruction.

These proposals were considered, generally approved by the Governor-General in Council and formally communicated to the Phulkian Chiefs assembled in Darbar at Patiala, on the 17th of November 1888, by the Marquess of Dufferin, in the following words—

* * * * *

" And now, before I leave this assembly, I wish to say a few words regarding a subject of the utmost importance. You are all aware that three years ago, when war seemed imminent upon our North-West Frontier, the Native Princes of India, both in the south and in the north, both Hindus and Muhammadans came forward in a body to place at the disposal of His Majesty's Government the whole resources of their States. Hostilities were then happily averted, but the feeling shown by the Native Chiefs could not be misunderstood; and I am convinced that their attitude in this crisis of our affairs not only created a very favourable impression in England, but produced a very striking effect in other countries. Again, last year, the year of the Jubilee of Her Most Gracious Majesty the Queen-Empress, the Rulers of many Native States seized the opportunity of offering to contribute in a very liberal manner towards the defence of the Empire, and their offers excited universal approval both at Home and abroad.

"Prominent among the Princes who came forward on both occasions were the Chiefs of the Punjab Frontier Province, who had already stood by the British Government more than once in the hour of trouble, and whose brave troops had fought and bled by the side of their English fellow-subjects. I remember with deep gratification, and they must remember with pride, that only ten years ago a contingent from the Punjab States marched to the Afghan Frontier, and did its duty well under circumstances of great hardship and difficulty. Some among those around me wear on their breasts the medals earned by them for the service they then rendered to their Sovereign and country.

"The Government of India has not failed to give earnest attention to the offers of the Native Princes, and, well knowing them to be as sincere as they were generous, has endeavoured to work out a scheme by which they might be turned to advantage in a manner both gratifying to the Princes themselves and of material value to the Empire. I believe we have succeeded in working out such a scheme, and this Darbar seems to me to afford a fitting opportunity for its public inauguration.

The Government of India does not think it necessary, or in all respects desirable, to accept from the Native States of India the pecuniary assistance which they have so freely tendered. But in one very important particular we wish to enlist their co-operation.

"The armies of the Native States are strong in numbers, but at present of various degrees of efficiency. Among many of them there exist warlike traditions and fine soldierly materials, while some already contain regiments well worthy to share in any active operations which Her Majesty's troops may be called upon to undertake. What we propose, in a few words, is that we should ask those Chiefs who have specially good fighting material in their armies to raise a portion of those armies to such a pitch of general efficiency as will make them fit to go into action side by side with the Imperial troops. For this purpose, some extra exertions will be necessary, as troops in the present day, to be thoroughly fit for service, require very complete arrangements in the way of arms, transport, equipment and organization generally. But we shall in no case ask a Native State to maintain a larger force of this description than it can well afford to support, and we do not doubt that under these conditions the Chiefs, knowing that the Government of India has no desire to take undue advantage of their loyalty in order to throw upon them an excessive burden, will be glad of the opportunity of making good their words by providing troops for the defence of the Empire. I trust that the Chiefs selected will in any case regard the acceptance of their offers as an honourable distinction, while those whose armies it is not found possible to utilize in the same manner will understand that if they cannot usefully contribute to the fighting strength of the Empire, they can in other ways render services equally meritorious and equally sure to win the approval of Her Majesty the Queen-Empress.

"To help these Chiefs in setting on foot and maintaining the troops selected for service a few English officers will be appointed as advisers and inspectors. These officers will have their headquarters at some central point in British territory, and will visit the several States in turn. Capable Native Drill Instructors will also be lent to the Native States from our own regiments. The selected troops will be armed with breech-loading weapons presented to the several States by the British Government. These will be carbines for the cavalry and Snider rifles for the infantry.

"It is hoped that in this way, while each force will remain a purely State force recruited in the territories of its Chief, and serving within them, the troops composing it will gradually be made so efficient as to enable the Imperial Government to use them as part of its available resources to meet any external danger.

"The principal States of the Punjab and others elsewhere have, I am happy to say, expressed their full concurrence in this scheme, and arrangements will be made to carry it into effect as far as they are concerned. I cannot but feel that I have been very fortunate in being able to announce before I leave India the inauguration of this important measure, which will, I hope serve to show the world in what estimation Her Majesty the Queen-Empress holds the Native States of India, and how she appreciates the conspicuous loyalty and attachment of her Chiefs."

* * * * *

Directly the policy of the Government of India became known, definite offers of military aid were received from other States in India.

Each case was dealt with separately, careful enquiries being made into the circumstances of the particular State, and the precise wishes of the Chief being ascertained. The result was the computation that the Punjab, Kashmir and Rajputana would furnish in time of war 15,000 good troops, 4,000 being cavalry; also that the numbers would rise to 25,000 when other States came forward.

Since the inauguration of the title "Imperial Service Troops," the names Hunza, Nagar, Chitral Tirah and China blazon the colours of some of these regiments, whilst despatches record the good services of the cavalry, infantry, sappers or transport employed. State after State volunteered the use of its troops for employment in China, but His Excellency the Viceroy, whilst expressing the gratification of Government at the loyal offers, declared his regret at his inability to utilize more than one brigade.

Material aid was however afforded in 1899 by the Indian States in sending some 1,200 horses to South Africa for Mounted Infantry. These were accompanied by small parties of non-commissioned officers and men of the Imperial Service regiments, who with few exceptions remained until the conclusion of the war.

From all sides, commendation on their work and behaviour was received, and they had the satisfaction of enjoying Lord Kitchener's approval in a farewell message :—

> "Please express to the Indian Details about to return to India Lord Kitchener's appreciation of the good work they have done in South Africa during the last two and-a-half years. In wishing them Good-bye Lord Kitchener wishes them good fortune in India."

Since then on the North-West Frontier and in Somaliland, the Imperial Service Troops have rendered excellent service.

We have seen that immediately on the outbreak of the Great War the Indian Princes placed their personal services, their troops and the entire resources of their States at the disposal of the King-Emperor.

The extent of their contributions, up to the Armistice, was as follows :—

Indian States	No. of Combatants sent overseas	REMARKS
Alwar	1,502	1 Squadron of Cavalry and 1 Battalion of Infantry.
Bahawalpur	326	Detachments from the Camel Corps and Camel Transport.
Bharatpur	1,581	1 Battalion Infantry and 1 Transport Corps.
Bikaner	1,164	1 Camel Corps.
Faridkot	444	1 Sapper Company.
Gwalior	2,597	2 Battalions of Infantry and Detachment Transport Corps.
Hyderabad	1,075	1 Regiment of Cavalry.
Indore	681	1 Squadron of Cavalry and 1 Transport Corps.
Idar	20	Despatch Riders.
Jaipur	1,256	1 Transport Corps.
Jhind	1,116	1 Battalion of Infantry.
Jodhpur	1,342 .	1 Regiment of Cavalry.
Kathiawar	472	Detachments of Cavalry.
Kapurthala	689	1 Battalion of Infantry.
Kashmir	4,983	Detachments of Cavalry, 1 Battery of Mountain Artillery and 3 Battalions of Infantry.
Khairpur	147	Detachments of Infantry and Transport Corps.
Malerkotla	520	1 Company and detachments of Sappers.

Indian States	No. of Combatants sent overseas	Remarks
Mysore	1,355	1 Regiment of Cavalry and 1 Transport Corps.
Nabha	538	1 Battalion of Infantry.
Patiala	2,695	1 Regiment of Cavalry and 1 Battalion of Infantry.
Rampur	567	1 Battalion of Infantry.
Rutlam	5	Despatch Riders.
Sinnur	561	2 Companies of Sappers, the second company replacing the first which was captured at Kut-el-Amarah.
Tehri	457	Detachment of Infantry and 1 company of Sappers.
Udaipur	6	Detachment of Cavalry.
Total	26,099	

Note.—In addition to the above the following Imperial Service Units were employed on Imperial Service in India :—

2 Squadrons, Alwar Lancers.

Bahawalpur Camel Corps (proceeded on Field Service on the North-West Frontier).

Bhopal Victoria Lancers.

Detachments, 1st Gwalior Lancers.

2 Squadrons, 2nd Gwalior Lancers.

3rd Gwalior Lancers.

1 Squadron, Navanagar Lancers.

2-2nd Kashmir Rifles.

Khairpur Transport Corps (proceeded on Field Service on the North-West Frontier).

Detachments, Rampur Lancers.

Detachments, Udaipur Lancers.

In addition to the contingents of State troops lent for Imperial purposes, the Indian States contributed a large number of combatant and non-combatant emits for service in the Regular Indian Army and it is a matter for regret that complete figures are not immediately available. But the following table affords an indication of the part played by certain States in providing recruits up to the date of the Armistice:—

Indian State	Combatant recruits enlisted	Non-combatants recruits enlisted	TOTAL
Hyderabad	7,830	5,058	12,888
Mysore	3,503	3,028	6,531
Baroda	268	751	1,019
Kashmir	20,722	8,806	29,528
Central India	7,198	3,540	10,738
Rajputana	48,611	5,656	54,267
Sikkim	826	94	920
TOTAL	88,958	26,933	115,891

*These figures relate only to states directly associated with the Foreign and Political Derailment of the Government of India. Figures for other states were unfortunately included in Provincial totals.

With regard to the new constitution of the Imperial Service Troops under the title of Indian State Forces, the Foreign and Political Department of the Government of India issued the following notice on 7th January 1922 :—

> "A recent notification by the Government of India has introduced a change in the designation of the Imperial Service Troops maintained by the Ruling Princes. These troops are henceforth to be known as 'Indian State Forces,' and the Inspecting Officers as 'Military Advisers.'

The new term 'Indian State Forces' however, embraces not only those troops which are expressly intended for war service, but also those which are maintained for internal security. The change therefore is not to be regarded merely as one of name since it signifies the growth of a new idea. The State Forces are for the first time recognised in their entirety as an Imperial asset. When the Ruling Princes, on the outbreak of war, showed their loyalty and attachment to His Majesty the King-Emperor by the offer of their whole resources this offer included the local troops, as well as those expressly maintained for Imperial Service, and in most instances, casualties in the Imperial Service Troops were replaced by drafts from the local force. Further, it was realised that the preservation of internal security was as truly 'Imperial Service' as the more conspicuous assistance rendered by the State troops which left India for the various theatres of war. Actual experience has thus shown that the distinction between the two classes of troops implied in the old nomenclature was misleading. It has also shown the importance of improving the second-line troops from which, in case of need, the reinforcements will be drawn. The lessons of war have been turned to account and a committee of Ruling Princes and political and military officers made a number of recommendations involving the reorganisation of the military strength of the darbars. The main proposals made by this committee, and approved by the Government of India, were sanctioned by the Secretary of State towards the end of 1920. Since then Major-General Sir H.D. Watson, with Brigadier-General K. Wigram and subsequently Lieutenant-Colonel P.T.L. Thompson, have toured the States in order to explain the scheme, and to discuss questions of organisation. By November last 31 States had been visited and the committee had been consulted by representatives of 8 others. Some of the darbars have already formulated their proposals under the new scheme. The replies of the remainder are awaited and it is hoped that, when they are received, it will be possible to give full effect to the new policy, which affords the sincerest recognition of the military services rendered by the States in the past by providing for the greater efficiency of their forces in the future."

The following table shows the casualties sustained by the Imperial Service Troops during the Great War and the North-West Frontier operations:—

	Killed and died from all causes	Wounded	Missing	TOTAL
Great War	1.529[1]	1,011[2]	2	2,542
North-West Frontier	170[3]	42[4]		212
TOTAL	1,699	1,053	2	2,754

[1] Includes 16 British Officers attached to Imperial Service Troops.

[2] Includes 13 British Officers attached to Imperial Service Troops.

[3] Includes 2 British Officers attached to Imperial Service Troops.

[4] Includes 3 British Officers attached to Imperial Service Troops.

The following table shows the decorations awarded to effective recipients of the Imperial Service Troops:—

Military Cross	4
Order of British India, 1st Class	37
Order of British India, 2nd Class	78
Indian Order of Merit	49
Indian Distinguished Service Medal	164
Indian Military Service Medal	240
TOTAL	572

CHAPTER VII

The Indian Defence Force

Mention has been made of the fact that the only form of compulsory military service employed in India during the war was applied to European British subjects.

In 1820 an Act was passed empowering the East India Company to raise contingents of volunteer infantry, but it was not until 1869 that the scope of the Volunteer Force, under the Government of India, was expanded and defined.

Prior to the outbreak of war it had been realised that the volunteer system in India was unsatisfactory and as the war progressed it became obvious that equality of sacrifice was necessary despite the fact that the small non-official British community in the country were for the most part engaged in essential occupations.

From the beginning of the war the volunteers had been freely used, especially in Bombay, for a variety of duties normally performed by garrison troops, such as embarkation work and as escorts to prisoners of war; and numbers of them joined the army and the Indian

Army Reserve of Officers. Also a Volunteer Battery went to Mesopotamia and a Volunteer Machine Gun Section to East Africa. But of the force as a whole no compulsory use could be made so long as the Indian Volunteers' Act, prescribing local limits of service, remained in existence.

From time to time various resolutions were passed by Chambers of Commerce and other bodies favouring some form of compulsory service for able-bodied Europeans, but it was not until the beginning of 1916 that the depletion of British troops in India made it necessary to formulate a scheme by which the Europeans remaining in the country could be employed for its defence.

On the 2nd February 1917 the Registration Ordinance was published by which every male European British subject between the ages of 16 and 50 was compelled to register his name; place of residence; date of birth; whether single, married or widower; number of dependents, if any; as well as various details regarding his profession or occupation. The exceptions to the above included persons not ordinarily resident in British India; members of His Majesty's naval and military forces, other than volunteers enrolled under the Indian Volunteers' Act; and certain minor categories.

The process of registration was carried out with little difficulty and shortly afterwards the Indian Defence

Force Act came into operation and remained in force during the continuance of the war and for a period of 12 months thereafter. Briefly, by the terms of this Act, every male European British subject, with the exceptions outlined above, between the ages of 18 and 41 was deemed to have been enrolled for general military service and thereby liable to serve in any part of India; whilst those between the ages of 41 and 50 were deemed to have been enrolled for local military service. Youths of from 16 to 18 were liable to military training only. Corps of the Indian Defence Force normally consisted of active, reserve and cadet companies. Speaking generally, and provided they were physically fit, men of the first category composed the active companies and were liable for service anywhere in India; men of the second category composed the reserve companies and were liable to local service; whilst youths of the third category were formed into cadet companies for military training only. In the autumn of 1918 three amendments to the Act were introduced whereby men over 50 were permitted to volunteer for service in the Defence Force; men under 41 were made liable to service in any part of the world; and all persons deemed to be enrolled for military service under the Act might be called upon to take up or continue any employment in any industrial concern under Government control, declared to be of national importance by the Governor-General in Council. This latter amendment, however, was never enforced owing to the termination of the war. In addition to the compulsory enrolment of European British subjects, the Indian Defence Force Act contained a clause whereby Indians might gratify their frequently expressed longing to join the Volunteer Force.

> "The Governor-General in Council may, by notification in the Gazette of India constitute, in any local area which he may specify in the notification corps or units for the enrolment in the Indian Defence Force of persons other than European British subjects, who satisfy the prescribed conditions and, within six months from the commencement of this Act, offer themselves for enrolment for general military service, and such persons may be enrolled accordingly in the prescribed manner."

But the response was meagre. During the first two months after the passing of the Act only 300 men were enrolled out of the 6,000 for whom arrangements had been made as a preliminary step. In May 1917 the Government of India recorded their disappointment in a Resolution of which the following is an extract:—

> "It is felt that all who take an interest in the Defence Force and believe those sentiments of patriotism which have brought it into being, and who have the good name of India at heart will be disheartened to learn that out of the six months for which recruiting is open so much time should have elapsed without any adequate response being made."

At the end of the six months only 2,432 had been enrolled, which figure was afterwards increased to 5,634, including men subsequently rejected, but the

Indian Branch of the Defence Force as a whole never became effective.

When introducing the Indian Defence Force Bill in the Indian Legislative Council on the 21st February 1917, His Excellency the Commander-in-Chief (Sir Charles Monro) spoke as follows :—

> "It is a matter of general anticipation that the Central Powers will make a great effort to resume the offensive in the ensuing spring. With this object in view, they are straining every nerve to increase their man-power and augment their output of munitions. The Allied Powers, on their side, are doubtless doing the same, and to ensure for our armies in the field that superiority in men and munitions which is the surest guarantee of victory, it is essential that His Majesty's Government should have the support of every portion of the Empire, and that all should unite in developing their resources in men, munitions and money to the utmost, so as to put forth their fullest strength in what we all hope will be the last phase of this war. India has rendered great service in the struggle of the last three years, and her armies have gained distinction in many fields. She has not, however, felt the burden of the war to the same extent as other portions of the Empire, and the past two years have, as a matter of fact, been years of great material prosperity. The virile population of the Punjab has filled the ranks of our regiments and given us thousands of gallant soldiers, but there are several provinces which so far have not yielded a single recruit, so that the man-power of India, as a whole, can hardly be said to have been touched. In the same way, the resources of the country have not been drawn upon to anything like their full capacity, and, given a suitable organization, I believe that much more could be done to utilize her production and

develop her manufactures for military purposes.

* * * * * *

"The Volunteer Force in India is now some 40,000 strong, and a large proportion of its members have the makings of excellent soldiers. The potential military value of the Force is thus considerable. It suffers, however, from lack of organization and insufficient training, while its local character detracts from its military utility by restricting the range and scope of its employment. To derive full value from the fine material of which it is composed, it is necessary to organise it as a second line force ready to take the place of a portion of the Regular Army for local defence. In other words, building up on the basis of the existing Volunteer Force, we want to improve and expand the latter into an Indian Defence Force. As this Defence Force will serve as an auxiliary to the Regular Army, we consider that it should, like the latter, be composed partly of British and partly of Indian units. In this way all classes of His Majesty's subjects in India will be afforded opportunities of rendering personal service during the war.

* * * * * *

"We have, of course, no previous experience to guide us, but there appears to be a widespread desire among His Majesty's Indian subjects to assist in the defence of the Empire, and we have, therefore, no reason to suppose that there will be any difficulty in obtaining by voluntary enrolment the numbers we shall want to complete Indian units of the Defence Force. As we do not want recruitment for the Defence Force to interfere with recruitment for the Regular Army, the enrolment of Indian subjects in the former will be restricted, as a rule, to classes or individuals who, in ordinary circumstances, would not be available for enlistment in the latter.

* * * * * *

> "I will conclude my remarks by observing that, though the Indian Defence Force will be a second line force, it will be in no sense a second rate force, for we mean to make it a model of its kind. Its members must realise that we are dealing now with serious soldiering, and that personal convenience and other considerations must yield to military efficiency and to the creation of the spirit of discipline upon which that efficiency so largely depends. The old Volunteer Force has become an anachronism. It has been replaced at Home by the Territorial Force, and will now be replaced in India by a Defence Force, designed to suit local requirements, whose development and progress will be watched with the keenest interest."

The maximum number of enrolments in the European Branch of the Indian Defence Force amounted to 44,500, and the net effective strength, after allowing for men granted commissions in the Regular Army, or who had been permitted to leave the country, to approximately 35,000.

On 1st October 1920 the Indian Defence Force was replaced by voluntary organizations called the Auxiliary Force, India, for European British subjects, and the Indian Territorial Force for non-European British subjects.

On 1st October 1921 the strength of the former was 30,603, but in the latter, enrolment had not extended beyond the University Training Corps, action in the matter of raising provincial battalions on a militia basis having been of a preliminary nature.

CHAPTER VIII

THE ROYAL INDIAN MARINE

THE East India Company was authorised by Charters of Charles II and James II to maintain an armed naval force for the defence of its possessions and for the prevention of interference with its trade monopoly. This force eventually developed into the Indian Navy, with its headquarters at Bombay and was, subject to the supreme control of the Government of India, immediately under the Bombay Government.

Another marine service, called the Bengal Marine, was also established, with headquarters at Calcutta, and was immediately under the Bengal Government. The above organizations remained in existence from 1830 to 1863, when it was decided to transfer to the Royal Navy such duties as were of a warlike character, the transport of troops and stores and other civil duties being relegated to a local service not subject to martial law.

The local service thus constituted was designated the Indian Marine and was split up into two divisions, the

Eastern and Western, with a Superintendent of Marine to each Division, and stationed at Calcutta and Bombay respectively.

In 1877 the title of the service was altered to Her Majesty's Indian Marine, which was brought as a whole, including the Dockyards, under the direct control of the Government of India and was administered by a Royal Naval Officer called Director of the Indian Marine, with headquarters at Bombay. In 1892 its designation was changed to Royal Indian Marine.

In peace time the ships of the Royal Indian Marine are unarmed, their normal duties being to convey troops and stores from port to port in India (including Burma and Aden) and from India to Colonial stations and *vice versa* in Indian waters, which connotes for this purpose the high seas between the Cape of Good Hope on the west and the Straits of Magellan on the east, and all territorial waters between those limits. They were also liable to convey troops between India and England, when such a course was authorised by the Secretary of State for India. Amongst their other normal duties were to furnish station vessels for Aden, Port Blair and Rangoon; to survey the coasts and harbours of India and Burma and the Indian Ocean between certain defined limits; to visit lighthouses; to relieve distressed or wrecked vessels; to be in charge of the lights and buoys in the Persian Gulf; to supply trained and efficient officers to maritime local Governments for employment as Port Officers and Engineer and Shipwright Surveyors; to maintain and keep in efficient condition dockyards at Bombay and Calcutta; to construct and maintain in efficient condition vessels for military duty at Aden, Bombay, Calcutta, Karachi and Rangoon; to construct and repair vessels required for other Government purposes; to carry out repairs required from time to time by naval vessels on the East Indies Station; and to suppress piracy. Such were amongst the various duties entrusted to the Royal Indian Marine up to July 1914.

Royal Indian Marine Ships "Hardinge" and "Dufferin" had been specially constructed with a view to their employment as Auxiliary Cruisers should occasion arise, and arrangements had been made beforehand whereby they would be transferred to the Royal Navy, in accordance with Section 6 of the Indian Marine Service Act, 1884, in the event of war with a foreign power. On the outbreak of war, however, in addition to the vessels above-mentioned, the "Northbrook," "Minto," "Dalhousie" and "Lawrence"[1] were also transferred to the Royal Navy; as was the "Comet" when hostilities commenced with Turkey. The "Comet" was mainly employed as a gun-boat in the Mesopotamian waterways, and was captured by the

[1] Now called "Canning".

Turks after the battle of Ctesiphon. The remaining vessels were employed as Auxiliary Cruisers, commanded by Royal Navy officers, but officered and manned mainly by Royal Indian Marine personnel.

In this capacity they performed very useful service, assisting, in the early stages of the war, the East Indies Squadron in escorting convoys of troops from India overseas, and later on in carrying out various duties, mainly on the East Indies Station, falling to vessels of the Royal Navy.

A very heavy and important task which fell to the Royal Indian Marine on the outbreak of war was that of arranging for the fitting out and despatch of vessels conveying the various expeditionary forces overseas. Although the number of troops and animals, and the quantities of stores, to be despatched was without precedent in this country, the Royal Indian Marine rose splendidly to the occasion and, by utilising all local resources available, succeeded in having the requisite numbers of vessels fitted out and ready for troops to embark as soon as they reached the ports of embarkation. As an illustration of the work involved it may be mentioned that 240 were thus fitted out or refitted at the various ports in India during the first 4 months of the war, while the total number of vessels fitted and refitted at Bombay during the first three years amounted to 1,252, and at other ports to 324.

Considerable repairs to war ships on the East Indies Station were also carried out at the Royal Indian Marine Dockyard at Bombay, no less than 78 British and 2 Foreign war vessels being repaired there during the first three years.

The various enemy vessels detained or captured at Indian ports and Ceylon, amounting in all to 23 vessels, as well as 2 vessels transferred by the Australian Commonwealth, were originally administered and managed by the Royal Indian Marine, and were employed mainly as storeships and colliers. The management of these ships added considerably to the duties and responsibilities of the Royal Indian Marine staff who had to arrange for every detail connected with them, including the provision of officers and crews, until the control of the majority of these vessels was transferred to the India Office.

In normal times the Director, Royal Indian Marine, carries out, on behalf of the Admiralty, the duties of Resident Transport Officer, Bombay; Officer in charge of Admiralty Victualling Depot, Bombay; and Officer in charge of Naval Coal, Bombay; but on the outbreak of war he had also to assume additional naval duties as Naval Intelligence Officer; Registrar of the Royal Fleet Reserve; and Registrar of the Royal Naval Reserve.

To assist him in these duties the Assistant Paymaster in charge of the Royal Naval Depot at

Bombay (and his staff), was placed under his orders as Secretary for Naval and Transport duties. The Director, Royal Indian Marine, was likewise responsible for the control and economical utilization of all transport, storeships, etc., plying between India and the various theatres of operations in which troops from India were employed. This necessitated the despatch of Royal Indian Marine officers and establishments to the ports of disembarkation overseas, in addition to the provision of additional officers and staff to cope with the abnormal conditions prevailing at Indian ports, particularly at Karachi and Bombay.

The provision of rivercraft for Mesopotamia and of personnel to man them also devolved on the Royal Indian Marine in the earlier part of the war. This question was beset with many difficulties as craft above a certain draught were useless, whilst vessels within the draught limits fixed by the authorities in Mesopotamia were not only very scarce in India, but even when available were neither constructed nor intended for sea-going purposes. As, however, the demand was insistent such vessels as most nearly approximated to the required dimensions were taken up in India and despatched in tow to Mesopotamia over a distance varying between 1,600 to 3,000 miles, but not without some loss owing to the frail nature of many of the craft, which were unfitted to face sea conditions.

Moreover, it was not possible to provide officers for the vessels from the permanent cadre of the Royal Indian Marine, so local recruitment was resorted to and when this supply became exhausted officers were obtained from Home. Workshops had also to be erected for the repair of the vessels, a duty which was originally assigned to the Royal Indian Marine, and later to a specially selected officer, but there was always a tendency whenever any indent pertaining to the requirements of craft was received to pass it to the Director for compliance and he was invariably able to meet the demand.

As these vessels arrived in Mesopotamia they were organised into a river transport service by the Royal Indian Marine, who controlled this service most efficiently until the conduct of operations was taken over by the Inland Water Transport Department under the War Office in August 1916; but even then practically all the officers so employed, with the exception of the Administrative staff, were the permanent and temporary officers originally sent there by the Royal Indian Marine.

India, however, continued to be the base of supply of troops and stores for Mesopotamia and the fact that the War Office had taken over the conduct of operations in nowise relieved the Royal Indian Marine from the responsibility for the preparation of vessels for despatch from this country. During the first three years of the war a total of over 1,000 rivercraft were repaired or prepared for despatch, at the various ports in India, by the Royal Indian Marine, who also transferred 38 permanent and 175 temporary officers to the War Office for service in Mesopotamia, when the latter assumed charge of the operations.

Owing to the sowing of mines in Indian waters by an enemy minelayer in the early part of 1917, it became necessary to institute measures of protection at the various defended ports. The actual direction and responsibility of mine-sweeping and patrolling originally devolved on the Royal Indian Marine, who were, however, able to rely on the assistance and advice of the local naval authorities. After some months the direction of mine-sweeping at Bombay was placed under naval control, owing to the importance of the port and to the increasing scope of the measures necessary; but although this arrangement proved satisfactory, the Government of India considered that a central control of these operations, and undivided responsibility for the requirements of Indian ports as a whole, would ensure more efficient working and better results. The mine-sweeping and patrolling organisation was accordingly placed under the control and direction of the Naval Commander-in-Chief, East Indies, the Royal Indian Marine remaining responsible only for the provision of suitable vessels and the supply of the requisite personnel to man them.

The provision of vessels was a matter of considerable difficulty. Suitable craft were not available locally in the numbers required and to make up the deficiency three vessels were obtained from China, and nine trawlers, the designs and specifications for which were supplied by the Admiralty, were laid down. The construction of six of these trawlers was undertaken by the Royal Indian Marine Dockyards, the balance being laid down by a private Firm.

Reference has already been made to the transfer of certain Royal Indian Marine ships to the Royal Navy on the outbreak of war, and some of these took part in actions. Early in 1915, Royal Indian Marine ship "Hardinge" was struck by an 8-inch shell, whilst assisting in the defence of the Suez Canal, which carried away her fore funnel and part of the bridge; "Comet" was sunk by the Turks during the battle of Ctesiphon in 1916; and "Lawrence" (now "Canning") was in action on the Tigris at Qurna and was frequently under fire.

Out of its comparatively small establishment 21 officers, 9 warrant officers and approximately 300 ratings of the Royal Indian Marine gave their lives in the war.

The good work rendered by this service during the war has been the subject of mention in Parliament and has received recognition from the Government of India.

The number of officers and warrant officers who have been the recipient of honours in connection with the war is as follows:—

—	Officers	Warrant Officers
Companions of the Order of St. Michael and St. George	5	...
Companions of the Order of the Indian Empire	9	...
Commanders of the Order of the British Empire	6	...
Officers of the Order of the British Empire	20	...
Members of the Order of the British Empire	3	2
Companions of the Distinguished Service Order	13	...
Distinguished Service Cross	10	...
Distinguished Service Medal	...	1
Foreign Orders—		
Legion of Honour	1	...
Croix de Guerre	1	...
Camendador of the Order d'Aviz	1	...
Greek Military Cross	1	...
4th Class Egyptian Order of the Nile	1	...
TOTAL	71	3

The ships of the Royal Indian Marine are as given below:—

		Tons
Troopship	"Dufferin"	6,315
Do.	"Hardinge"	5,467
Do.	"Northbrook"	5,048
Station Ship	"Dalhousie"	1,524
Do.	"Clive"	1,474
Do.	"Minto"	960
Despatch Vessel	"Lawrence"	1,125
Do.	"Canning"	903
Surveying Ship	"Investigator"	1,014
Do.	"Palinurus"	300
Lighthouse Tender	"Nearchus"	491
River Gunboat	"Sladen"	270
Do.	"Bhamo"	172

In addition to the above there are some 40 small steamers and launches, as well as 2 Tender Flats, and a number of lesser craft such as gigs.

CHAPTER IX

Results of India's efforts, directly on the conduct of the war, and indirectly on her national development

We have traced in some measure the contributions and sacrifices made by the Indian Empire to the war and it now remains to endeavour to assess the direct and indirect results of her efforts.

With regard to her troops, the Indian Corps reached France in the nick of time and helped to stem the great German thrust towards Ypres and the Channel Ports during the autumn of 1914. These were the only trained reinforcements immediately available in any part of the British Empire and right worthily they played their part.

In Egypt and Palestine, in Mesopotamia, Persia, East and West Africa and in subsidiary theatres they shared with their British and Dominion comrades the attainment of final victory.

But meanwhile India had to face a grave peril nearer home. The collapse of Russia towards the end of 1917 had thrown an additional burden on the Allies, which subsequently became immensely aggravated by Germany's exploitation of the Bolshevik Government with the object of carrying the war into the East. On the 2nd April 1918, the Prime Minister addressed a telegram to the Viceroy containing the following extract:—

"At this time, when the intention of the rulers of Germany to establish a tyranny, not only over all Europe but over Asia as well, has become transparently clear, I wish to ask the Government and people of India to redouble their efforts. Thanks to the heroic efforts of the British armies, assisted by their Allies, the attempt of the enemy in the west is being checked but if we are to prevent the menace spreading to the East and gradually engulfing the world, every lover of freedom and law must play his part. I have no doubt that India will add to the laurels it has already won, and will equip itself on an even greater scale than at present to be the bulwark which will save Asia from the tide of oppression and disorder which it is the object of the enemy to achieve."

The Viceroy, on behalf of all India, replied on 5th April as follows :—

"Your message comes at a time when all India is stirred to the depths by the noble sacrifices now being made by the British people in the cause of the world's freedom and by the stern unalterable resolution which those sacrifices evince. India anxious, yet confident, realises to the full the great issues at stake in this desperate conflict, and your trumpet call at this crisis will not fall upon deaf ears. I feel confident that it will awaken the princes and the peoples' leaders to a keener sense of the grave danger which, stemmed in Europe, now threatens to move eastwards. I shall look to them for the fullest effort and the fullest sacrifice to safeguard the soil of their motherland against all attempts of a cruel and unscrupulous enemy, and to secure the final triumph of those ideals of justice and honour for which the British Empire stands."

A War Conference, including certain Ruling Chiefs and all the non-official members of the Imperial Legislative Council, was promptly summoned at Delhi with a view to inviting the co-operation of all classes to meet the crisis.

The conference was opened by the Viceroy (Lord Chelmsford) in a speech explaining the menace to which the Prime Minister referred and pointing out how German agents were already at work on disintegration and that the collapse of Russia into anarchy had opened a door for Germany leading up to the actual frontiers, of India.

In plain words the position was this. Hitherto the fate of India, in common with that of the world in general, had been in process of decision on the battlefields of France and Belgium; now there was grave peril of the actual invasion of India itself.

The response of the conference was immediate. Committees were appointed on man-power and resources; the Central Recruiting Board and Munitions Board redoubled their activities; a Central Publicity

Board was established to undertake active propaganda for the information of the public; a Central Communications Board was constituted to co-ordinate the working of the railways; a Central Food Stuffs and Transport Board was designed to facilitate the equitable distribution of supplies; and the Central Employment and Labour Board aimed at furnishing Government with the necessary labour and at utilising the many offers of voluntary service which poured in.

The results of the Delhi Conference, in manpower especially, surpassed all expectations. India undertook to contribute half a million recruits during the twelve months commencing on 1st June 1918, although during the previous year, only 270,000 combatant recruits had been obtained. By the date of the Armistice (11th November 1918) some 200,000 had been enrolled and there is reason to believe that the balance would have been forthcoming in due time had recruiting continued, despite the terrible epidemic of influenza which ravaged the country during the autumn causing a mortality of some six million souls. The special effort thus made by India to meet the menace of invasion relieved, in no small measure, the anxiety and embarrassment of the Imperial Government.

In weighing the extent of her contribution in men it should be remembered that the great bulk of her population are agriculturists, working with crude implements in order to produce sufficient food for themselves and for the non-agricultural population, with but a small margin for export when considered in the light of the enormous number of persons so employed.

And a further factor to be observed is that Indian women, from divers causes, are far less able than their European sisters to replace men required for military service.

But the most important point to be noted is that prior to the war India had maintained a highly trained army in being, a large portion of which became immediately available on the outbreak of war for service overseas.

In regard to material the Indian Empire's contribution to the war should not be measured by the standard of her territory and population. As already observed the vast majority of her peoples are, and have been from time immemorial, engaged in agricultural and pastoral pursuits. Beautiful as were the products of her old time looms and of her ancient arts and crafts, they were essentially limited in extent and severely confined to certain castes under the direct patronage of the various Indian courts.

In a previous chapter the main causes of her industrial stagnation have been outlined and owing to this lack of development India found herself, on the outbreak of war, not only ill-provided with the necessary machinery, but without the technically trained personnel required for her industrial expansion. Viewed in this light her output has been marvellous, and many new industries were created during the war in addition to the vast development of existing ones.

The direct effect of her efforts therefore were two-fold:—

(*a*) by utilising local resources she curtailed her demands on the energies of allied countries,

(*b*) by controlling material and developing industries she was able to export to allied countries large quantities of raw and manufactured articles, as well as foodstuffs, in addition to meeting her home requirements and most of the needs of her overseas forces that were based on India.

With regard to India's contribution in money we have seen that, owing to her poverty, the extent of her taxable capacity is severely limited. So, although the financial position of the country appears extremely strong, this result has been only attained by the Government of India exercising the most rigid economy in all directions.

Compared with most other countries the incidence of direct taxation in India is exceedingly small, indeed a very large proportion of her revenue is derived not from taxation of any kind, but from such sources as land revenue (which is *akin* to rent), opium, railways, forests, and irrigation.

On the outbreak of war there occurred in India, as elsewhere, a general dislocation of trade and finance, which was accompanied by a run on the savings bank deposits, some panic encashment of currency notes, and a considerable demand for the remittance of money to London. The measures necessary to maintain the exchange value of the rupee, resulting from this temporary want of confidence, cost India some £14 millions sterling, and the consolidation and conservation of her financial resources presented a vital problem during this period.

But though little could be done at the start in the form of direct financial assistance to Great Britain, India rendered such indirect help as was possible by refraining from drawing on the London market, and set herself, by the curtailment of expenditure, to meet possible military contingencies.

Towards the close of the following year the effects of the initial dislocation had subsided and a war demand for Indian products resulted in marked improvement of her export trade and consequently of her fiscal outlook.

To return to the direct financial help afforded by India at the beginning of the war we have seen that, under Parliamentary Resolutions of September and

November 1914, her net contribution amounted to £22.2 millions to the end of 1918-19 and to a total of £26.4 millions to the end of 1919-20. At the beginning of 1917 her position had sufficiently improved to enable her to make the mother-country a free gift of £100 millions, 75 per cent of which was raised by means of War Loans and as regards the balance the Government of India took over the liability for interest on an equivalent amount of the British Government War Loan.

The further contributions towards the expenses of the war, passed by the non-official members of the Legislative Council in September 1918, brought India's total net direct contribution up to about £160 millions by 1919-20.

To the above must be added the additional charges which India has borne as a necessary result of war conditions, thus bringing her total approximate expenditure, incurred specifically on account of the war up to 31st March 1921, to about £214 millions, including £39 millions for operations on the North-West Frontier.

India's contributions in men, material and money have proved therefore of incalculable assistance to Great Britain and her Allies. From a "frontier war" standard she so mobilized and developed her resources that she was able not only to defend her own borders, but to despatch and maintain large forces overseas.

Great, however, as has been her effort in matters which can be weighed and measured, we must never lose sight of her moral assistance, of her intense goodwill, enthusiasm and co-operation, which comprised an Imperial asset of the highest magnitude.

We now turn to the results of the war in relation to India's moral, material and economic development, in so far as their more prominent manifestations can at present be appraised.

In its moral effect the war has proved far reaching India's* rally to the Empire at the outbreak of hostilities was but the manifestation of a great wave of loyalty which swept over the country. The classes interested in politics realised, as never before that India was part of the Empire, that her very existence was intimately bound up with the Empire's survival. To the first feeling of enthusiasm there succeeded a steady determination to discharge whatever obligations the war might place upon the country. This again was followed by a widespread pride in the success of India's war efforts and in the generous recognition accorded to them by the Mother Country and the Dominions. As a consequence of this development, the politically-minded classes steadfastly set before their eyes the aim of asserting India's right to a place among the self-governing

* "India in the years 1917-18". Official Report by Prof. L.F. Rush-brook Williams.

Dominions of the British Commonwealth. The idea of responsible Government within the Empire came to the front in political discussions as never before, and afforded a marked stimulus to constructive constitutional activities. At no time was there any symptom of a desire for the severance of the ties which bound India to the Mother Country. There was on the contrary a demand for the strengthening of these ties, combined with a fixed resolve that India's position within the Empire should not fall short of that which was deemed to be rightfully her due. Satisfaction was felt at the recognition of India's status in the Empire through her admission to the Imperial War Conference and the Imperial Cabinet. This satisfaction was strengthened by the admission of representatives of India among the Imperial delegates at the Peace Conference. The removal of certain standing grievances has also helped to stiffen the growing feeling of self-respect and pride in India's war achievements. The acceptance by the Dominions' representatives of the principle of reciprocity of treatment, the grant of King's Commission to Indians, and other like developments have served at once to stimulate India's devotion to the Empire and to awaken her pride in her own growing national spirit.

The material effect of the war has been hardly less marked. There has been a notable stimulus to commerce and industry. The peculiar circumstances arising out of the war have introduced an atmosphere of economic protection in which the industries of India, both nascent and established, have flourished to an unprecedented degree. Great public interest has been aroused in the industrial development of the country, and it is noticed in the Report of the Indian Industrial Commission that there has been a definite demand for the adoption of the policy of State participation in industrial development, and of State assistance to industrial undertakings, which is likely to produce results stretching far into the future. As a consequence of this interest in industrial matters, there has been a growing desire on the part of the politically-minded classes that Government assistance should be directed towards the aim of making India more economically self-sufficing than has been the case hitherto. The report of the Indian Industrial Commission points out the grave danger to which India and the Empire are alike exposed, owing to the fact that the principal industries in India depend very largely upon certain key industries, which are not adequately developed in the country. Hence, any marked interruption of communications between India and the Empire, such as nearly resulted from the campaign of unrestricted submarinism, threatens to bring the industries of India to a standstill. There is every reason to hope that it will be found possible to take measures for the avoidance of any future danger upon this score. The Government of India has lost no time in considering the report of the Indian Industrial Commission and in consulting the local administrations on the proposals made therein. In the near future, we may confidently expect to see great and far-reaching industrial developments.

On the whole, then, it may be said that "both in the moral and in the material sphere, the war has acted as a great stimulus to India. It has broadened her outlook, it has deepened her interest in the Empire. It has aroused hundreds of people to a realisation of the problems lying outside their immediate environment. In short, it may well prove to be the beginning of a new era, not merely in the relations of India to the Empire, but also in the internal life of India herself."

In the United Kingdom one of the most striking results of the war, in its early stages, was the change in democratic opinion concerning the Home army and all that it connoted.

In pre-war days it had been somewhat the fashion in democratic circles to regard an army as an institution apart from and indeed almost inherently hostile to the mass of the population. They were inclined to look on it as a close preserve for certain classes, as a menace to the liberties of the people and so forth; not perhaps with any deep sincerity of feeling, but at any rate as affording a ready mark for political shibboleths. All this the war swept rapidly away. A new spirit of true democracy found vent in the fusion of all classes of the community in a common sense of national duty, and capitalists and workmen, aristocrats and artisans stood shoulder to shoulder in the new armies, under no other compulsion than their own voluntary determination to give their services and, if need be, their lives, for their country.

In India, too, although conditions differed, there had been a reflection of such political thought amongst a section of the educated classes, leading them by doctrinaire conceptions to miscontrue the significance of an army in a democratic state. And this, again, disappeared when the whole country rallied on the outbreak of war.

Amongst Indians, whose ideal is an united India there is a growing appreciation of the Indian Army as an institution which embodies in a large and effective measure the conception of Indian unity. In that army, as nowhere else in India, are found men of all races, creeds, castes and classes brought into the closest community of thought and action. Their different idiosyncracies are safeguarded and respected, but these very differences serve mainly to foster a generous emulation.

In this connection the late Mr. Gokhale is reported to have said, "I'm not sure that the Indian Army won't do more for us Indians than all the Royal Commissions in the world."

Amongst the many speeches made by non-official members in support of the Resolution on the War at the opening of the Legislative Council Session on the 8th September 1914, a quotation from one of them may be taken as containing a highly prophetic utterance:—

> " My Lord, this war, so terrible and so minatory to the whole fabric of European civilization, has its silver lining; it has demonstrated once for all the absolute solidarity of the Empire. The most perfect harmony exists among the various units, India included, on all large and important issues; the Empire is absolutely united in the presence of a common danger. The war may thus yet prove a blessing in disguise."

Much as India has done for the war, the war has done as much and more for India. A commonly observed fact in relation to human progress is that great ultimate good can seldom be attained without much present evil and that the incidence of immediate suffering is in direct proportion to the speed with which the wheel of progress is set in motion.

The times in which we now live are transitional, and changing conditions require a strong spirit of adaptability to environment if much needless discontent is to be avoided.

In the words of Robert Louis Stevenson, in order to dwell happily together folks must be versed in the niceties of the heart and endowed with the faculty for willing compromise.

CHAPTER X

Measures taken for improvement in the position of the Indian Soldier since the commencement of the Great War

Details regarding the various measures sanctioned for improving the position of the Indian Soldier, and for affording relief to those incapacitated by the war and to the dependents of those who fell in the war have been published in the Press from time to time. It will be of interest, however, briefly to recapitulate the main headings under which these improvements have been attained.

Commissions

In recognition of the services of the Indian Army during the Great War His Majesty the King-Emperor has been pleased to grant honorary King's Commissions as Captain or 2nd-Lieutenant to selected Indian Officers of the Indian Army who have rendered distinguished service during the war, and up to the 1st January 1923. 371 Commissions have been bestowed.

In addition, 39 Indian gentlemen, including certain Indian Officers, were granted King's Commissions as temporary 2nd-Lieutenants on probation after undergoing a course of training at the Training School for Indian Cadets, Indore. Of these, 32 have received permanent Commissions.

King's Commissions as 2nd-Lieutenants have been granted to 20 Indian Officers for specially distinguished services during the war, and 9 officers of the Indian Land Forces have been granted Commissions in the Indian Army.

Indian gentlemen of good family and education are now eligible for nomination for admission to the Royal Military College, Sandhurst, with a view to qualifying for the grant of King's Commissions, the number of Cadets from India being limited to 10 annually. So far 43 Cadets have been sent to the College.

In order to give men of the corps of Indian Coast Artillery and Indian drivers of Royal Horse, Royal Field and Heavy Artillery a prospect of attaining commissioned rank, an establishment of Indian Officers has been authorised.

Rewards

Two hundred special jagirs (hereditary assignments of land as a reward for service to Government) have been granted to selected Indian Officers in recognition of their distinguished services during the war.

Twenty thousand other rewards, consisting of grants of land or special pensions, have also been bestowed. (See work of the Indian Soldiers' Board below.)

The above were in addition to decorations, orders with increased monetary allowances, accelerated promotion, and the various rewards that could be earned for special service in the field. In this connection it should be mentioned that Indian Officers and Sub-Assistant Surgeons have been declared eligible for the Military Cross, and the grant of a special money allowance to accompany this decoration has been sanctioned by the Secretary of State, amounting to Rs. 40 per mensem for Indian Officers and Rs. 11 per mensem for Warrant Officers.

Pensions

The ordinary retiring and special pensions admissible to Indian Officers and men have been increased by amounts varying from 40 to 100 per cent, and the minimum qualifying service has been reduced from 18 to 15 years.

Similar increases have been made in connection with the rates of family pensions, up to a maximum of 135 per cent, with an added concession enabling the pension to be transferred to another dependent on the death (or on remarriage in the case of a widow) of the original nominee, and similarly in the case of the next heir if necessary, the principle being that the dependents of a deceased soldier shall never be left unprovided for until they can earn their own living.

New rules have also been introduced, with effect from the 4th August 1914, affecting the grant of gratuities and wound, injury and disability pensions to Indian Officers and other ranks, which are greatly in favour of the Indian soldier; and provision has likewise been made for the grant of disability pensions to Indian combatant ranks pronounced unfit for further service owing to illness or incapacity which, though not contracted on, or solely attributable to field service, has been so aggravated by the exigencies of such service as to necessitate invaliding from the army. Further, Indian combatant and non-combatant ranks, who sustained bodily injuries whilst prisoners of war, after due investigation, have had their pensions assessed as though the bodily injuries had been the result of wounds received in action.

Rations

Consequent on the introduction of free rations for the Indian Army, an extra Indian Officer (Jemadar Quartermaster) has been authorised for the purpose of their inspection and issue.

In addition to free rations a messing allowance of ten annas per man per mensem has been sanctioned for the provision of extra articles of diet in each mess, and General Officers Commanding have been authorised to increase Indian combatant rations in special circumstances when considered necessary by the medical authorities.

Special concessions, including the continuance of free rations on the enhanced field service scale, have been granted to Indian troops and followers returning sick, wounded or convalescent from the front.

All Government military servants are now allowed to purchase, for *bona fide* consumption by themselves and their families, any articles of Supply and Transport Corps supply, other than Hospital supplies. This concession benefits the individual by giving him the opportunity of buying at the favourable rates which the large wholesale army purchases render possible.

Interior Economy

Vast improvements have been effected in the barrack accommodation for Indian troops and followers.

Bathing compartments at the rate of one to every 27 men have been provided, washing places in all Indian Officers' and married quarters have been enlarged, and improved latrines arranged for masonry floors and glazed windows have been undertaken and in Indian Officers' quarters a durbar room with a verandah has been built outside the front wall of the courtyard; cook-houses have been improved by the addition of washing up places and special cooking facilities for single and married followers have been sanctioned; marked improvement has been made in the scale of accommodation and in the type of barracks, ample shelves and pegs being provided in all living rooms, whilst in the lines of Indian Cavalry regiments special saddle rooms and grain stores are provided for each troop.

Concessions by rail or sea

Substantial changes have been made in the regulations governing the free passages of Indian soldiers and their families, and when travelling by rail in India during the summer months and for journeys over 700 miles, Indian soldiers have been granted increased accommodation on the same scale as authorised for British troops *en route* by rail for embarkation to, or on disembarkation from, the United Kingdom or overseas and General Officers Commanding have been authorised to sanction, when necessary, the issue of hand fans and ice.

Pay and allowances

With a view to preventing any delay that might occur in the payment of family allotments and to expedite the settlement of accounts generally, the Government of India granted an extra office allowance of Rs. 200 per mensem to every combatant unit and depot in India, so as to enable them to employ extra accounts clerks. In addition, one head clerk for each division was sanctioned, whose duties were to tour round divisions and help to keep the accounts of units and depots in order.

With regard to batta, the monthly rates for field service were enhanced as a temporary war measure, the increase, in the case of a private soldier being from Rs. 1-8-0 to Rs. 5, and special field allowances, in addition to the above, were granted to all Indian troops and followers serving in East Africa, Mesopotamia, Egypt, Aden, Persia, etc. Indian troops and followers serving on the Continent of Europe, in the Balkans, at Salonika and the Dardanelles received a 25 per cent increase on pay as special field allowance.

With effect from 1st January 1917 the pay of all combatant Indian Officers and Non-commissioned Officers was increased by from 10 to 20 per cent according to rank.

Bonus

A bonus of Rs. 50 to combatant recruits was temporarily offered.

In addition recruits received a further Rs. 15 on completing their training, or on proceeding overseas.

From the 1st June 1918 a war bonus was given for every six months' service completed after that date, the rate for every such completed period being Rs. 24 in the case of Indian other ranks and amounting to Rs. 60 for the highest grades of Indian Officers. This war bonus, for which *quasi* combatants such as Muleteers and Army Bearer Corps personnel were also eligible to a lesser degree was subsequently given as a definite increase to the monthly rates of pay.

MEDICAL

Substantial measures were sanctioned with effect from 18th April 1917 in order to improve the conditions of service of military sub-assistant surgeons of the Indian Medical Department. Their rates of pay were increased by from 27 to 71 per cent, according to grade, and increases in the rates of field allowance were from 33 to 100 per cent. Free quarters, or compensation in lieu, were authorised for the families of those on field or foreign service and various grants of charge and sub-charge allowance were made admissible.

They also became eligible for the grant of Indian commissioned rank and of certain honorary ranks.

HOSPITALS AND SANITATION

Diets for Indian Station Hospitals have been introduced as a permanent measure, and accommodation is being brought up to the standard of modern requirements.

Large sums have been provided for purchase of extra equipment and furniture and for the supply, repair and renewal of artificial limbs for disabled pensioned soldiers and public followers.

Strenuous efforts have been made to check the spread of malaria at various stations and large schemes for draining nullahs, etc., have been undertaken.

Miscellaneous

Kit-money has been abolished and the Army Clothing Department has undertaken the supply of clothing, boots and necessaries as a free issue to units of the Indian Army to relieve them of the burden which the rise in prices, due to the war, would otherwise have thrown on them.

The issue of free civilian clothing, up to a maximum of Rs. 18, has been sanctioned for all Indian soldiers invalided from field service.

The conditions of service of mule transport drivers have been greatly improved, and they have received all the concessions admissible to Indian troops, but on a slightly lower scale. Camel and bullock personnel have been given a free ration of firewood and an increased scale of clothing.

With regard to blinded soldiers a scheme has been

sanctioned for their training either at the school for the blind at Lahore or the Victoria Memorial school at Bombay. Instruction at these schools, of course, is free and students receive free quarters and rations, free conveyance by rail for themselves and for an attendant and a monthly allowance of Rs. 6 from the Imperial Indian Relief Fund in addition to their pension. The duration of training is usually limited to nine months and any money earned by students during the course is treated as their own property.

For the benefit of soldiers and followers of the Indian Army, an Institution called "The Queen Mary's Technical School for Disabled Indian Soldiers" has been established at Bombay. Its aim is to take over for a period of 6 months, or more, soldiers and followers of the Indian Army of all ranks and classes, who have been disabled in war service, or who have been pensioned as unfit for further military service from any cause whatever. Its further object is to provide them with clothes, food and other necessaries, and to teach them a trade so that, after a course of training, they will have means of supplementing their pensions and will thus be able to live in comfort. The men are allowed to select the trade they would like to learn and the Committee endeavour to obtain employment for trained men when they have finished their course of training.

With regard to disciplinary measures the infliction of corporal punishment has been abolished for persons subject to the Indian Army Act, and an Act entitled the Indian Army (Suspension of Sentences) Act was passed under which sentences of punishment awarded to Indian soldiers may be held in suspense, and be ultimately remitted, in cases of good behaviour on the part of the soldier concerned.

The Indian Soldiers (Litigation) Act was introduced for the protection of Indian soldiers from civil and revenue litigation when unable to attend to their affairs while serving under war conditions.

In connection with the improvement of education in the Indian Army the regimental school establishments and allowances have been very greatly increased.

The principle has been accepted that education shall be an integral part of the training of the Indian Army, with a view to :—

- *(a)* facilitating the battle training of the soldier;
- *(b)* ensuring a supply of men sufficiently educated to undertake the duties of leaders of smaller units in the event of war necessitating an expansion of the forces;
- *(c)* ensuring the degree of mental fitness necessary in modern war;
- *(d)* ensuring the economic efficiency and employability of the short service soldier on return to civil life.

To this end an organisation has been created, under the direction of the General Staff Branch, Army Headquarters, India, with education staff officers at the Headquarters of each Command and District, which will supervise the work of the personnel of the Indian Wing of the Army Educational Corps attached to each unit.

This specialist personnel to be drawn from the martial classes and trained, under the direction of the General Staff, in a School of Education.

Reference has been made above to the work of the Indian Soldiers' Board. The activities of this Institution have been so varied and of such a useful and humane nature that a brief account of its work, compiled by its Secretary in the autumn of 1919, may fittingly be inserted.

> "The conclusion of the Armistice in November 1918 and the prospect of an early peace diverted attention from the problem of winning the war to the problem that would inevitably arise during the period of demobilization, when men released from the colours had not yet settled down to the ordinary conditions of peace. In England and in the Colonies special machinery was created to deal with the situation. In England, for example, as long ago as August 1917, a Ministry of Reconstruction was established, the functions of the minister being "to consider and advise upon the problems which may arise out of the present war and may have to be dealt with on its termination, and for the purpose aforesaid to initiate and conduct such enquiries, prepare such schemes and make such recommendations as he thinks fit."

"In India, too, similar problems were anticipated. From the demobilization of a large proportion of the Indian Army, no matter how excellently the military arrangements were conceived and how admirably they were carried out, difficulties were bound to ensue which could be dealt with satisfactorily by no existing Department of Government and for the immediate solution of which the establishment of an *ad hoc* transitional board was emphatically required. Finding employment for soldiers released from the colours, the grant of rewards to those who had rendered distinguished service, the relief of the dependents of those who had lost their lives in the war, or of those who were incapacitated for further service, the education of the soldiers' children, and safeguarding the general interests of soldiers whether serving or discharged, and of their dependents if deceased, were all matters demanding immediate and close attention.

Accordingly, the Indian Soldiers' Board was established in January 1919. The scope of its work was not of the same formidable character as that confronting the Ministry of Reconstruction in England but, on a smaller scale, its functions were similar. This Board, the lineal descendant of the Recruiting Board, was composed of the following members :—

The Hon'ble Sir George Lowndes, K.C.S.I., K.C., Bar-at-law (Law Member), President.

His Honour the Lieutenant-Governor of the Punjab.

The Hon'ble the Revenue Member.

The Hon'ble the Finance Member.

The Adjutant General in India.

The Secretary to the Government of India in the Army Department.

The Financial Adviser, Military Finance.

His Highness the Maharaja of Gwalior.

His Highness the Maharaja of Bikaner.

His Highness the Maharaja of Patiala.

A whole-time Secretary with a small office staff was also appointed.

At the outset it was obvious that the Central Board should, in the main, exercise advisory and deliberative functions, and that executive action in the numerous cases expected to arise should be delegated to similar organizations in the provinces.

The latter were accordingly invited to form boards of their own, and at present in every province (except Bengal where it was represented there was no need to set up a special organization, correspondence when necessary being carried on with the local Government) and in many Indian States boards have been established, working in co-operation with and carrying out the policy of the Central Board, and at the same time vigorously grappling with their own special problems.

The subjects chiefly dealt with fall under the following headings :—

(1) Rewarding officers and men of the Indian Army for distinguished service during the war.

(2) Employment.

(3) Education.

(4) The after-care of the wounded and incapacitated.

(5) Attention to the general interests and welfare of soldiers serving, discharged or deceased.

(6) Relief of distress among the dependents of soldiers.

(7) Commemoration of the exploits of the Indian Army.

A brief exposition follows in non-technical language of what has been accomplished under each heading.

The scheme of rewards is in effect to give grants of land to selected officers and men who have rendered distinguished service during the war. It is in some ways akin to the policy of settling discharged soldiers and sailors on the land which has been accepted in England and the Dominions. The Government of India, however, have looked primarily not to the opportunity of opening out fresh land for colonization but to the necessity of rewarding conspicuous merit in the Army. These rewards have been specially devised to meet the unique circumstances of the Great War, and are in addition to all the stereotyped forms of war rewards such as the rapid flow of promotion carrying with it the attendant advantages of increased pay, rewards for specific acts of gallantry carrying additional pecuniary benefit, war bonuses and the like. They are also in addition to all forms of pension whether service or war pensions. Thanks to the generosity of the major local Governments, and particularly of the Punjab, considerable areas of land have been made available for distribution and, though the grants will entail the obligations of tenancy, the conditions of tenure are very favourable to the grantees. While these conditions must of necessity vary in the several provinces, steps have been taken to ensure that the capital value of the grant is as nearly as possible equal in all provinces providing land.

It has, from the outset, been recognised that a grant of land was the most attractive form of reward, but owing to the limited amount of land suitable for cultivation and ready for early distribution a supplementary form of rewards has had to be devised in the form of a jangi inam or money allowance payable monthly for two lives.

The total number of rewards whether of land or money was fixed at 20,000, and one of the hardest tasks of the Board has been to make an equitable distribution to units. Such an allotment, however, has now been made, based on the number of men sent on service and the number of casualties sustained. In this distribution to units the Board has been advised by a committee of regimental commanding officers. No element of personal bias or judgment has entered into this calculation of the number of rewards assigned to each unit, and the Board confidently believes that the result achieved is as fair to all concerned as is possible in the circumstances. Officers Commanding Units have been invited to submit the names of the officers and men they select, subject to the final approval of the Board, as the recipients of these rewards. Everything possible is being done to secure a very early distribution among the men themselves; local Governments are ready to receive grantees on the land, and jangi inams will be payable from the 1st September 1919, while an orderly procedure for putting those selected in possession of their rewards has been devised in collaboration with local Governments. Much now depends on the promptitude with which Officers Commanding Units send in their names.

It must not be supposed that any distribution of rewards which can be made will not be productive of discontent among those whose names find no place in the final lists. Some grumbling of this sort is inevitable unless grants could be made to every soldier who has served during the war. But, however desirable this may appear upon sentimental grounds, it is obvious that in the case of an Indian Army amounting to nearly a million men it would be impossible to saddle the revenue of the country with the expenditure which would be entailed. Moreover, not more than half a million had enlisted in the pre-war army and in the period ending with 31st December 1917. The remaining half a million had served for less than a year before the termination of hostilities and consequently have far less claim to special consideration. The terms of enlistment in recent years have been so favourable to the soldier that he can have no legitimate cause for grumbling and all information received indicates a state of unusual prosperity among those who have been demobilized.

The natural expectation was that demobilization on a large scale would create an immediate and widespread demand for employment on the part of discharged soldiers and though this expectation has not been realized, steps were early taken to meet the contingency should it arise. In order that district officers might be prepared, they were informed in advance of the numbers of men being demobilized from time to time, and the latter were advised to consult the recruiting officer in cases of difficulty who, it was arranged; should act as a liaison officer between the soldier and the civil authorities. At the same time direct action has been taken by local Governments themselves. Instructions have been issued to give, where possible, a preference to ex-soldiers for vacancies in Government employment: lists of men desiring work have been maintained : district committees have, in many cases, been formed with the object of assisting soldiers to find work : the help and co-operation of business firms and Chambers of Commerce has been freely enlisted and readily and generously given. At the same time divisional recruiting officers keep lists of discharged soldiers desirous of finding occupation, and have acted as a link between the employer who wants workmen and the discharged soldier who seeks employment. Indian soldiers who possess technical qualifications have been dealt with by the Employment and Labour Board which has established provincial agencies for taking up individual applications. Thus though the demand for employment hitherto has been much less than was anticipated owing doubtless to the possession of accumulated savings, the natural desire for ease after a long period of arduous service and the fact that the majority of men demobilised, belonging as they do to the agricultural classes, can readily slip back into agricultural occupations, the Board feel confident that the organizations established throughout the country and the measures already adopted provide adequate safeguards against any extensive unemployment amongst the soldier class.

The necessity of providing educational facilities for the children of deceased and incapacitated soldiers has been fully recognised by all local Governments and generous concessions have been granted such as, speaking generally, free education in primary schools and at greatly reduced rates in secondary schools with, in many cases, money allowances for books, etc. The concessions vary in different provinces but there is little profit in a detailed enumeration of them. Suffice it to say there has been little for the Central Board to do in this direction beyond noting with satisfaction the generous measures adopted in the provinces.

There is perhaps no member of the community who has a greater claim upon the State than the incapacitated soldier. The pension provided by the Government is some guarantee against destitution, but it is now recognised that the State owes a still further duty and must, as far as possible, provide treatment for the incapacitated which will give them back to a limited extent the use of their disabled limbs, and instruction in suitable trades by which their means of livelihood may be increased. India is well equipped with institutes at which training and treatment are provided—the institute at Dehra Dun and the training schools at Bombay and Lahore, to say nothing of military orthopaedic hospitals at Cawnpore and Ambala, spring at once to the mind. Experience, however, has shown that the provision of institutes is not in itself sufficient; it is still necessary to overcome the greater reluctance exhibited by Indian incapacitated soldiers to avail themselves of the opportunities offered. It is to their popularization, therefore, that the Board has devoted considerable attention. Wide publicity in simple language has been given to the facilities that exist and the concessions that are offered. Army Instructions are not always easy to understand and therefore, on discharge, each soldier now receives a pamphlet in his own vernacular describing how he can secure medical treatment at the nearest military hospital should his wounds break out afresh, how he can obtain replacement of artificial limbs, boots and other medical appliances when such replacement has become necessary, how he can procure admission to a training school, and the inducements offered such as free quarters and free food, free railway travelling and permission to bring his wife with him, for whom accommodation also is provided.

While the dependents of soldiers were during the years of war treated with every consideration, it was recognized by the Board that this class would be likely to require special protection in the immediate future, especially in those districts in which the soldier who has gone on service belongs to the agricultural classes. Long absence on service may have laid up for him special difficulties on his return—it may be with regard to boundaries, it may be in connection with money lender's claims: while in some cases, it was felt, the troubles may be more intimately connected with family relations. A special duty was thought to be owing to the widows and children who, where the bread-winner has fallen in the war, may be in a particularly defenceless position. Accordingly, it has been widely made known through provincial boards that the dependents of soldiers will be taken under the special protection of district officers. The spirit of this policy has been universally followed : both in general attitude and in particular in the careful, prompt and sympathetic disposal of the many petitions that have been received. Especially in regard to litigation it was felt that a further measure of protection could, with advantage, be extended to soldiers and their dependents when in necessitous circumstances. The incapacitated and the widows and minor children would often have little means at their disposal to resist unscrupulous attempts to take advantage of their helplessness. The suggestion was accordingly made to local Governments that the benevolence of lawyers in each centre of litigation might be enlisted in their behalf, who would give free legal advice in necessitous 'soldier' cases. A prompt and generous response has been made to this suggestion; though at the same time its dangers—the possible encouragement of litigation and the opportunity afforded of causing embarrassment to an enemy—have been fully recognized and guarded against.

The interests of another important class, the pensioners, have not been forgotten. The hardship entailed by the system in force in some parts of India, under which pensioners often have to undertake a long journey to the district or tahsil headquarters in order to receive payment of their pensions has been recognized, and a committee has been appointed to consider whether a more convenient system cannot be devised, such as an extension of the system now in force in the Punjab where pension payments are made through the agency of the Post Office. It is impossible to anticipate their recommendations: but it may be confidently anticipated that an improvement will be effected.

Finally, mention must be made of the steps taken by the Board to allay the anxiety of soldiers serving overseas caused by the absence of news from their families in India. Communication from this country is never, at the best of times, an easy matter owing to the general illiteracy of the relatives left behind and ignorance as to the whereabouts of their kinsmen on service; moreover, the fears due to this absence of information were still more accentuated in the minds of the soldier overseas by his consternation at the reported ravages of the influenza epidemic in the autumn of 1918. To ensure a certain means of communication, post cards with the addresses of the regiments printed on them are now issued by depots free of cost to the relatives in India, and are accepted free of charge by the post office. If this concession is made use of, the soldier overseas will have no complaint on the score of absence of news from his family in India.

At its first meeting the Board recognized that one of its main duties was to bring to light and relieve cases of distress among the dependents of Indian soldiers. When it was created it had no funds at its disposal, but it was early seen that its activities would be hampered unless it could dispense relief. Accordingly, an arrangement was made whereby the Board took over the administration of the portion of the Imperial Indian Relief Fund devoted to the relief of Indian classes. Since then money has been freely spent—partly in making allotments to Brigade Area Committees which pay two and in some cases three donations of Rs. 50 each to the nominated heir of every Indian soldier killed or who has died on active service and also donations to the incapacitated; and partly in placing money at the disposal of local Governments for the relief of all cases of necessity among the dependents of soldiers which can be directly ascribed to the war or to the influenza epidemic.

This transfer of administration to the Board has resulted in a wide extension of discretionary relief. Early in the year it was represented that acute distress was prevailing in the Punjab especially among the widows and dependents of Indian soldiers : the position of the following classes was shown to be particularly hard:—

(*a*) Widows receiving small pensions with no adult male relative able and willing to help them, who possess no land or other resources, or whose land is now barren, and who are consequently unable to maintain themselves and those dependent upon them.

(*b*) Widowed mothers of sons who have been killed or have died on service whose circumstances are similar to those of class (*a*).

(c) Pensionless widows and widowed mothers of men who have been in the Army during the war and have died in India without acquiring pension rights on behalf of their wives and mothers, whose circumstances in respect of land or crops or male relatives able to win bread by labour are similar to those of the women described under *(a)* and *(b)*.

Local Governments were accordingly invited to submit applications for the money they thought to be necessary for the immediate relief of these unfortunate widows and dependents. Whatever funds were asked for were immediately made available.

Later in the year the high cost of living and general distress in parts of the Punjab induced the Board to consider the adequacy of existing arrangements for distributing discretionary relief. The classes mentioned above were by no means exhaustive and donations given by Brigade Area Committees only extended to nominated heirs of soldiers. It is true that these committees were empowered to grant discretionary relief in certain cases: but the amount so distributed was small, and they had no means of getting into touch with dependents other than the nominated heirs or of making enquiries about them. As the district authorities were in a better position to find out and investigate the claims of individual cases, the distribution of discretionary relief in all cases of necessity among dependents of soldiers and especially among widows, was made over to the Civil authorities, and any funds they have asked for have been immediately placed at their disposal. There is good reason to believe that the most urgent cases have in all provinces been in receipt of this discretionary relief. It has enabled them to get through a year of high prices and to avoid the incubus of debt that otherwise would have been their portion.

Further assistance in the form of a *post bellum* distribution especially among the very hard cases, the totally incapacitated and the blinded is under contemplation, and it is hoped that the necessary preliminary measures will shortly be completed. The case of blinded soldiers of whom happily there are only 48 in India has been under the special care of an institution known as St. Dunstans with whose work the Board has kept in close touch and it is hoped that funds may be available to provide special annuities in all their cases.

This compendious sketch of the activities of the Board has hitherto been confined to a description of what has been accomplished on behalf of serving or discharged soldiers, and the dependents of soldiers who have lost their lives in the war. But no account of its work would be- complete without a reference to the memorials it proposes to erect in order to commemorate the achievements of the Indian Army and to pay tribute to the memory of the brave men who have fallen. An Imperial memorial is being erected in Delhi, and in each theatre of war in which Indian troops have been engaged a memorial will be set up to commemorate their exploits in battle. War commemoration tablets will be presented to all villages in India which have supplied a large number of fighting men for the army. These tablets containing a simple inscription will be placed at suitable sites in the villages selected.

Such in brief is the main work accomplished by the Board. It has set itself steadfastly to be both in word and deed the soldier's friend to help him in his troubles, and to assist his dependents when in distress."

The Imperial Memorial at Delhi is estimated to cost Rs. 6 lakhs. The foundation stone was laid by His Royal Highness the Duke of Connaught on the 10th February, 1921. Drawn up in hollow square facing the dais were the colours of some 60 Indian and Imperial Service units and behind them chosen representatives of every unit in India.

His Excellency the Viceroy, in asking the Duke of Connaught to lay the foundation stone, said:—

"We are assembled here in the presence of representatives of all the units of the Indian Army to lay the foundation-stone of the All-India War Memorial. The immortal story of the endurance and valour of the sons of India in the cold and mud of Flanders, the heat of Mesopotamia, indeed in every land where the soldiers of the Empire fought and bled, is a legacy which their sons and their sons' sons will treasure above all the wealth that the world can offer. The stirring tales of individual heroism, which Your Royal Highness has no doubt read, will live for ever in the annals of this country, but the story of the no less heroic endurance of hardships and discomforts, of suffering and death in the field and in captivity, is known only to those who suffered and their comrades in arms. It is as a tribute to the memory of these heroes, known and unknown, that we are erecting the All-India War Memorial. May it serve to keep their memory green and to inspire us, for whom they fought and died, that we may endure hardships with like silent fortitude, may fight the battle of life with no less valour, and if Providence so wills may lay down our lives, content like them with a duty honourably done, and a cause nobly vindicated."

The Duke of Connaught, in performing the ceremony, said:—

"Officers and men of the Indian Army, and of the Imperial Service Troops, His Majesty the King-Emperor has commanded me on this solemn occasion to convey a message of his Royal thanks to the Indian army, and to the Imperial Service Troops furnished by Indian States. It is as follows:—

"The Great War, from which our Empire has emerged victorious, involved the most powerful nations of the earth and spread over vast seas and continents. From the crowded record, here and there certain leaders, here and there certain features, stand clearly out arresting the attention and admiration of the world to-day, and claiming with confidence the verdict of posterity. In this honourable company the Indian Army has an assured place. Scattered far and wide under alien skies, in adversity and in triumph, they played their part with stout and gallant hearts. True to their tradition they answered to the Empire's call with soldierly discipline and fortitude. Staunch in the loyalty they have ever displayed to the Throne and person of their King-Emperor, they made his cause their own, and willingly laid down their lives for their Sovereign. Gratitude for loyalty such as this lies deep in my heart, and is beyond the power of words. They did their duty. Can the King for whom they fought give higher praise to his soldiers? I have great pleasure in announcing that, in recognition of the distinguished services and gallantry of the Indian Army during the Great War, His Majesty the King-Emperor has been graciously pleased to confer the title Royal on the following units :—

The Deccan Horse.
3rd Sappers and Miners.
6th Jat Light Infantry.
34th Sikh Pioneers.
39th Garhwal Rifles.
59th Scinde Rifles (Frontier Force).
117th Mahrattas.
5th Gurkha Rifles (Frontier Force).

His Majesty has also been graciously pleased to nominate

me as Colonel-in-Chief of the 47th Sikhs, a regiment which served with great distinction in the war. I greatly value an honour which will strengthen the many ties I have with my old friends, the soldiers of the Khalsa."

"Officers and men of the Indian Army and of the Imperial Service Troops, many of us here to-day must have ringing in our ears the glowing tribute paid to the Indian Army by His Royal Highness the Prince of Wales when unveiling the testimony of affection and gratitude erected by the citizens of Brighton in memory of the Indian soldiers who died there in the days of the war. India knows full well, I trust, how generously and how tenderly the people of Brighton discharged their self-allotted task of receiving and sheltering the wounded Indian soldiers brought to their care from the battle fields of France. I am sure that throughout India the message of goodwill from the marble chattri at Brighton will awaken a grateful and responsive echo here on Indian soil. We are assembled to discharge a similar debt of honour. On this spot, in the central *vista* of the Capital of India, there will stand a memorial archway designed to keep present in the thoughts of the generations that follow after, the glorious sacrifice of the officers and men of the Indian Army, who fought and fell in the Great War. The men were nobly led, and the officers were bravely followed, and we give thanks to Almighty Providence that the cause for which they fought was the cause which prevailed, and that our memorial is not one of lives lost in vain, but a monument of great and overwhelming victory."

"To-day's simple ceremony would surely appeal to those gallant soldiers who have fought their last fight, and to whom we are gathered here to pay tribute, for it is a soldiers' ceremony. Before me there are assembled from far and wide men of the Indian Army of to-day, many of them once comrades of those who are at this hour foremost in our thoughts, but who will never again answer our reveille. Let us try to think that those absent comrades are with us here to-day, back from their distant and scattered graves, standing in our ranks once again, helping us to do them honour in the spirit they themselves would wish, inspiring us with their clearer vision to understand a soldier's duty."

"I am deeply touched to find that my visit to India should enable me to take part in to-day's solemn ceremony, for my admiration and affection for the Indian Army go back many years. I belong to the older generation among soldiers. The chances of service brought me into the closest touch with the Indian Army of former days, the army which Lord Roberts fathered, the army which Lord Kitchener schooled. I well remember those veteran regiments whose war medals told of service far from their Indian homes in China, East Africa, West Africa, South Africa, Somaliland, Egypt and the frontiers of India and Burma. It was an Army of great traditions and splendid discipline, but little did I dream in those days what remoter echoes the Indian bugle-call would awaken, to what still more distant fields the Indian Army would one day be called or to what immense expansion that great organization would be brought by the strong impulse of loyalty and patriotism."

To-day we know that more than a million Indians left these shores to serve abroad, of whom nearly 60,000 including 850 Indian Officers, gave up their lives in the Empire's cause. The many campaigns in which the units of the Indian Army took part are written in history. The honours they won were many, but on these I shall not dwell now. Some indeed are proudly worn by those who stand here before me, but the sole honour we commemorate here is the honour of the great sacrifice, the supreme honour of a soldier's death. What though the world sometimes seems to us dark with trouble, and the sky overcast, let us look back with pride, and forward with hope, for these men showed us the true heart of

India. Through them we know that the soul of India has only to be touched aright and India will respond to her King-Emperor's call."

"In this hour of crowding memories, let us have no sombre thoughts, but recapture once again that thrill which passed through us all when we first heard in those far off days of 1914 that the Indian troops had landed at Marseilles and were pressing on towards our thinly held battle lines in France and Flanders. That is the vision which the glorious dead would wish us to have to-day. Their tradition lives, the Army goes on fortified by their example to face whatever task the future may have in store. You men of the Indian Army know when a fine regiment marches through the streets of a busy town how everyone quits his work, and looks in admiring silence, or marches along with you. Is it merely because of your glittering array or the rhythm of your march ? No, it is something far deeper than that. It is the spirit of the Army, making itself felt, the spirit of discipline, of unity, of brave tradition of comradeship till death. In the presence of that moral force men turn from the sordid cares of every-day life, and pay you uplifting reverence, as though some uplifting influence had passed through their work-a-day world. You enjoy a great heritage of honour. Strive then always to uphold the honour of your regiments, and be faithful to the memory of these gallant soldiers who have added lustre to your name and fame. I like to recall the simple tribute paid by the Indian Corps Commander in France. He wrote: 'The discipline of this Corps has been above reproach. They have behaved like gentlemen, and French and British both knew it well. Had they done nothing else, they would still leave Europe with a clean sheet as citizens of the Empire.' 'They behaved like gentlemen.' I do not think that those who gave up their lives would wish for an epitaph more eloquent than this. May the spirit of the Indian Army ever remain bright and untarnished, and one of the great examples which we commemorate here to-day. May new and great traditions be founded, and the Indian Army of the future, through them re-consecrated and re-inspired, be the worthy heir of those who fought and died under its colours in the Great War."

The Colour Parties and representatives stood to attention after the foundation-stone had been declared truly laid. They presented arms and massed buglers sounded the Last Post.

His Excellency the Commander-in-Chief, in thanking the Duke of Connaught, said :—

" All ranks of the Indian Army pay their most respectful gratitude for the eulogistic terms in which you have so graciously referred to their deeds during the Great War."

" They welcome with delight the presence of their well beloved Field Marshal once more amongst them and remember with pride and gratification the many occasions in the past when they have had the honour of serving under Your Royal Highness' personal command. They wish to assure Your Royal Highness of their constant attention to duty, and of their unswerving loyalty to the Empire, and to His Majesty the King-Emperor."

A march past and three ringing cheers by the troops brought the ceremony to a close.

The speech made by His Royal Highness the Prince of Wales, when unveiling the memorial at Brighton, and referred to by His Royal Highness the Duke of Connaught, was as follows :—

"We are met to dedicate a memorial to brave men, our

fellow-subjects who, after the fire and stress of Flanders, received the last sacred rites of their religion on this high eminence. It is befitting that we should remember, and that future generations should not forget, that our Indian comrades came when our need was highest,—free men and voluntary soldiers who were true to their salt and gave their lives in a quarrel of which it was enough for them to know that the enemy were the foes of their sahibs, the Emperor and their King. This monument marks, too, another fact. When the wounded Indian soldiers were brought to England there was no place ready for their reception; your generous town came to the rescue, and, with a hospitality which will ever be remembered in India, gave not only the finest buildings but also her friendship and respect to these gallant men. Brighton has created this memorial to the Hindus and Sikhs who died in her beautiful hospitals, and has testified to the affection and admiration she felt for the men who fought so gallantly and bore themselves so patiently and so nobly during the long months they lay by the sea thinking of their village homes so far away.

"I can assure you, Mr. Mayor, that India never forgets kindness and sympathy, and from this Chattri a wave of goodwill will pass to India. In conclusion—though this is purely a memorial to the Hindu and Sikh soldiers—I am thinking, too, of the Mahomedan soldiers who passed away in your care. These were buried with all military honour at Working and I hear that before long a gate of Oriental character, the gift of Indians, will adorn the Pavilion. May these two memorials, so historical and so instinct with compassion and mutual regard, strengthen the ties between India and our country."

APPENDIX A.

Units.

Units.	Existing before the war.	Raised during the war.	Total existing or raised during the war.	Reduction during the war.	Remaining on Indian establishment.	Total units despatched overseas.	Received from overseas.	Balance remaining in India.	REMARKS.
Cavalry.									
British (Squadrons)	36	..	36	..	36	32	4	8	
Indian (Squadrons)	155⅔	43⅓	199	2	197	147	43	93	
Imperial Service (Squadrons).	39	..	39	..	39	29	3	13	
Artillery.									
Royal Horse Artillery Batteries.	11	..	11	..	11	10	1	2	
Ammunition Column	9	..	9	3	6	5	1	2	
Royal Field Artillery (Batteries).	45	..	45	13*	32	50*	33	19	* Includes 4 lost at Kut and not replaced.
Ammunition Column	12	2	14	2†	12	9†	..	4	† Includes 1 lost at Kut and not replaced.
Mountain Batteries (British).	8	..	8	..	8	2	..	6	
Mountain Batteries (Indian) (6 guns).	12	7	19	2	17	13⅓	5	8⅔	
Mountain Batteries (Indian) (4 guns).	..	9	9	..	9	4	..	5	

Special for Internal Security.								
Batteries . . .	..	2	2	..	2	..	..	2
Sections . . .		8	8	..	..	..	..	8
Royal Garrison Artillery (Companies).	21	..	21	5	16	6	3	13
Volunteer Batteries .	..	2	2	..	2	2	..	..
Anglo-Indian Batteries .	..	1	1	..	1	1	..	..
Mountain Artillery Section Divisional Ammunition Column.	..	1	1	..	1	1	..	..
Infantry.								
British Battalions . .	52	4	56	4	52	71	42	23
Indian Battalions . .	138	155½	293½	14	279½	192½	47	134
Garrison Battalions .	..	..	..	..	..	1	22	21
Special Indian Companies	..	76½	76½	54	22½	..	..	22½
Indian Garrison Companies	..	15½	15½	..	15½	..	..	15½
Machine Gun Corps.								
Machine Gun Squadron .	..	3	3	..	3	..	..	3
Machine Gun Companies, British.	..	19	19	..	19	7	..	12
Machine Gun Companies, Indian.	..	3	3	..	3	3	..	..
Volunteer Machine Company.	..	1	1	..	1	1	..	..
Motor Machine Gun Batteries.	..	1	1	..	1	..	4	5
Armoured Motor Batteries	..	16	16	..	16	..	..	16
Sappers and Miners.								
Field Squadrons . .	..	2	2	..	2	..	..	2
Field Troops . . .	1	9	10	1	9	3	..	6
Field Companies . .	19	41*	60*	2†	58*	31¾	1	27¼

* Including 4 Imperial Service companies.
† 2 lost at Kut.

Units—contd.

Units.	Existing before the war.	Raised during the war.	Total existing or raised during the war.	Reduction during the war.	Remaining on Indian establishment.	Total units despatched overseas.	Received from overseas.	Balance remaining in India.	REMARKS.
Sappers and Miners—contd.									
Bridging Trains	..	5	5	..	5	5	1	1	
Engineer Field Parks	6	2	8	..	8	4	..	4	
Railway Companies	2	3	5	..	5	4	3	4	
Electrical and Mechanical Companies.	..	1	1	..	1	1	..	..	
Printing Sections	5	5	10	..	10	8	..	2	
Litho Sections	5	3	8	..	8	6	..	2	
Searchlight Company	..	1	1	..	1	1	..	..	
Volunteer Armoured Train Detachment.	..	1	1	..	1	1	..	..	
Signal Units.									
Corps Signal Companies	..	3	3	1	2	1	..	1	
Divisional Signal Companies.	4	17	21	2	19	10*	..	10	* 1 lost at Kut.
Brigade Signal Sections	..	8	8	2	6	4†	2	4	† Includes 2 returned from East Africa and absorbed in other formations.
Signal Squadron	..	1	1	1	..	1	..	..	
Signal Troops	..	9	9	..	9	3	..	6	
Wireless Squadron	1	1	2	..	2	1	..	1	
Signal Park and Depot	..	1	1	..	1	1	..	..	
Medical Units.									
British Field Ambulances	(a) 21¼	1½	22¾	..	22¾	13¾	½	9½	(a) 24¾ sanctioned of which—

Indian Field Ambulances	(*b*) 44	38¾	82¾	..	82¾	50¼	..	32½	¼ converted into ¼ B.C.H. ¼ converted into ¼ I.C.H. ⅓ converted into 2½ I.F.A.
Sanitary Sections	8	24⅓	32⅓	..	32⅓	13⅓	..	19	
British Clearing Hospitals	(*c*) 3¼	3¼	6½	..	6½	2½	..	4	(*b*) 41⅓ sanctioned to which was added 2½ B.F. As. by conversion.
Indian Clearing Hospitals	(*d*) 12¼	14½	26¾	..	26¾	12¼	..	14½	(*c*) 3 sanctioned —¼ added by converting ¼ B.F.A.
British Stationary Hospitals.	40	8	48	(*e*)1	47	3	(*e*) 1	45	(*d*) 12 sanctioned—¼ added by converting ¼ B.F.A.
Indian Stationary Hospitals	40	86	126	..	126	46	..	80	
Advance Depôts, Medical	8	11	19	..	19	11	..	8	(*e*) Sent to Port Blair—on return unit was abolished.
British General Hospitals	(*f*) 3	5 3/16	8 3/16	..	8 3/16	3 1/16	..	5⅛	(*f*) 4 sanctioned 1 converted into I.G.H.
Indian General Hospitals	(*g*) 9	35⅝	44⅝	..	44⅝	(*h*) 38⅝	..	16	(*g*) 8 sanctioned —1 added by converting 1 B.G.H.
X-Ray Sections	15	13	28	..	28	10	..	18	
General Medical Store Depot.	..	1	1	(*j*) 1	..	1	..	..	(*h*) 2 of these had no equipment.
Base Depôts, Medical stores.	..	¼	¼	..	¼	¼	..	..	(*j*) Absorbed in Force "D."
Hospital ships	..	6	..	3	3	6	(*k*) 3	3	(*k*) Surrendered from Hospital service.

APPEN

Distribution of Indian

—	At Outbreak of War.												
	Cavalry.				British Battalions.					Imperial Service Units.			
	British.	Indian.	Mobile Guns.	Sapper and Miner Companies.	Regular.	Territorial.	Garrison.	Indian Battalions.	Nepalese Battalions.	Cavalry Regiments.	Guns.	Sapper and Miner Companies.	Battalions.
(a) Sent overseas independently.	..	..	..	..	..	..	..	..	..	..	..	..	..
(b) In France	..	..	..	..	..	..	..	..	..	..	..	..	..
(c) In Mesopotamia	..	..	..	..	..	..	..	..	..	..	..	..	..
(d) In Egypt and the Mediterranean.	..	..	6	..	..	..	..	..	..	..	..	..	..
(e) In East Africa	..	..	..	..	..	..	..	..	..	..	..	..	..
(f) In South Persia and the Persian Gulf.	..	..	..	..	..	..	..	1	..	..	..	..	..
(g) In East Persia	..	..	..	..	..	..	..	..	..	..	..	..	..
(h) In Aden	..	¼	14	1	1	..	..	1	..	..	..	..	..
(i) In Colonies	..	..	6	..	..	..	..	7	..	..	..	..	..
(j) In Siberia	..	..	..	..	..	..	..	..	..	..	..	..	..
Total sent overseas	..	¼	26	1	1	..	..	9	..	..	..	..	..
In India :—													
(k) Field Army and Frontier Brigades	8	28	396	18	27	..	..	97	..	6	..	4	7½
(l) Internal Security.	1	11	78	1	24	..	..	32	..	5	8	..	3
(m) Unallotted Units.	..	..	..	..	..	..	..	..	..	..	..	..	..
Total in India	9	39	474	19	51	..	..	129	..	11	8	4	10½
Grand Total	9	39¼	500	20	52	..	..	138	..	11	8	4	10½
Deduct—Units received from *Ex*-India.	..	..	..	..	..	..	..	..	..	..	..	..	..
Net total of Units furnished by India.	9	39¼	500	20	52	..	..	138	..	11	8	4	10½

DIX B

Units at different periods of the War

NOVEMBER 1914.												
CAVALRY.				BRITISH BATTALIONS.					IMPERIAL SERVICE UNITS.			
British.	Indian.	Mobile Guns.	Sapper and Miner Companies.	Regular.	Territorial.	Garrison.	Indian Battalions.	Nepalese Battalions.	Cavalry Regiments.	Guns.	Sapper and Miner Companies.	Battalions.
..	..	126	..	32	..	..	..	..	..	..	..	..
6	14	162	4	6	..	..	20	..	1	..	..	..
..	1	30	2	3	..	..	10	..	..	..	..	..
..	..	12	..	1	..	..	21	..	4*	..	..	3
..	..	12	..	1	..	..	7	..	..	..	1	4
..	..	..	..	..	..	..	2	..	..	..	..	..
..	..	..	..	..	..	..	..	..	..	..	..	..
..	½	20	1	..	1	..	2	..	..	..	..	..
..	..	6	..	..	..	..	8	..	..	..	..	..
..	..	..	..	..	..	..	..	..	..	..	..	..
6	15½	368	7	43	1	..	70	..	5	..	1	7
2	10	136	10	9	..	..	37	..	4	..	3	..
1	14	134	2	..	34	..	31	..	2	8	..	3½
..	..	..	..	..	..	..	..	..	..	..	..	..
3	24	270	12	9	34	..	68	..	6	8	3	3½
9	39½	638	19	52	35	..	138	..	11	8	4	10½
..	..	116	..	..	35	..	..	..	..	..	..	..
9	39½	522	19	52	..	..	138	..	11	8	4	10½

* Includes Bikaner Camel Corps.

Distribution of Indian

	JULY 1916.												
	CAVALRY.				BRITISH BATTALIONS.					IMPERIAL SERVICE UNITS.			
— —	British.	Indian.	Mobile Guns.	Sapper and Miner Companies.	Regular.	Territorial.	Garrison.	Indian Battalions.	Nepalese Battalions.	Cavalry Regiments.	Guns.	Sapper and Miner Companies.	Battalions.
(a) Sent overseas independently.	..	..	180	..	33	1	..	..	..	..	..	..	..
(b) In France . .	6	12	36	..	..	..	..	..	..	1	..	..	..
(c) In Mesopotamia .	1	6½	180	10	10	7	..	52½	..	2	..	2	..
(d) In Egypt and the Mediterranean.	..	..	18	1	..	..	..	4	..	3*	..	..	3
(e) In East Africa .	..	¼	12	..	1	..	..	10	..	..	..	1	4
(f) In South Persia and the Persian Gulf.	..	¼	2	..	..	..	..	2	..	..	..	..	..
(g) In East Persia .	..	..	..	..	..	..	..	..	..	..	..	..	..
(h) In Aden . .	..	½	25	2	..	1	..	4	..	..	..	..	..
(i) In Colonies .	..	..	..	..	..	..	..	3	..	..	..	..	..
(j) In Siberia . .	..	..	..	..	..	..	..	..	..	..	..	..	..
TOTAL SENT OVERSEAS	7	19½	453	13	44	9	..	75½	..	6	..	3	7
In India:—													
(k) Field Army and Frontier Brigades.	2	8	120	7	8	11	..	35	3	4	..	..	..
(l) Internal Security .	..	11¼	114	2	..	20	16	21½	7	1	8	..	3½
(m) Unallotted Units	..	..	..	..	..	..	..	..	..	..	..	..	..
TOTAL IN INDIA .	2	19¼	234	9	8	31	16	56½	10	5	8	..	3½
GRAND TOTAL.	9	38¾	687	22	52	40	16	132	10	11	8	3	10½
Deduct—Units received from *Ex*-India.	..	..	128	..	..	40	16	..	10	..	..	..	..
NET TOTAL OF UNITS FURNISHED BY INDIA	9	38¾	559	22	52	..	..	132	..	11	8	3	10½

* Includes Bikaner Camel Corps.

Units at different periods of the War—contd.

JANUARY 1917.												
CAVALRY.				BRITISH BATTALIONS.					IMPERIAL SERVICE UNITS.			
British.	Indian.	Mobile Guns.	Sapper and Miner Companies.	Regular.	Territorial.	Garrison.	Indian Battalions.	Nepalese Battalions.	Cavalry Regiments.	Guns.	Sapper and Miner Companies.	Battalions.
..	..	180	..	33	2	..	..	..	..	..	..	..
5	10	36	..	..	..	..	..	..	1	..	..	..
2	8¼	180	11	10	7	..	56	..	1	..	2	..
..	..	18	1	..	..	..	4	..	3*	..	..	3
..	¼	12	..	1	..	..	10	..	..	4	1	4
..	¼	2	..	..	..	..	2	..	..	..	..	..
..	1	2	..	..	..	..	1	..	..	..	..	..
..	¾	25	2	..	1	..	4	..	..	..	..	..
..	..	..	..	..	..	..	3	..	..	..	..	..
..	..	..	..	..	..	..	..	..	..	..	..	..
7	20½	455	14	44	10	..	80	..	5	4	3	7
2	7	152	6	8	10	..	33½	5	3	..	..	..
..	11¼	77	1	..	20	16	22½	5	¼	..	..	..
..	..	..	2	..	..	..	15½	..	2¾	4	..	3½
2	18¼	229	9	8	30	16	71½	10	6	4	..	3½
9	38¾	684	23	52	40	16	151½	10	11	8	3	10½
..	..	128	..	..	40	16	..	10	..	..	..	..
9	38¾	556	23	52	..	..	151½	..	11	8	3	10½

* Includes Bikaner Camel Corps.

Distribution of Indian

—	JANUARY 1918.												
	CAVALRY.				BRITISH BATTALIONS.					IMPERIAL SERVICE UNITS.			
	British.	Indian.	Mobile Guns.	Sapper and Miner Companies.	Regular.	Territorial.	Garrison.	Indian Battalions.	Nepalese Battalions.	Cavalry Regiments.	Guns.	Sapper and Miner Companies.	Battalions.
(a) Sent overseas independently.	..	..	180	..	34	10	..	..	..	..	..	..	..
(b) In France . .	5	10	36	..	..	..	..	..	..	1	..	..	..
(c) In Mesopotamia .	3	11¼	186	16	10	13	..	86	..	1	..	3	..
(d) In Egypt and the Mediterranean.	..	..	18	1	..	..	..	8	..	3*	..	..	3
(e) In East Africa .	..	1	18	..	..	..	..	8	..	..	4	1	1
(f) In South Persia and the Persian Gulf.	..	1	2	..	..	..	..	3½	..	..	..	..	..
(g In East Persia .	..	½	..	..	..	..	..	1	..	..	..	..	..
(h) In Aden . .	..	¾	25	2	..	1	..	4	..	..	..	..	..
(i) In Colonies .	..	..	..	..	..	..	..	2	..	..	..	..	..
(j) In Siberia . .	..	..	..	..	..	..	..	..	..	..	..	..	..
TOTAL SENT OVERSEAS	8	24½	465	19	44	24	..	112½	..	5	4	4	4
In India:—													
(k) Field Army and Frontier Brigades.	2	9¼	158	8	8	7	..	34	8	3	..	..	..
(l) Internal Security.	..	8½	75	1	..	9	21	21	2	¼	..	..	2
(m) Unallotted Units.	..	½	2	8	..	..	..	36½	..	2¾	4	..	4½
TOTAL IN INDIA .	2	18¼	235	17	8	16	21	91½	10	6	4	..	6½
GRAND TOTAL .	10	42¾	700	36	52	40	21	204	10	11	8	4	10½
Deduct—Units received from *Ex*-India.	1	..	134	..	..	40	21	..	10	..	..	..	..
NET TOTAL OF UNITS FURNISHED BY INDIA.	9	42¾	566	36	52	..	..	204	..	11	8	4	10½

* Includes Bikaner Camel Corps.

Units at different periods of the War—contd.

ON DATE OF SIGNING OF ARMISTICE.												
CAVALRY.				BRITISH BATTALIONS.					IMPERIAL SERVICE UNITS.			
British.	Indian.	Mobile Guns.	Sapper and Miner Companies.	Regular.	Territorial.	Garrison.	Indian Battalions.	Nepalese Battalions.	Cavalry Regiments.	Guns.	Sapper and Miner Companies.	Battalions.
..	..	180	..	34	10	..	..	..	..	..	..	..
5	..	36	..	..	..	..	..	..	..	..	..	..
3	11¼	126	17	4	13	..	55	..	1	..	3	½
..	10	102	13	6	..	..	74	..	4*	..	..	5
..	..	6	1	..	..	..	..	..	..	..	..	..
..	1½	14	2	..	..	..	11	..	..	..	..	..
..	1½	..	..	..	..	..	3	..	..	..	..	..
..	¾	25	2	..	1	..	4	..	..	..	..	..
..	..	..	..	..	..	1	2	..	..	..	..	..
..	..	..	..	..	1	..	..	..	..	..	..	..
8	25	489	35	44	25	1	149	..	5	..	3	5½
2	14¾	164	10	8	4	..	54	8	3	..	1	..
..	8½	63	2	..	11	20	20	2	¼	6	..	..
..	1	5	9	..	..	1	57	..	2¾	4	1	7
2	24¼	232	21	8	15	21	131	10	6	10	2	7
10	49¼	721	56	52	40	22	280	10	11	10	5	12½
1	..	134	..	..	40	22	..	10	..	..	..	..
9	49¼	587	56	52	..	..	(a)280	..	11	10	5	12½

(a) Excluding 14 battalions lost in Kut.

* Includes Bikaner Camel Corps.

APPENDIX "C."

Recruitment by classes.

The number of Indian fighting men recruited up to the end of November 1918 was as follows :—

Classes.	Total obtained during the 1st year ending 31st July 1915.	Total obtained during the 2nd year ending 31st July 1916.	Total obtained during the 3rd year ending 31st July 1917.	Total obtained during the 4th year ending 31st July 1918.	Total from 1st August 1918 to 30th November 1918.	Grand total from 1st August 1914 to 30th November. 1918.
Pathans	5,712	5,958	4,647	8,412	3,128	27,857
Baluchis	118	294	116	1.877	454	2,859
Punjabi Mussalmans	15,597	23,302	23,938	54,460	19,229	136,126
Kashmiris	84	499	232	603	102	1,520
Hindustani Mussalmans	1,777	3,435	7,372	15,826	7,943	36,353
Rajputana and Central India Mussalmans.	2,113	2,811	2,751	4,506	2,043	14,224
Dekhani Mussalmans	992	1,261	1,392	3,039	1,434	8,118
Madrasi Mussalmans	1 267	677	901	2,605	1,002	6,452
Hazaras (Afghanistan and Meshed).	461	528	325	767	137	2,218
Sikhs	12,293	14,973	16,231	31,265	14,160	88,925
Dogras	3,699	3,954	5,391	7,836	2,611	23,491
Gurkhas	10,430	17,418	12,040	13,208	2,493	55,589
Jharuas	..	..	..	179	359	538
Garhwalis	1,139	1,165	1,231	2,761	871	7,167
Rajputs	4,755	5,364	7,122	20,499	11,346	49,086
Rajputs (Rajputana)	1,493	2,312	2,191	4,767	2,341	13,104
Jats	4,946	6,184	8,843	13,027	7,272	40,272
Jats (Rajputana)	1,361	3,265	2,748	4,991	2,602	14,967
Brahmans	558	500	2,090	11,884	5,350	20,382
Gaur Brahmans	143	601	2,023	2,408	1,670	6,845
Dekhani Mahrattas	1,155	1,556	2,488	4,759	2,308	12,266
Konkhani Mahrattas	1,320	1,984	3,705	4,482	1,547	12,038
Ahirs	487	2,158	3,797	8,691	4,403	19,546
Gujars	1,130	3,242	1,789	5,409	3,726	18,296
Mers, Minas, etc.	1,119	1,924	1,391	2,296	1,152	7,882
Tamils	2,822	2,117	2,964	6,302	2,595	16,390
Paraiyans	601	633	1,084	2,355	1,087	5,761
Christians	400	475	905	2,964	1,161	5,905
Punjabi Christians	169	858	679	1,978	557	3,681
Moplahs	247	175	232	519	195	1,368
Telegus	344	328	432	4,061	1,583	6,748
Tiyyans	..	..	169	978	496	1,638
Nayars	..	364	663	1,764	807	3,598
Coorgs	..	..	..	816	37	853
Burmans	..	..	489	9,191	2,483	12,163
Bengalis	..	..	1,019	2,933	1,634	5,586
Bishnois	..	..	129	237	80	446
Mahars	..	..	613	1,160	592	2,365
Kumaonis	..	..	267	1,499	947	2,713
Musallis	..	..	..	737	191	927
Other Hindus	..	..	1,076	22,229	15,241	38,546
Other Mussalmans	..	..	30	2,770	1,329	4,129
TOTAL	78,232	110,315	128,509	292,174	130,708	739,938

Recruitment by Provinces

Illustrates the share each province has taken in obtaining' combatant and non-combatant recruits up to the Armistice :—

Province	Combatant recruits enlisted	Non-combatant recruits enlisted	Total
Madras	51,223	41,117	92,340
Bombay	41,272	30,211	71,483
Bengal	7,117	51,935	59,052
United Provinces	163,578	117,565	281,143
Punjab	349,688	97,288	446,976
North-West Frontier Province	32,181	13,050	45,231
Baluchistan	1,761	327	2,088
Burma	14,094	4,579	18,673
Bihar and Orissa	8,576	32,976	41,552
Central Provinces	5,376	9,631	15,007
Assam	942	14,182	15,124
Ajmer-Merwara	7,341	1,632	8,973
TOTAL	683,149	414,493	1,097,642

In addition, a total of 58,904 recruits have been obtained from Nepal.

Total recruitment

Including the 115,891 recruits provided by the Indian* States directly under the Government of India, the total recruitment up to the Armistice was as follows:—

Combatants	826,855
Non-combatants	445,582

Turning now to British other ranks, it was not to be expected that India could make any important contribution under this category from her very limited resources of British manpower. It may be mentioned, however, that 411 ex-soldiers

* See p. 200.

were re-enlisted in India and sent home for duty with the New Armies; 373 ex-soldiers were re-enlisted for service in India; 900 civilians were enlisted for general service, and 60 for the Royal Engineers; and 793 members of Indian Volunteer Corps units were enlisted for special purposes. An Anglo-Indian contingent was also raised consisting of a battery of artillery, three Cavalry Brigade Signal Troops and half a battalion of infantry. In addition it must be remembered that up to the Armistice no less than 5,307 British Commissions were given in the Indian Army Reserve, as Officer reinforcements for the Indian Army, and that all British born civilian subjects residing in India were liable for compulsory service in the Indian Defence Force, with certain reservations.

The following table shews the pre-war establishment of Indian combatant personnel (excluding Imperial Service units) in each branch of the service, and the increase in establishment effected during the war :—

Arm	Pre-war establishment, including reservists	Establishment on November 1st, 1918	Increase per cent
Artillery	10,457	52,410	400
Cavalry	25,727	33,650	31
Engineers, Sappers and Miners	4,802	17,518	264
Signal Service	352	7,733	2,000
Infantry	151,915	437,000	100

Adherence to establishment was not, however, insisted on when recruits were obtainable readily, and the actual strength of Indian Infantry at the beginning of November 1918, amounted to 520,000 men.

APPENDIX D

List of principal ordnance stores issued up to the 31st October 1918 to meet specific demands from the War Office and India Office.

Items		Quantity
Brass pig	Tons.	1,100
Tents, I.P. complete (all descriptions)	No.	9,000
Cordite (all descriptions)	Tons.	450
Gunpowder	lbs.	120,000
Fuzes (all descriptions) :—		
Filled	No.	124,530
Empty	No.	278,750
Tubes (all descriptions) :—		
Filled	No.	238,000
Empty	No.	86,000
Projectiles (all descriptions) :—		
Filled	No.	130,817
Empty	No.	147,931
Cartridges, filled (all descriptions)	No.	289,095
Cases, Q. F., empty (all descriptions)	No.	28,002
Guns and Howitzers (all descriptions)	No.	205
Guns and Howitzers carriages and vehicles (all descriptions)	No.	811
Rifles and Carbines (Early patterns, part worn)	No.	49,530
Lance Staves	No.	15,000
Binoculars	No.	2,800
Saddlery, Universal, sets	No.	15,000
Cartridges, S. A. Ball, ·303-inch	Millions	107
Cartridges, Dummy Drill, ·303-inch	Millions	150,000

In addition to the above, H. E. empty shells were manufactured under arrangements made by the Munitions Branch. The following shell were reported as ready for despatch up to 30th June 1916 :—

Q. F. 4·5-inch	75,332
Q. F. 18-pr.	77,828
Q. F. 13-pr.	112,464
TOTAL	265,624

APPENDIX E

Some of the more important items of ammunition and explosives supplied to Mesopotamia.

Item	Demands up to November 1915	Demands from December 1915 to August 1916	Demands from 1st September 1916 to 31st August 1917	Demands from 1st September 1917 to 31st October 1918	Total
Complete rounds of ammunition consisting of cartridge, shell, fuze, tube or primer—					
B. L. 10-pr.	10,840	6,500	..	..	17,340
B. L. 15-pr.	4,620	8,500	..	..	18,120
B. L. 4-inch gun	1,040	2,178	..	..	3,218
B. L. 5-inch gun	3,000	1,350	..	..	4,350
B. L. 5-inch howitzer	2,374	13,451	..	..	15,825
Q. F. 13-pr. gun	6,000	11,500	1,000	100	18,600
Q. F. 18-pr. gun	31,500	91,100	105,600	172,166	400,366
Q. F. 4-5-inch howitzer	*Nil.*	3,400	10,000		18,400
Cartridges, B. L., filled, 10-pr.	*Nil.*	12,000	..	..	12,000
Shell, B. L., filled, 15-pr.	*Nil.*	5,000	..	..	5,000
Blasting Gelatine	22,000	40,000	..	..	62,000
Dynamite	9,000	3,000	6,000	36,000	54,000
Guncotton—					
Dry Primers	10,060	10,000	24,000	..	44,060
Wet Slabs	7,008	5,140	800	24,000	36,948
Detonators	13,550	37,200	53,000	69,000	172,750
Grenades—					
Hand	500	154,334	..	..	154,864
Rifle	100	40,000	..	..	40,100
Cartridges, S. A. Ball—					
Pistol, Webley, Mark II	30,600	100,000	350,000	1,500,000	1,980,600
·303-inch, Mark VI	20,600,000	15,000,000	5,000,000	..	70,600,000
·303-inch, Mark VII			5,000,000	..	5,000,000

APPENDIX F

Some of the more important general stores supplied to Mesopotamia

Item		Demands up to November 1915	Demands from December 1915 to August 1916	Demands from 1st September 1916 to 31st August 1917	Demands from 1st September 1917 to 31st October 1918	Total
Bottles, water		703	10,623	..	39,150	50,481
Items of accoutrements		47,600	203,600	641,493	1,143,266	2,035,959
Buckets, water		6,715	9,995	82,006	61,100	159,816
Jhools (Rugs, horse)		2,345	10,458	51,300	86,200	150,303
Lanterns, tent		3,203	13,180	30,538	50,050	96,971
Items of Intrenching tools		74,400	214,900	289,952	662,839	1,242,091
Items of line gear		29,400	72,700	144,100	495,546	741,746
Tents, I.P., complete		6,426	21,710	27,785	29,706	85,627
Bags, nose, I.P.		20,962	88,216	111,800	110,000	330,978
Whips, drivers, I.P.		600	11,910	7,070	20,850	40,430
Items of:—						
Harness, P.D.G.S.		2,000	29,900	69,030	72,427	173,357
Stable necessaries		17,000	200,200	308,200	441,341	966,741
Packsaddlery		13,700	33,400	36,891	48,513	132,504
Saddlery, Universal		22,800	183,700	225,777	273,835	706,112
Blankets, saddle		3,867	18,793	41,700	37,100	101,460
Saddles		665	4,273	10,758	11,517	27,218
Leather		6,960	17,004	22,700	42,700	89,364
Tools	No.	18,000	76,000	94,801	60,058	248,859
Cordage hawser	fms.	18,875	21,460	378,420	945,491	1,364,246
Ropes, galvanized steelwire		12,800	17,478	47,040	..	77,318
Items of Visual Signalling equipment		8,300	44,400	19,881	71,839	144,426
Compasses		159	1,312	1,385	408	3,264
Lubricants	galls.	1,600	11,500	11,595	122,228	146,923
Lubricants	lbs.	23,000	85,100	223,450	657,970	989,520

Some of the more important general stores supplied to Mesopotamia—contd.

Stores		Demands up to November 1915	Demands from December 1915 to August 1916	Demands from 1st September 1916 to 31st August 1917	Demands from 1st September 1917 to 31st October 1918	Total
Shoes, horse	prs.	4,857	57,150	103,900	23,000	188,907
Pawlins		1,236	5,141	6,620	33,285	46,282
Stretchers ambulance		334	3,835	6,000	13,000	23,169
Vehicles and Mountings, complete		105	519	1,021	457	2,102
Components		9,800	54,300	36,455	70,842	171,397
Binoculars		383	2,354	3,162	15	5,914
Clinometers		9	426	..	..	435
Directors		10	130	60	..	200
Mekometers	prs.	62	541	200	..	803

Some of the more important general stores supplied to Mesopotamia—conoid.

Stores.	Demands up to November 1915	Demands from December 1915 to August 1916	Demands from 1st September 1916 to 31st August 1917	Demands from 1st September 1917 to 31st October 1918	Total
Telescopes	117	631	207	..	955
Belts, ammunition, maxim.	548	3,720	420	..	4,688
Boxes, belt, ammunition	2,083	9,020	1,749	..	12,852
Barrels	30	490	600	..	1,120
Side arms, tackles, etc.	537	4,200	32	10	4,779
Cable, electric D. Miles	467	2,618	130	..	3,215
Cells, electric	2,076	9,450	11,950	..	23,476
Wire, electric, T-3	1,136	4,454	2,720	..	8,310
Apparatus, telephone, Portable—					
Carriers, drum	109	636	650	..	1,395
Drums cable, 12"	215	1,187	1,700	800	3,902
Telephones	194	832	95	10	1,131
Telegraphs sets, vibrating, R.E.	24	175	21	..	220
Tools, electricians sets	41	92	100	..	233
Bags, sand	342,480	3,300,000	7,200,000	10,000,960	20,843,440
Pumps, lift and force	38	347	750	700	1,835
Tube wells, $1\frac{1}{4}$"	4	40	80	70	194
Rifles and pistols	1,419	10,509	22,390	5,490	39,808
Swords, lances and sword bayonets	781	4,510	19,370	24,350	49,011

APPENDIX G

Mechanical Transport units raised in India since the outbreak of war

——	Personnel.					Vehicles.				Remarks.
	Officers.	British ranks.	Indian ranks.	Supply lorries.	Stores lorries.	Workshop lorries.	Motor cars.	Motor cycles.	Motor ambulance.	
For Service in India—										
No. 1 Mechanical Transport Company.	5	142	104	72*	3	5	5	6	..	* Include 16 in reserve.
No. 2 Mechanical Transport Company.	5	142	104	72*	3	3	5	6	..	
No. 3 Mechanical Transport Company.	5	157	91	44	..	..	28	14	34	
No. 4 Mechanical Transport Company.	4	30	72	7	2	1	4	7	23	
No. 6 Mechanical Transport Company. (Attached No. 2 M. A. Convoy).	2	31	83	9	2	1	4	7	50	
No. 1 Advance Repair Workshops.	4	66	..	..	..	..	..	..	..	
Central Mechanical Transport Workshops.	1	4	34	..	..	..	..	..	..	
Nushki Mechanical Transport Section.	2	33	27	3	..	..	10	1	..	
For Service in Aden—										
Aden Mechanical Transport Section.	2	33	53	11	..	..	17	17	7	1 tractor attached.
For service with South Persia Rifles— Mechanical Transport Section equipped with Ford vans.	3	13	39	30	..	..	1	2	..	Also certain equipment for Stationary Workshops.
For service with East Persia Cordon—										
No. 5 Mechanical Transport Company (Ford Vans).	6	23	198	135	2	2	7	7	..	

Mechanical Transport units raised in India since the outbreak of war—contd.

—	Personnel.					Vehicles.				Remarks.
	Officers.	British ranks.	Indian ranks.	Supply lorries.	Stores lorries.	Workshop lorries.	Motor cars.	Motor cycles.	Motor ambulance.	
Motor Lorry Section	1	80	..	24	1	1	1	1	..	
Motor Ambulances Convoy Section.	1	87	..	..	..	..	..	..	15	
For service at Bushire—										
Mechanical Transport Section equipped with Ford vans.	3	7	37	22	..	..	1	2	..	Also certain equipment for Stationary Workshops.
For service in Mesopotamia—										
No. 1 Burma Ford Van Company.	6	23	213	..	..	..	..	..	..	
No. 2 Burma Ford Van Company.	6	8	228	..	..	..	..	..	..	
No. 3 Burma Ford Van Company.	6	8	228	..	..	..	..	..	..	
No. 4 Burma Ford Van Company.	6	8	228	..	..	..	..	..	..	
No. 5 Burma Ford Van Company.	6	8	228	..	..	..	..	..	..	

APPENDIX H

Theatres in which Indian units served during the Great War up to the Armistice

A.=Aden	F.=France.
Af.=Africa.	G.=Gallipoli.
B.S.=Black Sea.	I.=India and Burma.
C.=Colonies.	M.=Mesopotamia.
Ch.=China.	P.=Persia,
E.=Egypt.	S.=Salonika.

Cavalry

1st Lancers	I.	25th Cavalry	I.; Af.; I.
2nd Lancers	F.; E.	26th Cavalry	I.; A. (2); P. (1)
3rd Horse	F.; I.	27th Cavalry	I.; P. (1).
4th Cavalry	F.; M.; I.	28th Cavalry	I.; P.
5th Cavalry	I.; M.	29th Lancers	F.; E.; F.; I.
6th Cavalry	F.; E.	30th Lancers	F.; L.
7th Lancers	I.; M.; I.	31st Lancers	I.
8th Cavalry	I.	32nd Lancers	I.; M.
9th Horse	F.; E.	33rd Cavalry	M.; I.
10th Lancers	I.; M.	34th Horse	F.; E.
11th Lancers	I.; M.	35th Horse	I.
12th Cavalry	I.; M.	36th Horse	F.; E.
13th Lancers	I.; M.	37th Lancers	I.
14th Lancers	I.; M.	38th Horse	F.; E.
15th Lancers	F.; M.; P	39th Horse	I.
16th Cavalry	I.; M.; I.	40th Cavalry	I.
17th Cavalry	I. (1 sqdn. Af.).	41st Cavalry	I.; P. (2).
18th Lancers	F.; E.	42nd Cavalry	I.
19th Lancers	F.; E.	43rd Cavalry	I.
20th Horse	F.; E.	44th Cavalry	I.
21st Cavalry	I.; M.	45th Cavalry	I.
22nd Cavalry	I.; M.	Guides Cavalry	I.; M.
23rd Cavalry	I.; M.		

Infantry and Pioneers

1-1st Brahmans	I.; A.	1-6th Jats	F.; E.; M.
2-1st Brahmans	I.	2-6th Jats	I.
1-2nd Rajputs	E.; M.; S.	1-7th Rajputs	M.; A.
2-2nd Rajputs	I.	2-7th Rajputs	I.
3-2nd Rajputs	I.	1-8th Rajputs	I.; M.
1-3rd Brahman	E.; M.; P.	2-8th Rajputs	I.
2-3rd Brahman	I.	1-9th Infantry	F.; E.; M.
1-4th Rajputs	I.; M.	2-9th Infantry	I.; M.
2-4th Rajputs	I.	3-9th Infantry	I.; M.
1-5th Infantry	C.; Af.; I.	4-9th Infantry	I.
2-5th Infantry	I.	1-10th Jats	I.; M.

Infantry and Pioneers—contd.

2-10th Jats	I.	36th Sikhs	Ch.; I.; M.
1-11th Rajputs	I.; M. I.	37th Dogras	I.; M.
2-11th Rajputs	I.	38th Dogras	I.; A.; E.
1-12th Pioneers	I.	1-39th Garhwalis	F.; E.; I.; M.
		2-39th Garhwalis	F.; E.; I.; B. S.
2-12th Pioneers	I.	.3-39th Garhwalis	I.
13th Rajputs	Af.; I.; M.	4-39th Garhwalis	I.
14th Sikhs	E.; G.; M.	1-40th Pathans	C.; F.; Af.; I.
1-15th Sikhs	F.; E.; I.	2-40th Pathans	I.
2-15th Sikhs	I.	1-41st Dogras	F.; E.; M.; I.
16th Rajputs	I.; P.	2-41st Dogras	I.
1-17th Infantry	C.; Af.; I.; E.	1-42nd Deolis	I.; M.
2-17th Infantry	I.	2-42nd Deolis	I.; E.
1-18th Infantry	I.; C.	1-43rd Erinpuras	I.; M.
2-18th Infantry	I.; E.	2-43rd Erinpuras	I.
1-19th Punjabis	I.; P.	1-44th Infantry	I.; M.
2-19th Punjabis	I.; E.	2-44th Infantry	I.
20th Punjabis	M.; E.	45th Sikhs	I.; M.
1-21st Punjabis	I.; E.	46th Punjabis	I.; E.
2-21st Punjabis	I.	47th Sikhs	F.; M.; E.
1-22nd Punjabis	M.; P	1-48th Pioneers	M.; L.; M.
2-22nd Punjabis	I.	2-48th Pioneers	I.
1-23rd Pioneers	A.; E.	49th Bengalis .	I.; M.
2-23rd Pioneers	E.	1-50th Kumaon Rifles	I.; E.
3-23rd Pioneers	I.	2-50th Kumaon Rifles	I.
24th Punjabis	E.; M.; B. S.; S	51st Sikhs	E.; A.; M.
1-25th Punjabis	C.; I.; M.; S.	52nd Sikhs	I.; M.
2-25th Punjabis	I.	53rd Sikhs	E.; A.; M.
1-26th Punjabis	C.; M.	1-54th Sikhs	I.; E.
2-26th Punjabis	I.	2-54th Sikhs	I.
1-27th Punjabis	E.; F.; M.	1-55th Rifles	I.; Af.; I.
2-27th Punjabis	I.	2-55th Rifles	I.
1-28th Punjabis	C.; M.; E.	1-56th Rifles	E.; A.; M.
2-28th Punjabis	I.	2-56th Rifles	I.
29th Punjabis	Af.; E.	1-57th Rifles	F.; E.; Af.; I.
1-30th Punjabis	I.; Af.; I.	2-57th Rifles	I.
2-30th Punjabis	I.; E.	58th Rifles	F.; E.
3-30th Punjabis	I.	59th Rifles	F.; M.; E.
4-30th Punjabis	I.	1-61st Pioneers	Af.; I.
31st Punjabis	I.; M. B. S.	2-61st Pioneers	I.
1-32nd Pioneers	I.; M.	62nd Punjabis	E.; A.; M.
2-32nd Pioneers	I.; E.	1-63rd Infantry	Af.; I.
3-32nd Pioneers	I.	2-63rd Infantry	I.
1-33rd Punjabis	E.; F.; A.; Af.; I	64th Pioneers	I.; M.
2-33rd Punjabis	I.	1-66th Punjabis	I.; M.
1-34th Pioneers	F.; M.; E.	2-66th Punjabis	I.
2-34th Pioneers	I.	1-67th Punjabis	I.; M.; B. S.
3-34th Pioneers	I.	2-67th Punjabis	I.
1-35th Sikhs	I.	1-69th Punjabis	E.; G.; F.; A.
2-35th Sikhs	I.	2-69th Punjabis	I.

Infantry and Pioneers—contd.

1-70th Burma Rifles	I.; E.
2-70th do.	I.
3-70th do.	I.
4-70th do.	I.
21st Punjabis	I.; P.
1-72nd Punjabis	I.; E.
2-72nd do.	I.
1-73rd Infantry	I.; M.
2-73rd do.	I.
7-4th Punjabis	C.; I.; E.
1-75th Infantry	I.; A.
2-75th do.	I.
1-76th Punjabis	E.; M.; I.
2-76th do.	I.
79th Infantry	I.; M.
1-80th Infantry	I.; C; M.
2-80th do.	I.
1-81st Pioneers	I.; P.
2-81st do.	I.
82nd Punjabis	I.; M.
83rd Infantry	I.; P.; M.; E. S.
84th Punjabis	P.; I.; M.; I.
85th Burma Rifles	I.; M.
1-86th Infantry	I.
2-86th do.	I.
87th Punjabis	I.; M.
1-88th Infantry	I.; M.
2-88th do.	I.
1-89th Punjabis	E.; G.; F.; I.; M.; B. S.
2-89th Punjabis	I.
1-90th Punjabis	I.; M.
2-90th Punjabis	I.
1-91st Punjabis	I.; M.; E.
2-91st Punjabis	I.
92nd Punjabis	E.; M.
93rd Burma Infy.	E.; F.; M.
1-94th Infantry	P.; I.; M.
2-94th do.	I.
1-95th Infantry	P.; I.; M.; B.; S.
2-95th do.	I.
1-96th Infantry	I.; P.; M.
2-9 6th do.	I.
1-97th Infantry	I.; M.
2-97th do.	I.; E.
1-98th Infantry	Af.; I.; P.
2-98th do.	I.
1-99th Infantry	I.; M.
2-99th do.	I.
1-101st Grenadiers	Af.; E.

2-101st Grenadiers	E.; I.
1-102nd do.	P.; I.; M.
2-102nd do.	I.
1-103rd Infantry	M.; I.
2-103rd do.	I.
3-103rd do.	I.
104th Rifles	M.
1-105th Infantry	I.; M.; E.
2-105th do.	I.
106th Pioneers	I.; M.
1-107th Pioneers	F.; M., I.; P
2-107th do.	I.; E.
108th Infantry	I.; P.; M.
1-109th Infantry	A,; I.
2-109th do.	A.; I.
110th Mahrattas	M.; E.; I.
111th Mahars	I.
1-112th Infantry	I.; M.
2-112th do.	I.
1-113th Infantry	I.; M.
2-113th do.	I.
114th Mahrattas	I.; M.
1-116th Mahrattas	I.; M.
2-116th do.	I.
1-117th Mahrattas	M.; P.
2-117th do.	I.
1-119th Infantry	M.
2-119th do.	I.
120th do.	M.; I.; P.
121st Pioneers	I.; M.; E.
122nd Infantry	I.; M.
1-123rd Rifles	I.; E.
2-123rd do.	I.
1-124th Baluch. Infy.	I.; M.; I.
2-124th do.	P.; M.; E.
3-124th do.	I.; P.
1-115th Riflcs	F.; E.; M.
2-125th do.	I.
126th Baluchis Infy.	E.; P.(2); A(2) I.; M
1-127th Baluchis	I.; Af.
2-127th do.	I.: E.
1-128th Pioneers	E.; M.
2-128th do.	I.
1-129th Baluchis	E.; Af.; I.
2-129th do.	I.
1-130th Baluchis	I.; Af.; E
2-130th do.	I.
1-131st Infantry	I.
2-131st do.	I.

289 Infantry and Pioneers—contd.

1-132nd Infantry	I.
2-132nd do.	I.
133rd Infantry	I.
140th Infantry	I.
141st Infantry	I.
142nd Infantry	I.
143rd Infantry	I.
144th Infantry	I.
1-150th Infantry	M.
2-150th do.	M.
3-150th do.	M.
1-151st Infantry	I.
2-151st do.	E.
3-151st Punjabi Rifles	E.
1-152nd Punjabis	M.; E.
2-152nd do.	M.; E.
3-152nd do.	E.
1-153rd Punjabis	M.; E.
2-153rd do.	E.
3-153rd Rifles	E.
1-154th Infantry	I.
2-154th do.	M.; E.
3-154th do.	M.; E.
1-155th Pioneers	M.; E.
2-155th do.	E.
156th Infantry	I.
Burma Mily. Police, Mtd. Infy.	I.; P.
1-1st Gurkha Rifles	F.; M.; E.
2-1st do.	I.
3-1st do.	I.
1-2nd Gurkha Rifles	I.; M.
2-2nd Gurkha Rifles	F.; E.; I.
3-2nd do.	I.
1-3rd Gurkha Rifles	I.; M.
2-3rd do.	F.; E.
3-3rd do.	E.
4-3rd do.	I.
1-4th Gurkha Rifles	F.; G.; E.; I.
2-4th do.	I.; M.; S.
1-5th Gurkha Rifles	E.; G.; I.
2-5th do.	I.; M.
3-5th do.	I.
1-6th Gurkha Rifles	E.; G.; I.; M.
2-6th do.	I.; M.
3-6th do.	I.
1-7th Gurkha Rifles	I.; M.
2-7th do.	E.; M.; I.
3-7th do.	I.
1-8th Gurkha Rifles	I.; M.; E.
2-8th do.	F.; E.; I.
3-8th do.	I.
1-9th Gurkha Rifles	F.; M.; I.
2-9th do.	I.; M.
3-9th do.	I.
1-10th Gurkha Rifles	I.; M.
2-10th do.	E.; G.; M.
1-11th Gurkha Rifles	M.
2-11th do.	M.
3-11th do.	M.
4-11th do.	E.
1st Guides Infantry	T; M.; E.
2nd do.	I.; E.
3rd do.	I.

Sappers and Miners

1st S. & M.	A.; E.; F.; I. M.; P.
2nd S. & M.	Af.; E.; F.; I.; M.; P.
3rd S. & M.	A.; Af.; E.; F.; I.; M.; P.

Railways Companies, Sappers and Miners

No. 25 Rly. Coy.	Af.; I.; E.
No. 26 Rly. Coy.	Af.; I.
No. 27 Rly. Coy.	Af.; I.
No. 28 Rly. Coy.	I.; Af.
No. 29 Rly. Coy.	I.; E.
Hd. Qrs. Rly. Battn.	I.

Signals.

Companies, troops and Wireless Squadrons — A.; Af.; E.; F.; I., M.; P.

Mountain Artillery

Unit	Service
21st Pack Batty.	E.; G.; M.
22nd Pack Batty.	I.; Af.
23rd Pack Batty.	M.; I.; P.
24th Pack Batty.	C.; I.; Af.; I.
25th Pack Batty.	I.; M.
26th Pack Batty.	E.; G.; M.
27th Pack Batty.	Af.; I.
28th Pack Batty.	Af.; I.
29th Pack Batty.	I.; E.
30th Pack Batty.	M.; I.
31st Pack Batty.	I.; M.
32nd Pack Batty.	I.; E.
33rd Pack Batty.	I. P.; I.
34th Pack Batty.	I.; M.
35th Pack Batty.	I.; P.
36th Pack Batty.	P.
37th Pack Batty.	I.
38th Pack Batty.	I.; E.
39th Pack Batty.	I.; E.
40th Pack Batty.	I.
41st Pack Batty	I.
42nd Pack Batty	I.
43rd Pack Batty	I.
44th Pack Batty	I.
45th Pack Batty	I.
49th Pack Batty	M.
50th Pack Batty	M.

A. = Aden
Af. = Africa
B.S. = Black Sea
C. = Colonies
Ch. = China
E. = Egypt
F. = France
G. = Gallipoli
I. = India and Burma
M. = Mesopotamia
P. = Persia
S. = Salonika

Imperial Service Troops

Cavalry

Unit	Service
Alwar Lancers	F.; I.
Bhavnagar Lancers	E.; M.; I.
Bhopal Lancers	I.
1st Gwalior Lancers	F.; M.; I.
2nd Gwalior Lancers	I.
3rd Gwalior Lancers	Af.; I.
1st Hyderabad Lancers	I.
2nd Hyderabad Lancers	I.
Indore Mounted Escort	F.; I.; M.
1st Jodhpur Lancers	F.; E.
2nd Jodhpur Lancers	E.
Junagadh Lancers	F.; I.
Kashmir Lancers	E.; M.
Mysore Lancers	E.
Navanagar Lancers	E.; I.
Patiala Lancers	E.; I.; M.
Rampur Lancers	I.
Ratlam Despatch Riders	E.
Udaipur Lancers	I.

Infantry

Unit	Service
Alwar Infantry	E.; I.
Bharatpur Infantry	Af.
3rd Gwalior Infantry	I.
4th Gwalior Infantry	E.
Jind Infantry	Af; I.
Kapurthala Infantry	Af.; I,
1st Kashmir Infantry	E.; I.
2nd Kashmir Rifles	Af.; E.; 1.
3rd Kashmir Rifles	Af. : I.
Nabha Infantry	M.; I.
Patiala Infantry	E; I.
Rampur Infantry	Af.; I.

Artillery

Unit	Service
1st Kashmir Mountain Battery	Af.; I.
2nd Kashmir Mountain Battery	I.; P.

Sappers

Unit	Service
Faridkot Sappers	Af. I.
Maler Kotla Sappers	F.; I.; M.
Sirmoor Sappers	I.; M.
Tehri (Garhwal) Sappers	E.; F.; M.

Transport

Unit	Service
Bahawalpur Mounted Rifles and Camel Transport	Af.; E.; I.
Bharatpur Transport Corps	F.; I.; M.
Gwalior Transport Corps	F.; I.; M.
Indore Transport Corps	F.; G.; I.; M.
Khairpur Mounted Rifles and Camel Transport	Af.; E.; F.; M,
Mysore Transport Corps	M.

APPENDIX " I."

Dates of Entry, etc., of the various powers into the war.

Date.	Country.	Remarks.
1914		
28th June	Austria	Assassination of Heir Presumptive of, at Serajevo.
28th July	Serbia	Austria-Hungary declared war on.
1st August	Russia	Germany declared war on. Concluded Peace with Central Powers, 2nd March, 1918.
3rd August	France	Germany declared war on.
4th August	Great Britain	Declared war on Germany.
4th August	Belgium	Germany declared war on.
5th August	Montenegro	Declared war on Austria-Hungary.
12th August	Great Britain	Declared war on Austria-Hungary.
23rd August	Japan	Declared war on Germany.
1st November	Turkey	Commenced hostilities with Great Britain.
1915		
23rd May	Italy	Declared war on Austria.
3rd June	San Marino	Declared war on Austria.
1916		
1 January	Albania	Essad Pasha declared war on Austria.
9th March	Portugal	Germany declared war on.
7th June	Hedjaz	Arab rising began at Medina.
27th August	Rumania	Declared war on Austria. Concluded Peace with Central Powers, 7th May, 1918. Re-entered war, 10th November 1918.
1917		
(12th March	Russia	Revolution.)
6th April	United States	Declared war on Germany.
7th April	Panama	...
7th April	Cuba	....

Dates of Entry, etc., of the various powers into the war—contd.

Date	Country	REMARKS
13th April	*Bolivia	....
27th June	Greece	....
22nd July	Siam	
4th August	Liberia	....
14th August	China	....
7th October	*Uruguay	....
7th October	*Peru	
26th October	Brazil	
7th November	Ecuador	
1918		
2nd March	....	Russo-German Peace at Brest.
23rd April	Guatemala	Broke off relations, 27th April 1917.
16th May	Nicaragua	Broke off relations, 19th May 1917.
23rd May	Costa Rica	Broke off relations, 22nd September 1917.
12th July	Hayti	Broke off relations, 15th June 1917.
19th July	Honduras	Broke off relations, 17th May 1917.
31st July	Onondago Indians	....
13th August	Czecho-Slovaks	Recognised by Great Britain as Allies on this date.
12th October	Polish National Army	Recognized by Great Britain on this date as autonomous, allied, and co-belligerent.

*States which broke off relations but did not declare war.

APPENDIX "J"

Dates of the signing of the Armistices and Treaties, etc.

1918

29th September	Armistice between the Allies and Bulgaria.
30th October	Armistice between the Allies and Turkey.
3rd November	Armistice between the Allies and Austria-Hungary.
9th November	Abdication of the Kaiser.
11th November	Armistice between the Allies and Germany.
13th December	Armistice between the Allies and Germany prolonged to 17th January 1919.

1919

16th January	Armistice between the Allies and Germany prolonged to 17th February 1919.
16th February	Armistice between Allies and Germany prolonged.
4th April	Protocol and Annexe to protocol between Allies and Germany, signed.
7th May	The Allies' Peace terms handed to the German representative.
2nd June	The Allies' Peace terms handed to the Austrian representatives.
28th June	The Allies' Peace terms signed by the Germans.
10th September	The Allies' Peace terms signed by the Austrians.
27th November	The Allies' Peace terms signed by the Bulgarians.

1920

10th January	Ratification of the Treaty with Germany signed.
11th May	Peace Treaty handed to Turkish delegates.

APPENDIX K

Comparative statistics for the British Empire, and a note regarding India's Naval contribution.

I. *Men.*—During the Great War, India was fighting as much for her individual liberty and salvation as was any other nation or people in the world. Germany's bid for world dominion envisaged the creation of an Asiatic Empire beneath the heel of the Prussian jackboot.

The collapse of Russia towards the close of 1917 and Germany's efforts in the following spring to exploit the Bolshevik government with a view to the invasion of India, resulted in the summoning of a special War Conference at Delhi which brought home to Indian thought the intimacy of this country's connection with the war and gave a wonderful fillip to recruitment. Throughout the war the recruitment of Indians was effected on a purely voluntary basis, the principle of compulsion being applied to European British subjects only. The question of enforcing conscription on India as a whole need not be enquired into here, beyond stating the bare fact that no machinery would have been available to deal with the enormous number of persons so involved.

Another point to be remembered is that no true comparison can be made between India's efforts and those of the self-governing Dominions which ignores the fact that, for many years prior to the war, India had maintained a large and highly trained army in being, a great part of which became immediately available for Imperial purposes on the outbreak of hostilities.

Arranged in order of geographical extent the position with regard to contributions in men up to the Armistice is as follows:—

	Area in sq. miles	Population in 1911	Numbers supplied	Ratio
Canada	3,729,665	7,206,643	640,886	1 in 11½
Australia	3,063,041	4,455,005	416,809	1 in 10½
India	1,802,657	315,156,396	1,401,350	1 in 225 (224·8)
Union of S. Africa	473,100	5,973,394	136,070	1 in 44
Newfoundland 42,750 } Labrador Coast 120,000 }	162,750	242,619 (3,949 from Labrador Coast)	11,922	1 in 22
The British Isles, including the Channel Islands.	121,377	45,370,530	6,184,416	1 in 7¼ (7·33)
New Zealand	103,860	1,083,508	220,099,	1 in 5 (4·92)

The figures for the British Isles refer only to their military contribution and take no account of the large naval forces maintained during the war, nor of the mercantile marine. The figures for India are based on the total population, including that of the Indian States, as the contribution of the States in manpower is included in the total numbers supplied.

II. *War expenditure.* The total war expenditure from public funds, so far as figures are immediately available is approximately as below :—

	£
Canada	*435,370,611 to 1920.
Australia	381,149,019 to 1920.
India	†207,500,000 to 1922.
Union of S. Africa	39,092,028 to 1920.
Newfoundland and Labrador	....
United Kingdom	8,742,000 000 to 1919.
New Zealand	80,089,025 to 1919.

* Calculated at 3·845 = £1.

†Including £50 millions for operations on N.-W. Frontier up to 31st March 1922 and £100 millions lump sum contribution.

During the six years, from 1914-15 to 1919-20, India's revenue and expenditure have approximately balanced at an annual average of £106 millions sterling, the gross revenue during this period increasing by about 67 per cent.

The main sources of increase were derived from new taxes which took the general form of an addition to the tariff. That is to say the general import duty was raised, the free list reduced and special (*i.e.*, higher) tariffs arranged for wines, spirits and tobacco. Export duties were also imposed on tea and jute, and the income-tax was raised, and a super-tax added in respect of incomes exceeding Rs. 50,000. But incomes derived from agriculture were exempt. *Pari passu* with increased taxation, rigid economy was exercised in the capital programme, the railway budget during the second year of war being reduced from £8 to £4.9 millions and considerable reduction effected in expenditure on irrigation.

The burden of taxation per head of population was as follows:—

—	In 1913-14			In 1920		
	£	*s.*	*d.*	£	*s.*	*d.*
Canada	8	16	$11^1/_2$	36	12 (1919)	6
Australian Commonwealth and States	4	14	0	8	18 (1919)	3
India (including land tax)	0	3	10	0	4	$2^1/_4$
Union of S. Africa				2	10	0
Newfoundland and Labrador figures not available		...			...	
United Kingdom	3	10	10	22	0	6
New Zealand including Maoris	5	5	2	11	17	1
New Zealand excluding Maoris	5	10	0	*12	7 (1919)	8

* £14-2-9 in 1920 excluding Maoris.

III. *Naval Contribution.*—The total length of India's frontiers amount to nearly 13,000 miles; of which the land frontier (including Kashmir but excluding Nepal and Bhutan) accounts for 7,053, and her sea frontier (excluding Ceylon) for 5,854 miles. Throughout the war India's naval contribution has remained fixed at the pre-war figure of £100,000 per annum, plus cost of coal of His Majesty's ships employed in Indian waters, making an approximate total of £140,000 per annum.

The pre-war average annual value of India's sea-borne trade amounted to £247 millions and in 1919-20 to £370 millions; whilst the pre-war quinquennial average of net register tonnage of all vessels and craft entering and clearing Indian ports with cargoes and in ballast was 16,216,000 tons. If to this be added the security of overseas passengers and mails, not to mention the very existence of India herself, it must be admitted that her naval insurance has been effected for an exceedingly moderate figure.